Building Tools with GitHub

Customize Your Workflow

Chris Dawson with Ben Straub

Beijing · Boston · Farnham · Sebastopol · Tokyo

Building Tools with GitHub

by Chris Dawson and Ben Straub

Copyright © 2016 Chris Dawson, Ben Straub. All rights reserved.

Printed in the United States of America.

Published by O'Reilly Media, Inc., 1005 Gravenstein Highway North, Sebastopol, CA 95472.

O'Reilly books may be purchased for educational, business, or sales promotional use. Online editions are also available for most titles (*http://oreilly.com/safari*). For more information, contact our corporate/institutional sales department: 800-998-9938 or *corporate@oreilly.com*.

Editors: Brian MacDonald and Meghan Blanchette	**Indexer:** WordCo Indexing Services, Inc.
Production Editor: Nicholas Adams	**Interior Designer:** David Futato
Copyeditor: Christina Edwards	**Cover Designer:** Randy Comer
Proofreader: Kim Cofer	**Illustrator:** Rebecca Demarest

February 2016:   First Edition

Revision History for the First Edition
2016-02-05:   First Release
2016-12-16:   Second Release

See *http://oreilly.com/catalog/errata.csp?isbn=9781491933503* for release details.

The O'Reilly logo is a registered trademark of O'Reilly Media, Inc. *Building Tools with GitHub*, the cover image, and related trade dress are trademarks of O'Reilly Media, Inc.

While the publisher and the authors have used good faith efforts to ensure that the information and instructions contained in this work are accurate, the publisher and the authors disclaim all responsibility for errors or omissions, including without limitation responsibility for damages resulting from the use of or reliance on this work. Use of the information and instructions contained in this work is at your own risk. If any code samples or other technology this work contains or describes is subject to open source licenses or the intellectual property rights of others, it is your responsibility to ensure that your use thereof complies with such licenses and/or rights.

978-1-491-93350-3

[LSI]

Table of Contents

Preface

This book contains stories about building software tools.

If you write software on a daily basis, you realize the act of writing software is the craft of creating tools. Software is nothing more than a tool. A spreadsheet is fundamentally a tool to add and subtract numbers. A video game is fundamentally a tool to alleviate boredom. Almost immediately after people started writing software tools we then discovered we needed more tools to permit us to write the tools we set out to build in the first place. Let's call these tools that are strictly to support writing software (rather than software tools for the general population) meta-tools.

One of the most important meta-tools in the software development world is Git. Git is a meta-tool that helps software developers manage the complexity that comes from writing software. Git allows software developers to store snapshots of their programs (and then easily restore those snapshots if necessary) and to easily collaborate with other programmers (a surprisingly complicated problem). Git is called a source code management (SCM) tool and though there were many other SCMs before Git, Git has taken the software world by storm like no other before it and now dominates the SCM landscape.

GitHub is a company that saw the immense potential of Git early on and built a layer of web services on top of the existing features found in Git. Not surprisingly, one of the factors behind its success was that GitHub employees embraced the ethos of writing meta-tools from the beginning. Building meta-tools requires the courage to take a little extra time to build a meta-tool rather than taking the easy route to get the public-facing software out the door. GitHub employees are proud of this prioritization and have written extensively about the benefits, which include easy on-boarding of new hires and a transparent workflow visible to all employees.

This book looks at the tools GitHub uses internally. The GitHub.com website is itself a meta-tool, and we discuss the many facets of the GitHub service. Specifically these technologies are the GitHub API and related GitHub technologies, Gollum wiki,

Jekyll static page generator, and the chat robot called Hubot (if you are not familiar with any of these, we'll explain them fully in their respective chapters).

To reiterate, this book is not a reference of those technologies. This book is a story-book, a book that relates the process of building software meta-tools, explaining not only the technology specifics, but also the compromises, the realities of refactoring, and the challenges inherent to writing meta-tools in long narrative story form.

Meta-tools require a different mindset than what comes from building software available to the general population. Meta-tools are generally open source, which requires a different level of responsibility and usage. One could argue that software engineers are more demanding of quality than general users because software developers know they can take action to improve or fork software that does not work for them. Meta-tools enforce a higher level of contributory involvement, which makes automated tests almost a requirement. All of these concepts constitute the background story behind meta-tools, and we show you how they play out when building your own.

Why APIs and Why the GitHub API?

Using an API to back an application is a common practice today: this is the future of application development. APIs provide a great pattern for making data accessible to the multiscreen world. If your application is backed by a remote service API, the first application could be a mobile app running on Apple's iOS operating system. Critically, if that business model does not turn out to be correct, you can respond quickly to changing requirements and iterate to build another application for an Android wearable. Or, perhaps you'll build an integrated car application, or any other console (or even nonconsole) application. As long as your applications can send and receive data using calls to a remote API you are free to build whatever user interface you want on whatever platform you want.

As an author, you could write and host your own API. Many frameworks for popular languages like Ruby, Go, or Java support building APIs using standard architectural styles like REST. Or, you could use a third-party API. In this book we'll focus on a third-party API: the GitHub API.

Why the GitHub API? The GitHub API is exceedingly relevant if you are building software because you are probably using GitHub to manage your software code. For those that aren't, you might be using Git without GitHub, and the GitHub API is useful to know there as well, as it layers the functionality of Git into a networked programming interface.

The GitHub API is perhaps the best designed API I've ever used. It is a Hypermedia API, which is an arguably successful attempt to make API clients resilient to API changes—a tricky problem. The API is well versioned. It is comprehensive, mapping closely to most features of Git. It is consistent across sections and well organized. The

GitHub API is a great API on which to build applications, serving as a case study for a well-designed API.

Structure of This Book

The GitHub API is extremely comprehensive, permitting access and modification of almost all data and metadata stored or associated with a Git repository. Here is a grouped summary of the sections of the API ordered alphabetically as they are on the GitHub API documentation site (*https://developer.github.com/v3/*):

- Activity: notifications of interesting events in your developer life
- Gists: programmatically create and share code snippets
- Git Data: raw access to Git data over a remote API
- Issues: add and modify issues
- Miscellaneous: whatever does not fit into the general API categorization
- Organizations: access and retrieve organizational membership data
- Pull Requests: a powerful API layer on the popular merge process
- Repositories: modify everything and anything related to repositories
- Search: code-driven search within the entire GitHub database
- Users: access user data
- Enterprise: specifics about using the API when using the private corporate GitHub

In addition, though not a part of the API, there are other important technologies you should know about when using GitHub that are not covered in the API documentation:

- Jekyll and "gh-pages": hosting blogs and static documentation
- Gollum: wikis tied to a repository
- Hubot: a programmable chat robot used extensively at GitHub

Each of these sections of the GitHub technology stack are covered in various chapters (with two exceptions, which we explain next). The GitHub API documentation is a stellar reference you will use constantly when writing any application that talks to the API, but the chapters in this book serve a different purpose: these chapters are stories about building applications on top of the technologies provided by GitHub. Within these stories you will learn the trade-offs and considerations you will face when you use the GitHub API. Chapters in this book often cover multiple pieces of the API when appropriate for the story we are telling. We've generally tried to focus on a major API section and limit exposure to other pieces as much as possible, but most chapters do need to bring in small pieces of more than one section.

Here is a short synopsis of each chapter:

Chapter 1

This chapter covers a first look at the API through the command-line HTTP client called cURL. We talk a bit about the response format and how to parse it within the command line, and also document authentication. This is the only chapter that does not build an application from the technologies presented. Chapter 2: This chapter covers the Gist API, as well as command-line tools and the Ruby language "Octokit" API client. We then take this API and build a simple Ruby server that is stored as a gist and displays gists.

Chapter 3

This chapter explains usage of the Gollum command-line tool and associated Ruby library (gem), which is backed by Grit, the C-language bindings for accessing Git repositories. We also document some details of the Git storage format and how it applies to storing large files inside of a Git repository, and show how to use the Git command-line tools to play with this information. We use Gollum and the Grit libraries to build an image management tool that also functions as a regular Gollum wiki, which can be published to GitHub.

Chapter 4

In this chapter we explore the Search API and build a GUI tool to search repositories on GitHub using Python.

Chapter 5

This chapter covers a relatively new part of the API that documents the interactions between third-party tools and your code. This chapter builds an application using C# and the Nancy .NET GitHub API libraries.

Chapter 6

If you push a specifically organized repository into GitHub, GitHub will host a fully featured blog, equivalent in most ways to a Wordpress site (well, except for the complexity part). This chapter documents how to format your repository, how to use Markdown within Jekyll, how to use programmatic looping constructs provided by Liquid Templates, and then shows how to import an entire website from the Internet Archive into the Jekyll format using Ruby. We show how to respectfully spider a site using caching, a valuable technique when using APIs or third-party public information.

Chapter 7

In this chapter we create a mobile application targeting the Android OS. Our application reads and writes information into a Jekyll repository from the Git

Data section of the API. We show how to create user interface tests for Android that verify GitHub API responses using the Calabash UI testing tool.

Chapter 8

Hubot is a JavaScript (NodeJS) chat robot enabling technologists to go beyond developer operations ("DevOps") to a new frontier called "ChatOps." This chapter illustrates using the Activity and Pull Requests section of the API. In addition, we show how you can simulate GitHub notifications and how to write testable Hubot extensions (which is often a challenge when writing JavaScript code). We string all these pieces together and build a robot that automates assigning pull request review requests.

Chapter 9

Did you know you can host an entire "single-page application" on GitHub? We show how you can build a coffee shop information app backed by a flat file database hosted on GitHub written in the JavaScript language. Importantly, we show how you can write a testable JavaScript application that mocks out the GitHub API when needed.

We don't cover the Organizations API: this is a small facet of the API with only the ability to list organizations and modify metadata about your organization; once you have used other parts of the API this nook of the API will be very intuitive.

We also don't cover the Users section of the API. While you might expect it to be an important part of the API, the Users API is really nothing more than an endpoint to list information about users, add or remove SSH keys, adjust email addresses, and modify your list of followers.

There is not a specific chapter on issues. GitHub originally grouped issues and pull requests into the same API section, but with the growing importance of pull requests GitHub has separated them in the API documentation. In fact, they are still internally stored in the same database and pull requests are, at least for now, just another type of issue. Chapter 8 documents using pull requests and is a good reference for issues in that way.

The Enterprise API works almost exactly the same as the GitHub.com site API. We don't have a chapter telling a story about an Enterprise version of the API, but we do provide an appendix that contains a few notes about how the examples work when using an Enterprise server. We also provide the specific syntax for each of the languages used in the chapters that will make any of the examples provided work with an Enterprise server.

Through these stories about the technologies behind GitHub we hope to give you an inside look at the inner workings of the brain of a developer building on top of the GitHub API.

Who You Are

This book should be an interesting source of information for people who have used Git or GitHub and want to "level-up" their skills related to these technologies. People without any experience using GitHub or Git should start with an introductory book on these technologies.

You should have good familiarity with at least one imperative modern programming language. You don't need to be an expert programmer to read this book, but having some programming experience and familiarity with at least one language is essential.

You should understand the basics of the HTTP protocol. The GitHub team uses a very standard RESTful approach for its API. You should understand the difference between a GET request and POST request and what HTTP status codes mean at the very least.

Familiarity with other web APIs will make traversing these chapters easier, although this book simultaneously aspires to provide a guide showing how a well-thought-out, well-designed, and well-tested web API creates a foundation for building fun and powerful tools. If you have not used web APIs extensively, but have experience using other types of APIs, you will be in good company.

What You Will Learn

Much of the book focuses on the technical capabilities exposed by GitHub and the powerful GitHub API. Perhaps you feel constrained by using Git only from within a certain toolset; for example, if you are an Android developer using Git to manage your app source code and want to unlock Git in other places in your life as a developer, this book provides a wider vista to learn about the power of Git and GitHub. If you have fallen into using Git for your own projects and are now interested in using Git within a larger community, this book can teach you all about the "social coding" style pioneered and dogfooded by the GitHub team. This book provides a stepping stone for software developers who have used other distributed version control systems and are looking for a bridge to using their skills with Git and within a web service like GitHub.

Like any seasoned developer, automation of your tools is important to you. This book provides examples of mundane tasks converted into automated and repeatable processes. We show how to do this using a variety of languages talking to the GitHub API.

To make this book accessible to everyone, regardless of their editor or operating system, many of the programming samples work within the command line. If you are unfamiliar with the "command line" this book will give you a firm understanding of how to use it, and we bet you will find great power there. If you have hated the command line since your father forced you to use it when you were five, this is the perfect book to rekindle a loving relationship with the bash shell.

If you absorb not only the technical facets of using GitHub but also pay attention to the cultural and ideological changes offered behind the tools, you'll very likely see a new way of working in the modern age. We focus on these "meta" viewpoints as we discuss the tools themselves to help you see these extra opportunities.

Almost every chapter has an associated repository hosted on GitHub where you can review the code discussed. Fork away and take these samples into your own projects and tools!

Finally, we help you write testable API-backed code. Even the most experienced developers often find that writing tests for their code is a challenge, despite the massive body of literature connecting quality code with tests. Testing can be especially challenging when you are testing something backed by an API; it requires a different level of thinking than is found in strict unit testing. To help you get past this roadblock, whenever possible, this book shows you how to write code that interacts with the GitHub API and is testable.

GitHub "First Class" Languages

There are two languages that are so fundamentally linked to GitHub that you do need to install and use them in order to get the most out of this book.

Ruby
> A simple, readable programming language the founders of GitHub used extensively early in the life of the company.

JavaScript
> The only ubiquitous browser-side programming language; its importance has grown to new heights with the introduction of NodeJS, rivaling even the popularity of Ruby on Rails as a server-side toolkit for web applications, especially for independent developers.

Undoubtedly, many of you picking up this book already have familiarity with Ruby or JavaScript/NodeJS. So, the basics and installation of them are in appendices in the back of the book. The appendices don't cover syntax of these languages; we expect you have experience with other languages as a prerequisite and can read code from any imperative language regardless of the syntax. Later chapters discuss facets of the API and go into language details at times, but the code is readable regardless of your familiarity with that particular language. These explanatory appendices discuss the history of these tools within the GitHub story as well as important usage notes like special files and installation options.

Your time will not be wasted if you install and play with these two tools. Between them you will have a solid toolset to begin exploration of the GitHub API. Several chapters in this book use Ruby or JavaScript, so putting in some time to learn at least a little bit will make the journey through this book richer for you.

Operating System Prerequisites

We, the authors, wrote this book using MacBook Pros. MacBooks have a ubiquitous shell ("BASH") that works almost identically to the one found on any Linux machine. If you use either of these two operating systems, you will be able to run the code from any chapter.

If you use a Windows machine (or an OS that does not include the BASH shell) then some of the commands and code examples may not work without installing additional software.

An easy remedy is to use VirtualBox and Vagrant. VirtualBox is a freely available virtualization system for x86 hardware. Vagrant is a tool for managing development environments: using VirtualBox and Vagrant you can quickly install a Linux virtual machine. To do this, visit the downloads page for VirtualBox (*https://www.virtual box.org/wiki/Downloads*) and Vagrant (*https://www.vagrantup.com/downloads.html*). Once you have installed these two tools, you can then install an Ubuntu Linux virtual machine with these two commands:

```
$ vagrant init hashicorp/precise32
$ vagrant up
```

Who This Book Is Not For

If you are looking for a discussion of the GitHub API that focuses on a single language, you should know that we look at the API through many different languages. We do this to describe the API from not only the way the GitHub team designed it to work, but the aspirational way that client library authors made it work within diverse programming languages and communities. We think there is a lot to learn from this approach, but if you are interested in only a specific language and how it works with the GitHub API, this is not the book for you.

This book strives to prove that API-driven code is testable and that there is a benefit to doing so. This book does not intend to provide a manual on how to write perfectly tested code. We cover too many languages to end the healthy debates happening within each community about the right test frameworks. Instead, given our contention that most software projects have zero test coverage, this book tries to help you get past this significant roadblock. There is something transformational about writing tests if you have never done so before. Having these examples in hand, we hope, will allow you to transition to writing testable code for APIs, especially if you have not done so before. Some of the associated repositories have much greater test suites than are documented in this book, but we don't cover all the entire set of edge cases in every situation.

Conventions Used in This Book

The following typographical conventions are used in this book:

Italic
> Indicates new terms, URLs, email addresses, filenames, and file extensions.

`Constant width`
> Used for program listings, as well as within paragraphs to refer to program elements such as variable or function names, databases, data types, environment variables, statements, and keywords.

`Constant width italic`
> Shows text that should be replaced with user-supplied values or by values determined by context.

This icon signifies a general note.

This icon indicates a warning or caution.

Using Code Examples

Supplemental material (code examples, exercises, etc.) is available for download at *https://github.com/xrd/building-tools-with-github*.

This book is here to help you get your job done. In general, if example code is offered with this book, you may use it in your programs and documentation. You do not need to contact us for permission unless you're reproducing a significant portion of the code. For example, writing a program that uses several chunks of code from this book does not require permission. Selling or distributing a CD-ROM of examples from O'Reilly books does require permission. Answering a question by citing this book and quoting example code does not require permission. Incorporating a significant amount of example code from this book into your product's documentation does require permission.

We appreciate, but do not require, attribution. An attribution usually includes the title, author, publisher, and ISBN. For example: "*Building Tools with GitHub* by Chris Dawson and Ben Straub (O'Reilly). Copyright 2016 Chris Dawson and Ben Straub, 978-1-491-93350-3."

If you feel your use of code examples falls outside fair use or the permission given above, feel free to contact us at *permissions@oreilly.com*.

O'Reilly Safari

 *Safari* (formerly Safari Books Online) is a membership-based training and reference platform for enterprise, government, educators, and individuals.

Members have access to thousands of books, training videos, Learning Paths, interactive tutorials, and curated playlists from over 250 publishers, including O'Reilly Media, Harvard Business Review, Prentice Hall Professional, Addison-Wesley Professional, Microsoft Press, Sams, Que, Peachpit Press, Adobe, Focal Press, Cisco Press, John Wiley & Sons, Syngress, Morgan Kaufmann, IBM Redbooks, Packt, Adobe Press, FT Press, Apress, Manning, New Riders, McGraw-Hill, Jones & Bartlett, and Course Technology, among others.

For more information, please visit *http://oreilly.com/safari*.

How to Contact Us

Please address comments and questions concerning this book to the publisher:

O'Reilly Media, Inc.
1005 Gravenstein Highway North
Sebastopol, CA 95472
800-998-9938 (in the United States or Canada)
707-829-0515 (international or local)
707-829-0104 (fax)

We have a web page for this book, where we list errata, examples, and any additional information. You can access this page at *http://bit.ly/building-tools-with-github*.

To comment or ask technical questions about this book, send email to *bookquestions@oreilly.com*.

For more information about our books, courses, conferences, and news, see our website at *http://www.oreilly.com*.

Find us on Facebook: *http://facebook.com/oreilly*

Follow us on Twitter: *http://twitter.com/oreillymedia*

Watch us on YouTube: *http://www.youtube.com/oreillymedia*

Acknowledgments

Chris wants to thank his lovely wife, Nicole. I hope that I have added to this book even a tiny bit of the wit and wisdom you provide to me and our family every day. My son Roosevelt's energy continues to inspire me and keep me going even when I am at my limits. To my daughter Charlotte, you are my little smiling Buddha. To my mother, who showed me how to write and, most importantly, why to write, which is something we need more of in the technology world. To Tim O'Brien who invited me into this project, thank you, and I hope we can collaborate again. To Bradley Horowitz, who demonstrates how small acts of kindness can have immeasurable impact. And, to David J. Groom, though we have never met face to face, your suggestions and excitement about the book early on came at a critical moment in the life of this book, and I thank you for channeling the excitement I hoped to cultivate with people who would one day pick up this book.

Ben would like to thank his wife, Becky, for her ongoing support and (when needed) push from behind. None of this would have happened without you.

CHAPTER 1

The Unclad GitHub API

This chapter eases us into reading and writing data from the GitHub API. Successive chapters show you how to access information from the GitHub API using a variety of client libraries. These client libraries, by design, hide the nuts and bolts of the API from you, providing streamlined and idiomatic methods to view and modify data inside a Git repository hosted on GitHub. This chapter, however, gives you a naked viewpoint of the GitHub API and documents the details of the raw HTTP requests and responses. It also discusses the different ways to access public and private data inside of GitHub and where limitations exist. And it gives you an overview of the options for accessing GitHub data when running inside a web browser context where network access is restrained.

cURL

There will be times when you want to quickly access information from the GitHub API without writing a formal program. Or, when you want to quickly get access to the raw HTTP request headers and content. Or, where you might even question the implementation of a client library and need confirmation it is doing the right thing from another vantage point. In these situations, cURL, a simple command-line HTTP tool, is the perfect fit. cURL, like the best Unix tools, is a small program with a very specific and purposefully limited set of features for accessing HTTP servers.

cURL, like the HTTP protocol it speaks intimately, is stateless: we will explore solutions to this limitation in a later chapter, but note that cURL works best with one-off requests.

Installing cURL

cURL is usually installed on most OS X machines, and can easily be installed using Linux package managers (probably one of `apt-get install curl` or `yum install curl`). If you are using Windows or want to manually install it, go to *http://curl.haxx.se/download.html*.

Let's make a request. We'll start with the most basic GitHub API endpoint found at *https://api.github.com*:

```
$ curl https://api.github.com
{
    "current_user_url": "https://api.github.com/user",
    "current_user_authorizations_html_url":
    "https://github.com/settings/connections/applications{/client_id}",
    "authorizations_url": "https://api.github.com/authorizations",
    "code_search_url":
    "https://api.github.com/search/code?q={query}{&page,per_page,sort,order}",
    "emails_url": "https://api.github.com/user/emails",
    "emojis_url": "https://api.github.com/emojis",
    ...
}
```

We've abbreviated the response to make it more readable. A few salient things to notice: there are a lot of URLs pointing to secondary information, parameters are included in the URLs, and the response format is JSON.

What can we learn from this API response?

Breadcrumbs to Successive API Paths

The GitHub API is a hypermedia API. Though a discussion on what constitutes hypermedia deserves an entire book of its own (check out O'Reilly's *Building Hypermedia APIs with HTML5 and Node*), you can absorb much of what makes hypermedia interesting by just looking at a response. First, you can see from the API response that each response contains a map with directions for the next responses you might make. Not all clients use this information, of course, but one goal behind hypermedia APIs is that clients can dynamically adjust their endpoints without recoding the client code. If the thought of GitHub changing an API because clients *should* be written to handle new endpoints automatically sounds worrisome, don't fret too much: GitHub is very dilligent about maintaining and supporting its API in a way that most companies would do well to emulate. But you should know that you can rely on having an API reference inside the API itself, rather than hosted externally in documentation, which very easily could turn out to be out of date with the API itself.

These API maps are rich with data. For example, they are not just URLs to content, but also information about how to provide parameters to the URLs. Looking at the previous example, the `code_search_url` key references a URL that obviously allows you to search within code on GitHub, but also tells you how to structure the parameters passed to this URL. If you have an intelligent client who can follow this programmatic format, you could dynamically generate the query without involving a developer who can read API documentation. At least that is the dream hypermedia points us to; if you are skeptical, at least know that APIs such as GitHub encode documentation into themselves, and you can bet GitHub has test coverage to prove that this documentation matches the information delivered by the API endpoints. That's a strong guarantee that is sadly missing from many other APIs.

Now let's briefly discuss the format of all GitHub API responses: JSON.

The JavaScript Object Notation (JSON) Format

Every response you get back from the GitHub API will be in the JSON (JavaScript Object Notation) format. JSON is a "lightweight data interchange format" (read more on the JSON.org website (*http://www.json.org/*)). There are other competing and effective formats, such as XML (Extensible Markup Language) or YAML (YAML Ain't Markup Language), but JSON is quickly becoming the de facto standard for web services.

A few of the reasons JSON is so popular:

- JSON is readable. JSON has a nice balance of human readability when compared to serialization formats like XML.
- JSON can be used within JavaScript with very little modification (and cognitive processing on the part of the programmer). A data format that works equally well on both the client and server side was bound to be victorious, as JSON has been.

You might expect that a site like GitHub, originally built on the Ruby on Rails stack (and some of that code is still live), would support specifying an alternative format like XML, but XML is no longer supported. Long live JSON.

JSON is very straightforward if you have used any other text-based interchange format. One note about JSON that is not always obvious or expected to people new to JSON is that the format only supports using double quotes, not single quotes.

We are using a command-line tool, cURL, to retrieve data from the API. It would be handy to have a simple command-line tool that also processes that JSON. Let's talk about one such tool next.

Parsing JSON from the Command Line

JSON is a text format, so you could use any command-line text processing tool, such as the venerable AWK, to process JSON responses. There is one fantastic JSON-specific parsing tool that complements cURL that is worth knowing: *jq*. If you pipe JSON content (using the | character for most shells) into jq, you can then easily extract pieces of the JSON using *filters*.

 Installing jq

jq can be installed from source, using package managers like brew or apt-get, and there are binaries on the downloads page (*http:// stedolan.github.io/jq/download/*) for OS X, Linux, Windows, and Solaris.

Going deeper into the prior example, let's pull out something interesting from the API map that we receive when we access *api.github.com*:

```
$ curl https://api.github.com | jq '.current_user_url'
  % Total    % Received % Xferd  Average Speed   Time    Time     Time  Current
                                 Dload  Upload   Total   Spent    Left  Speed
100  2004  100  2004    0     0   4496      0 --:--:-- --:--:-- --:--:--  4493
"https://api.github.com/user"
```

What just happened? The jq tool parsed the JSON, and using the .current_user_url filter, it retrieved content from the JSON response. If you look at the response again, you'll notice it has key/value pairs inside an associative array. It uses the current_user_url as a key into that associative array and prints out the value there.

You also will notice that cURL printed out transfer time information. cURL printed this information to *standard error*, which is a shell convention used for messaging errors and an output stream that jq will correctly ignore (in other words, the JSON format stream will not be corrupted by error messages). If we want to restrict that information and clean up the request we should use the -s switch, which runs cURL in "silent" mode.

It should be easy to understand how the jq filter is applied to the response JSON. For a more complicated request (for example, we might want to obtain a list of public repositories for a user), we can see the pattern for the jq pattern parameter emerging. Let's get a more complicated set of information, a user's list of repositories, and see how we can extract information from the response using jq:

```
$ curl -s https://api.github.com/users/xrd/repos
[
  {
    "id": 19551182,
    "name": "a-gollum-test",
    "full_name": "xrd/a-gollum-test",
    "owner": {
      "login": "xrd",
      "id": 17064,
      "avatar_url":
```

```
            "https://avatars.githubusercontent.com/u/17064?v=3",
        ...
    }
]
$ curl -s https://api.github.com/users/xrd/repos | jq '.[0].owner.id'
17064
```

This response is different structurally: instead of an associative array, we now have an array (multiple items). To get the first one, we specify a numeric index, and then key into the successive associative arrays inside of it to reach the desired content: the owner id.

jq is a great tool for checking the validity of JSON. As mentioned before, JSON key/values are stored only with double quotes, not single quotes. You can verify that JSON is valid and satisfies this requirement using jq:

```
$ echo '{ "a" : "b" }' | jq '.'
{
  "a": "b"
}
$ echo "{ 'no' : 'bueno' }" | jq "."
parse error: Invalid numeric literal at line 1, column 7
```

The first JSON we pass into jq works, while the second, because it uses invalid single-quote characters, fails with an error. jq filters are strings passed as arguments, and the shell that provides the string to jq does not care if you use single quotes or double quotes, as you can see in the preceding code. The echo command, if you didn't already know, prints out whatever string you provide to it; when we combine this with the pipe character we can easily provide that string to jq through standard input.

jq is a powerful tool for quickly retrieving content from an arbitray JSON request. jq has many other powerful features, documented at *https://stedolan.github.io/jq/*.

We now know how to retrieve some interesting information from the GitHub API and parse out bits of information from that response, all in a single line. But there will be times when you incorrectly specify parameters to cURL or the API, and the data is not what you expect. Now we'll learn about how to debug the cURL tool and the API service itself to provide more context when things go wrong.

Debugging Switches for cURL

As mentioned, cURL is a great tool when you are verifying that a response is what you expect it to be. The response body is important, but often you'll want access to the headers as well. cURL makes getting these easy with the -i and -v switches. The -i switch prints out request headers, and the -v switch prints out both request and response headers (the > character indicates request data, and the < character indicates response data):

```
$ curl -i https://api.github.com
HTTP/1.1 200 OK
Server: GitHub.com
Date: Wed, 03 Jun 2015 19:39:03 GMT
Content-Type: application/json; charset=utf-8
Content-Length: 2004
Status: 200 OK
X-RateLimit-Limit: 60
...
{
  "current_user_url": "https://api.github.com/user",
  ...
}
$ curl -v https://api.github.com
* Rebuilt URL to: https://api.github.com/
* Hostname was NOT found in DNS cache
*   Trying 192.30.252.137...
* Connected to api.github.com (192.30.252.137) port 443 (#0)
* successfully set certificate verify locations:
*   CAfile: none
  CApath: /etc/ssl/certs
* SSLv3, TLS handshake, Client hello (1):
* SSLv3, TLS handshake, Server hello (2):
...
* CN=DigiCert SHA2 High Assurance Server CA
*       SSL certificate verify ok.
> GET / HTTP/1.1
> User-Agent: curl/7.35.0
> Host: api.github.com
> Accept: */*
>
< HTTP/1.1 200 OK
* Server GitHub.com is not blacklisted
...
```

With the -v switch you get everything: DNS lookups, information on the SSL chain, and the full request and response information.

 Be aware that if you print out headers, a tool like jq will get confused because you are no longer providing it with pure JSON.

This section shows us that there is interesting information not only in the body (the JSON data) but also in the headers. It is important to understand what headers are here and which ones are important. The HTTP specification requires a lot of these headers, and we can often ignore those, but there are a few that are vital when you start making more than just a few isolated requests.

Important Headers

Three headers are present in every GitHub API response that tell you about the GitHub API rate limits. They are X-RateLimit-Limit, X-RateLimit-Remaining, and X-RateLimit-Reset. These limits are explained in detail in "GitHub API Rate Limits" on page 14.

The X-GitHub-Media-Type header contains information that will come in handy when you are starting to retrieve text or blob content from the API. When you make a request to the GitHub API you can specify the format you want to work with by sending an Accept header with your request.

Now, let's use a response to build another response.

Following a Hypermedia API

We'll use the "map" of the API by hitting the base endpoint, and then use the response to manually generate another request:

```
$ curl -i https://api.github.com/
HTTP/1.1 200 OK
Server: GitHub.com
Date: Sat, 25 Apr 2015 05:36:16 GMT
...
{
  "current_user_url": "https://api.github.com/user",
  ...
  "organization_url": "https://api.github.com/orgs/{org}",
  ...
}
```

We can use the organizational URL and substitute "github" in the placeholder:

```
$ curl https://api.github.com/orgs/github
{
  "login": "github",
  "id": 9919,
  "url": "https://api.github.com/orgs/github",
  ...
  "description": "GitHub, the company.",
  "name": "GitHub",
  "company": null,
  "blog": "https://github.com/about",
  "location": "San Francisco, CA",
  "email": "support@github.com",
  ...
  "created_at": "2008-05-11T04:37:31Z",
  "updated_at": "2015-04-25T05:17:01Z",
  "type": "Organization"
}
```

This information allows us to do some forensics on GitHub itself. We get the company blog *https://github.com/about*. We see that GitHub is located in San Francisco, and we see that the creation date of the organization is May 11th, 2008. Reviewing the blog, we see a blog post from April (*https://github.com/blog/40-we-launched*) that indicates GitHub launched as a company a month earlier. Perhaps organizations were not added to the GitHub site features until a month after the company launched?

So far all of our requests have retrieved publicly available information. But the GitHub API has a much richer set of information that is available only once we authenticate and access private information and publicly inaccessible services. For example, if you are using the API to write data into GitHub, you need to know about authentication.

Authentication

There are two ways to authenticate when making a request to the GitHub API: username and passwords (HTTP Basic) and OAuth tokens.

Username and Password Authentication

You can access protected content inside GitHub using a username and password combination. Username authentication works by using the HTTP Basic authentication supported by the -u flag in cURL. HTTP Basic Authentication is synonymous with username and password authentication:

```
$ curl -u xrd https://api.github.com/rate_limit
Enter host password for user 'xrd': xxxxxxxx
{
  "rate": {
    "limit": 5000,
    "remaining": 4995,
    "reset": 1376251941
  }
}
```

This cURL command authenticates into the GitHub API and then retrieves information about our own specific rate limits for our user account, protected information only available as a logged-in user.

Benefits of username authentication

Almost any client library you use will support HTTP Basic authentication. All the GitHub API clients we looked at support username and passwords. And, writing your own specific client is easy as this is a core feature of the HTTP standard, so if you use any standard HTTP library when building your own client, you will be able to access content inside the GitHub API.

Downsides to username authentication

There are many reasons username and password authentication is the wrong way to manage your GitHub API access:

- HTTP Basic is an old protocol that never anticipated the granularity of web services. It is not possible to specify only certain features of a web service if you ask users to authenticate with username/passwords.

- If you use a username and password to access GitHub API content from your cell phone, and then access API content from your laptop, you have no way to block access to one without blocking the other.

- HTTP Basic authentication does not support extensions to the authentication flow. Many modern services now support two-factor authentication and there is no way to inject this into the process without changing the HTTP clients (web browsers, for example) or at least the flow they expect (making the browser repeat the request).

All of these problems are solved (or at least supported) with OAuth flows. Given all these concerns, the only time you will want to use username and password authentication is when convenience trumps all other considerations.

OAuth

OAuth is an authentication mechanism where tokens are tied to functionality or clients. In other words, you can specify what features of a service you want to permit an OAuth token to carry with it, and you can issue multiple tokens and tie those to specific clients: a cell phone app, a laptop, a smart watch, or even an Internet of Things toaster. And, importantly, you can revoke tokens without impacting other tokens.

The main downside to OAuth tokens is that they introduce a level of complexity that you may not be familiar with if you have only used HTTP Basic. HTTP Basic requests generally only require adding an extra header to the HTTP request, or an extra flag to a client tool like cURL.

OAuth solves the problems just described by linking tokens to scopes (specified subsets of functionality inside a web service) and issuing as many tokens as you need to multiple clients.

Scopes: specified actions tied to authentication tokens

When you generate an OAuth token, you specify the access rights you require. Though our examples create the token using HTTP Basic, once you have the token, you no longer need to use HTTP Basic in successive requests. If this token is properly issued, the OAuth token will have permissions to read and write to public repositories owned by that user.

The following cURL command uses HTTP Basic to initiate the token request process:

```
$ curl -u username -d '{"scopes":["public_repo"], "note": "A new authorization"}' \
https://api.github.com/authorizations
{
  "id": 1234567,
  "url": "https://api.github.com/authorizations/1234567",
  "app": {
    "name": "My app",
    "url": "https://developer.github.com/v3/oauth_authorizations/",
    "client_id": "00000000000000000000"
  },
  "token": "abcdef87654321
  ...
}
```

The JSON response, upon success, has a token you can extract and use for applications that need access to the GitHub API.

If you are using two-factor authentication, this flow requires additional steps, all of which are documented within Chapter 8.

To use this token, you specify the token inside an authorization header:

```
$ curl -H "Authorization: token abcdef87654321" ...
```

Scopes clarify how a service or application will use data inside the GitHub API. This makes it easy to audit how you are using the information if this was a token issued for your own personal use. But, most importantly, this provides valuable clarity and protection for those times when a third-party application wants to access your information: you can be assured the application is limited in what data it can access, and you can revoke access easily.

Scope limitations

There is one major limitation of scopes to be aware of: you cannot do fine-grained access to certain repositories only. If you provide access to any of your private repositories, you are providing access to all repositories.

It is likely that GitHub will change the way scopes work and address some of these issues. The great thing about the way OAuth works is that to support these changes you will simply need to request a new token with the scope modified, but otherwise, the application authentication flow will be unchaged.

Be very careful about the scopes you request when building a service or application. Users are (rightly) paranoid about the data they are handing over to you, and will evaluate your application based on the scopes requested. If they don't think you need that scope, be sure to remove it from the list you provide to GitHub when authorizing and consider escalation to a higher scope after you have developed some trust with your users.

Scope escalation

You can ask for scope at one point that is very limited, and then later ask for a greater scope. For example, when a user first accesses your application, you could only get the user scope to create a user object inside your service, and only when your application needs repository information for a user, then request to escalate privileges. At this point the user will need to approve or disapprove your request, but asking for everything upfront (before you have a relationship with the user) often results in a user abandoning the login.

Now let's get into the specifics of authentication using OAuth.

Simplified OAuth flow

OAuth has many variants, but GitHub uses OAuth2. OAuth2 specifies a flow where:

1. The application requests access
2. The service provider (GitHub) requests authentication: username and password usually
3. If two-factor authentication is enabled, ask for the OTP (one-time password) code
4. GitHub responds with a token inside a JSON payload
5. The application uses the OAuth token to make requests of the API

A real-world flow is described in full in Chapter 8.

Now let's look at the variety of HTTP status codes GitHub uses to communicate feedback when using the API.

Status Codes

The GitHub API uses HTTP status codes to tell you definitive information about how your request was processed. If you are using a basic client like cURL, it will be important to validate the status code before you look at any of the data retrieved. If you are writing your own API client, pay close attention to the status code before anything else. If you are new to the GitHub API, it is worth reviewing the response codes thoroughly until you are familiar with the various conditions that can cause errors when making a request.

Success (200 or 201)

If you have worked with any HTTP clients whatsoever, you know that the HTTP status code "200" means success. GitHub will respond with a 200 status code when your request destination URL and associated parameters are correct. If your request creates content on the server, then you will get a 201 status code, indicating successful creation on the server.

```
$ curl -s -i https://api.github.com | grep Status
Status: 200 OK
```

Naughty JSON (400)

If your payload (the JSON you send to a request) is invalid, the GitHub API will respond with a 400 error, as shown here:

```
$ curl -i -u xrd -d 'yaml: true' -X POST https://api.github.com/gists
Enter host password for user 'xrd':
HTTP/1.1 400 Bad Request
Server: GitHub.com
Date: Thu, 04 Jun 2015 20:33:49 GMT
Content-Type: application/json; charset=utf-8
Content-Length: 148
Status: 400 Bad Request
...

{
  "message": "Problems parsing JSON",
  "documentation_url":
  "https://developer.github.com/v3/oauth_authorizations/#create...authorization"
}
```

Here we attempt to generate a new gist by using the endpoint described at the Gist API documentation (*https://developer.github.com/v3/gists/#create-a-gist*). We'll discuss gists in more detail in a later chapter. This issue fails because we are not using JSON (this looks like it could be YAML, which we will discuss in Chapter 6). The payload is sent using the -d switch. GitHub responds with advice on where to find the documentation for the correct format at the documentation_url key inside the JSON response. Notice that we use the -X POST switch and value to tell cURL to make a POST request to GitHub.

Improper JSON (422)

If any of the fields in your request are invalid, GitHub will respond with a 422 error. Let's attempt to fix the previous request. The documentation indicates the JSON payload should look like this:

```
{
  "description": "the description for this gist",
  "public": true,
  "files": {
    "file1.txt": {
      "content": "String file contents"
    }
  }
}
```

What happens if the JSON is valid, but the fields are incorrect?

```
$ curl -i -u chris@burningon.com -d '{ "a" : "b" }' -X POST
https://api.github.com/gists
Enter host password for user 'chris@burningon.com':
HTTP/1.1 422 Unprocessable Entity
...

{
  "message": "Invalid request.\n\n\"files\" wasn't supplied.",
  "documentation_url": "https://developer.github.com/v3"
}
```

There are two important things to note: first, we get a 422 error, which indicates the JSON was valid, but the fields were incorrect. We also get a response that indicates why: we are missing the `files` key inside the request payload.

Successful Creation (201)

We've seen what happens when the JSON is invalid, but what happens when the JSON is valid for our request?

```
$ curl -i -u xrd \
-d '{"description":"A","public":true,"files":{"a.txt":{"content":"B"}}} \
https://api.github.com/gists
Enter host password for user 'xrd':
HTTP/1.1 201 Created
...

{
  "url": "https://api.github.com/gists/4a86ed1ca6f289d0f6a4",
  "forks_url":
  "https://api.github.com/gists/4a86ed1ca6f289d0f6a4/forks",
  "commits_url":
  "https://api.github.com/gists/4a86ed1ca6f289d0f6a4/commits",
  "id": "4a86ed1ca6f289d0f6a4",
```

```
    "git_pull_url": "https://gist.github.com/4a86ed1ca6f289d0f6a4.git",
    ...
}
```

Success! We created a gist and got a 201 status code indicating things worked properly. To make our command more readable we used the backslash character to allow parameters to span across lines. Also, notice the JSON does not require whitespace, which we have completely removed from the string passed to the -d switch (in order to save space and make this command a little bit more readable).

Nothing Has Changed (304)

304s are like 200s in that they say to the client: yes, your request succeeded. They give a little bit of extra information, however, in that they tell the client that the data has not changed since the last time the same request was made. This is valuable information if you are concerned about your usage limits (and in most cases you will be). We have not yet explained how rate limits work, so let's discuss that and then return to demonstrate triggering a 304 response code by using conditional headers.

GitHub API Rate Limits

GitHub tries to limit the rate at which users can make requests to the API. Anonymous requests (requests that haven't authenticated with either a username/password or OAuth information) are limited to 60 requests an hour. If you are developing a system to integrate with the GitHub API on behalf of users, clearly 60 requests per hour isn't going to be sufficient.

This rate limit is increased to 5000 requests per hour if you are making an authenticated request to the GitHub API, and while this rate is two orders of magnitude larger than the anonymous rate limit, it still presents problems if you intend to use your own GitHub credentials when making requests on behalf of many users.

For this reason, if your website or service uses the GitHub API to request information from the GitHub API, you should consider using OAuth and make requests to the GitHub API using your user's shared authentication information. If you use a token connected to another user's GitHub account, the rate limits count against that user, and not your user account.

 There are actually two rate limits: the *core* rate limit and the *search* rate limit. The rate limits explained in the previous paragraphs were for the core rate limit. For search, requests are limited to 20 requests per minute for authenticated user requests and 5 requests per minute for anonymous requests. The assumption here is that search is a more infrastructure-intensive request to satisfy and that tighter limits are placed on its usage.

Note that GitHub tracks anonymous requests by IP address. This means that if you are behind a firewall with other users making anonymous requests, all those requests will be grouped together.

Reading Your Rate Limits

Reading your rate limit is straightforward—just make a GET request to `/rate_limit`. This will return a JSON document that tells you the limit you are subject to, the number of requests you have remaining, and the timestamp (in seconds since 1970). Note that this timestamp is in the Coordinated Universal Time (UTC) time zone.

The following command listing uses cURL to retrieve the rate limit for an anonymous request. This response is abbreviated to save space in this book, but you'll notice that the quota information is supplied twice: once in the HTTP response headers and again in the JSON response. The rate limit headers are returned with every request to the GitHub API, so there is little need to make a direct call to the /rate_limit API:

```
$ curl https://api.github.com/rate_limit
{
  "resources": {
    "core": {
      "limit": 60,
      "remaining": 48,
      "reset": 1433398160
    },
    "search": {
      "limit": 10,
      "remaining": 10,
      "reset": 1433395543
    }
  },
  "rate": {
    "limit": 60,
    "remaining": 48,
    "reset": 1433398160
  }
}
```

Sixty requests over the course of an hour isn't very much, and if you plan on doing anything interesting, you will likely exceed this limit quickly. If you are hitting up against the 60 requests per minute limit, you will likely want to investigate making authenticated requests to the GitHub API. We'll show that when we discuss authenticated requests.

Calls to the /rate_limit API are not deducted from your rate limits. And, remember, rate limits are reset after 24 hours.

Conditional Requests to Avoid Rate Limitations

If you are querying the GitHub APIs to obtain activity data for a user or a repository, there's a good chance that many of your requests won't return much activity. If you check for new activity once every few minutes, there will be time periods over which no activity has occurred. These constant polls still use up requests in your rate limit even though there's no new activity to be delivered.

In these cases, you can send the conditional HTTP headers If-Modified-Since and If-None-Match to tell GitHub to return an HTTP 304 response code telling you that nothing has been modified. When you send a request with a conditional header and the GitHub API responds with an HTTP 304 response code, this request is not deducted from your rate limit.

The following command listing is an example of passing in the If-Modified-Since HTTP header to the GitHub API. Here we've specified that we're only interested in receiving content if the Twitter Bootstrap repositories have been altered after 7:49 PM GMT on Sunday, August 11, 2013. The GitHub API responds with an HTTP 304 response code that also tells us that the last time this repository changed was a minute earlier than our cutoff date:

```
$ curl -i https://api.github.com/repos/twbs/bootstrap \
        -H "If-Modified-Since: Sun, 11 Aug 2013 19:48:59 GMT"
HTTP/1.1 304 Not Modified
Server: GitHub.com
Date: Sun, 11 Aug 2013 20:11:26 GMT
Status: 304 Not Modified
X-RateLimit-Limit: 60
X-RateLimit-Remaining: 46
X-RateLimit-Reset: 1376255215
Cache-Control: public, max-age=60, s-maxage=60
Last-Modified: Sun, 11 Aug 2013 19:48:39 GMT
```

The GitHub API also understands HTTP caching tags. An ETag, or Entity Tag, is an HTTP header that is used to control whether or not content you have previously cached is the most recent version. Here's how your systems would use an ETag:

- Your server requests information from an HTTP server.
- Server returns an ETag header for a version of a content item.
- Your server includes this ETag in all subsequent requests:
  - If the server has a newer version it returns new content + a new ETag.
  - If the server doesn't have a newer version it returns an HTTP 304.

The following command listing demonstrates two commands. The first cURL call to the GitHub API generates an ETag value, and the second value passes this ETag value as an `If-None-Match` header. You'll note that the second response is an HTTP 304, which tells the caller that there is no new content available:

```
$ curl -i https://api.github.com/repos/twbs/bootstrap
HTTP/1.1 200 OK
Cache-Control: public, max-age=60, s-maxage=60
Last-Modified: Sun, 11 Aug 2013 20:25:37 GMT
ETag: "462c74009317cf64560b8e395b9d0cdd"

{
  "id": 2126244,
  "name": "bootstrap",
  "full_name": "twbs/bootstrap",
  ....
}

$ curl -i https://api.github.com/repos/twbs/bootstrap \
        -H 'If-None-Match: "462c74009317cf64560b8e395b9d0cdd"'

HTTP/1.1 304 Not Modified
Status: 304 Not Modified
Cache-Control: public, max-age=60, s-maxage=60
Last-Modified: Sun, 11 Aug 2013 20:25:37 GMT
ETag: "462c74009317cf64560b8e395b9d0cdd"
```

Use of conditional request headers is encouraged to conserve resources and make sure that the infrastructure that supports GitHub's API isn't asked to generate content unnecessarily.

At this point we have been accessing the GitHub API from a cURL client, and as long as our network permits it, we can do whatever we want. The GitHub API is accessible in other situations as well, like from within a browser context, and certain restrictions apply there, so let's discuss that next.

Accessing Content from the Web

If you are using the GitHub API from a server-side program or the command line then you are free to issue any network calls as long as your network permits it. If you are attempting to access the GitHub API from within a browser using JavaScript and the XHR (XmlHttpRequest) object, then you should be aware of limitations imposed by the browser's same-origin policy. In a nutshell, you are not able to access domains from JavaScript using standard XHR requests outside of the domain from which you retrieved the original page. There are two options for getting around this restriction, one clever (JSON-P) and one fully supported but slightly more onerous (CORS).

JSON-P

JSON-P is a browser hack, more or less, that allows retrieval of information from servers outside of the same-origin policy. JSON-P works because `<script>` tags are not checked against the same-origin policy; in other words, your page can include references to content on servers other than the one from which the page originated. With JSON-P, you load a JavaScript file that resolves to a specially encoded data payload wrapped in a callback function you implement. The GitHub API supports this syntax: you request a script with a parameter on the URL indicating what callback you want the script to execute once loaded.

We can simulate this request in cURL:

```
$ curl https://api.github.com/?callback=myCallback
/**/myCallback({
  "meta": {
    "X-RateLimit-Limit": "60",
    "X-RateLimit-Remaining": "52",
    "X-RateLimit-Reset": "1433461950",
    "Cache-Control": "public, max-age=60, s-maxage=60",
    "Vary": "Accept",
    "ETag": "\"a5c656a9399ccd6b44e2f9a4291c8289\"",
    "X-GitHub-Media-Type": "github.v3",
    "status": 200
  },
  "data": {
    "current_user_url": "https://api.github.com/user",
    "current_user_authorizations_html_url":
    "https://github.com/settings/connections/applications{/client_id}",
    "authorizations_url": "https://api.github.com/authorizations",
    ...
  }
})
```

If you used the same URL we used in the preceding code inside a script tag on a web page (`<script src="https://api.github.com/?callback=myCallback" type="text/javascript"></script>`), your browser would load the content displayed in the preceding code, and then a JavaScript function you defined called `myCallback` would be executed with the data shown. This function could be implemented like this inside your web page:

```
<script>
function myCallback( payload ) {
  if( 200 == payload.status ) {
    document.getElementById("success").innerHTML =
      payload.data.current_user_url;
  } else {
    document.getElementById("error").innerHTML =
      "An error occurred";
  }
```

```
    }
    </script>
```

This example demonstrates taking the `current_user_url` from the data inside the payload and putting it into a DIV, one that might look like `<div id="success">` `</div>`.

Because JSON-P works via `<script>` tags, only GET requests to the API are supported. If you only need read-only access to the API, JSON-P can fulfill that need in many cases, and it is easy to configure.

If JSON-P seems too limiting or hackish, CORS is a more complicated but official way to access external services from within a web page.

CORS Support

CORS is the W3C (a web standards body) approved way to access content from a different domain than the original host. CORS requires that the server be properly configured in advance; the server must indicate when queried that it allows cross-domain requests. If the server effectively says "yes, you can access my content from a different domain," then CORS requests are permitted. The HTML5Rocks website has a great tutorial explaining many details of CORS (*http://www.html5rocks.com/en/tutorials/ cors/*).

Because XHR using CORS allows the same type of XHR requests you get from the same domain origin, you can make requests beyond GET to the GitHub API: POST, DELETE, and UPDATE. Between JSON-P and CORS you have two options for accessing content from the GitHub API inside of web browsers. The choice is between the simplicity of JSON-P and the power and extra configuration of CORS.

We can prove using cURL that the GitHub API server is responding correctly for CORS requests. In this case we only care about the headers, so we use the `-I` switch, which tells cURL to make a HEAD request, telling the server not to respond with body content:

```
curl -I https://api.github.com
HTTP/1.1 200 OK
Server: GitHub.com
...
X-Frame-Options: deny
Content-Security-Policy: default-src 'none'
Access-Control-Allow-Credentials: true
Access-Control-Expose-Headers: ETag, Link, X-GitHub-OTP,
X-RateLimit-Limit, X-RateLimit-Remaining, X-RateLimit-Reset,
X-OAuth-Scopes, X-Accepted-OAuth-Scopes, X-Poll-Interval
Access-Control-Allow-Origin: *
X-GitHub-Request-Id: C0F1CF9E:07AD:3C493B:557107C7
Strict-Transport-Security: max-age=31536000; includeSubdomains;
preload
```

We can see the `Access-Control-Allow-Credentials` header is set to true. It depends on the browser implementation, but some JavaScript host browsers will automatically make a *preflight* request to verify this header is set to true (and that other headers, like the `Access-Control-Allow-Origin`, are set correctly and permit requests from that origin to proceed). Other JavaScript host browsers will need you to make that request. Once the browser has used the headers to confirm that CORS is permitted, you can make XHR requests to the GitHub API domain as you would any other XHR request going into the same domain.

We've covered much of the details of connecting and dissecting the GitHub API, but there are a few other options to know about when using it. One of them is that you can use the GitHub API service to provide rendered content when you need it.

Specifying Response Content Format

When you send a request to the GitHub API, you have some ability to specify the format of the response you expect. For example, if you are requesting content that contains text from a commit's comment thread, you can use the `Accept` header to ask for the raw Markdown or for the HTML this Markdown generates. You also have the ability to specify this version of the GitHub API you are using. At this point, you can specify either version 3 or beta of the API.

Retrieving formatted content

The `Accept` header you send with a request can affect the format of text returned by the GitHub API. As an example, let's assume you wanted to read the body of a GitHub Issue. An issue's body is stored in Markdown and will be sent back in the request by default. If we wanted to render the response as HTML instead of Markdown, we could do this by sending a different `Accept` header, as the following cURL commands demonstrate:

```
$ URL='https://api.github.com/repos/rails/rails/issues/11819'
$ curl -s $URL | jq '.body'
"Hi, \r\n\r\nI have a problem with strong...." ❶
$ curl -s $URL | jq '.body_html'
null ❷
$ curl -s $URL \
-H "Accept: application/vnd.github.html+json" | jq '.body_html'
"<p>Hi, </p>\n\n<p>I have a problem with..." ❸
```

❶ Without specifying an extra header, we get the internal representation of the data, sent as Markdown.

❷ Note that if we don't request the HTML representation, we don't see it in the JSON by default.

❸ If we use a customized `Accept` header like in the third instance, then our JSON is populated with a rendered version of the body in HTML.

Besides "raw" and "html" there are two other format options that influence how Markdown content is delivered via the GitHub API. If you specify "text" as a format, the issue body would have been returned as plaintext. If you specify "full" then the content will be rendered multiple times including the raw Markdown, rendered HTML, and rendered plaintext.

In addition to controlling the format of text content, you can also retrieve GitHub blobs either as raw binary or as a BASE64-encoded text. When retrieving commits, you can also specify that the content be returned either as a diff or as a patch. For more information about these fine-grained controls for formatting, see the GitHub API documentation.

 The GitHub team has already provided very thorough documentation on their API with examples using cURL. Bookmark this URL: *https://developer.github.com/v3/*. You'll use it often. Do note that this URL is tied, obviously, to the current API "version 3," so this URL will change when a new version is released.

Summary

In this chapter we learned how to access the GitHub API from the simplest client available: the command-line cURL HTTP tool. We also explored the API by looking at the JSON and played with a command-line tool (jq) that when paired with cURL gives us the ability to quickly find information in the often large body of data the GitHub API provides. We learned about the different authentication schemes supported by GitHub, and also learned about the possibilities and trade-offs when accessing the GitHub API from within a browser context.

In the next chapter we will look at gists and the Gist API. We'll use Ruby to build a gist display program, and host all source files for the application as a gist itself.

CHAPTER 2

Gists and the Gist API

GitHub revolutionized software development by responding to a deep desire to share information. But calling it just "sharing" does a disservice to the tools GitHub provides: these tools remove barriers to communication and streamline workflows. These tools also arose at exactly the moment when the information technology revolution forced companies to adopt more open technologies that assisted an emerging remote workforce.

Gists service part of this need: they permit intimate code sharing and reuse, refactoring, and experimentation in a way not served by the heavyweight tools predating it. In this chapter we will explore using gists to share code, and then build an application hosted as a gist that uses the Gist API.

Easy Code Sharing

Gists are straightforward to create. You copy a snippet of code into the large text box in the center, optionally enter in a description or filename, and then choose between a public or private gist. Once your gist has been created you are presented with a URL to share. Gists autodetect the language in most cases and syntax highlight according to the language when displayed as in Figure 2-1.

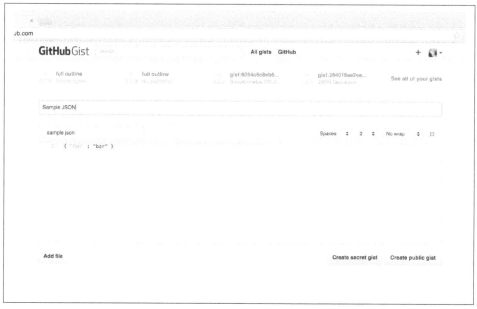

Figure 2-1. Documenting JSON using a gist

There are other services that do this: pastebin was the first, and there are many others that offer variances on code sharing. But gists by GitHub are not simply a pasting service. Gists are first-class repositories, forkable, editable, and expansive. We'll go over the basics of what gists are, and how to create them, and then show how they allow you to share code that is also a live application.

Gists Are Repositories

Every gist created is a tiny repository. You can update gists and see the history using `git log`. You can download gists, hack on the repository, and `git push` them back into the repository on *gist.github.com* (which will republish them onto the publicly facing web page). And, you can "fork" gists, just like any other repository.

You are allowed to branch within gist repositories; however, branches are not displayed inside of *gist.github.com/*. But if you need the benefits of branching when using gists you can branch normally inside a repository and the branch information is retained on the upstream repository after you push it up.

You can have an unlimited number of public and secret gists. Secret gists can, in many cases, replace private repositories, and these secret gists don't count against the limited amount of private repositories you have with paid GitHub accounts. Or, you can make a gist public, and share that URL to mailing lists or anywhere you need public feedback.

As there are two types of gists (public and secret), it is important to understand the differences between them. Public gists are searchable. Secret gists are not searchable, but they are accessible to anyone who knows the URL. Don't post any code to a gist you need to keep secret as once you put it there, it is only as safe as the URL is secret.

Most people share gists through the URL, but you can embed gists inside of other contexts (like blogs) and get a simple and pretty snippet of code.

Embedding Gists Inside HTML

To embed inside of an HTML page look for the "Embed this gist" box to the left of a gist. Copy the code listed there (which will look something like `<script src="https://gist.github.com/xrd/8923697.js"></script>`) and paste it into your HTML.

If you wish to include only a particular file from the gist (if it contains multiple files), then add `?file=hi.rb` to the end of the URL specified in the `src` attribute.

Embedding Inside Jekyll Blogs

Jekyll blogs (explained in Chapter 6) can easily host gists using a special syntax. The shortcut `{% gist 8138797 %}` will embed a private gist, which would be found at *http://gist.github.com/8138797*. If you want to use a specific file within the gist, add a filename to the gist code like `{% gist 8138797 hi.rb %}`. Secret gists can also be embedded. If you use a secret gist, prefix the username of the account holder in the gist like so: `{% gist xrd/8138797 hi.rb %}`.

Now let's look at creating gists from outside the GitHub.com site, using the command-line.

Gist from the Command Line

`gem install gist` will install a command line tool that helps create gists. You can use it simply by typing the command, and then entering the data you want to post as a gist:

```
$ gist
(type a gist. <ctrl-c> to cancel, <ctrl-d> when done)
{ "foo" : "bar" }
https://gist.github.com/9106765
```

The `gist` command will return the link to the gist just created. Gists are created anonymously by default. You can log in using the `--login` switch. Once you do this, your gists will be linked to your account:

```
$ gist --login
Obtaining OAuth2 access_token from github.
GitHub username: xrd
GitHub password:
2-factor auth code: 787878

Success! https://github.com/settings/applications
```

You can pipe text to the gist command to use the contents of that file:

```
$ echo '{ "foo" : "bar" }' | gist
https://gist.github.com/9106799
```

You can also cat a file to gist:

```
$ cat MyJavaFile.java | gist
https://gist.github.com/9345609
```

Gists are often used to show interesting or troublesome code, and there are times when you don't want to display the entirety of a file. In this case the command-line grep tool can be useful; grep searches for a specific piece of code and with the right switches can include several lines of context around that code inside a gist. This command looks for the function myFunction inside the *MyJavaFile.java* file and then prints the next 20 lines of context and stores it as a gist:

```
$ grep -A 20 myFunction MyJavaFile.java | gist
https://gist.github.com/9453069
```

Adding the -o switch automatically opens the gist inside your default web browser. You can also copy the gist URL to the clipboard using the -c switch. Or, you can copy the contents of your clipboard into a gist using the -P switch.

There are many other fun features of the gist command. To learn more run the gist command with the --help switch.

As gists are themselves repositories, you can use them for dual purposes: for hosting code samples, and for code samples that are themselves fully working and packaged applications inside a gist repository.

Gists as Fully Functioning Apps

Let's build a simple Sinatra application to showcase how code hosted as a gist can also be a living application. Sinatra is a Ruby library for creating dead-simple web servers. A Sinatra program can be as simple as this:

```
require 'sinatra'

get '/hi' do
  "Hello World!"
end
```

Create a gist for this by visiting *gist.github.com*. Enter in the text exactly as shown and then choose public gist.

You now have a share-friendly gist of code anyone can use to review. More importantly, this is a repository with executable code. To clone it, look for the Clone URL to the right of the gist itself. You will likely see a Git protocol URL and an HTTPS URL. If you are cloning the URL and intend only to read the gist, you can use the HTTPS URL. You technically can push changes once you have cloned a repository using the HTTPS URL but not if you have two-factor authentication enabled. In most cases it is easier and more flexible to use the Git protocol URL.

Let's clone it now:

```
$ git clone git@gist.github.com:8138797.git
```

Once you have cloned the repository, go inside it. You'll see a list of files, a list that right now includes only one file:

```
$ cd 8138797
$ ls
hi.rb
```

This code is exectuable: to run it enter `ruby hi.rb`.

If you have not used Sinatra with Ruby before, this will cause an error. This program requires a library called "sinatra" and you have not yet installed it. We could write a read me file, or add documentation into this file itself. Another way to guarantee the user has the proper files installed is to use a *Gemfile*, which is a file that tells which libraries are installed and from where. That sounds like the best way:

```
$ printf "source 'https://rubygems.org'\ngem 'sinatra'" > Gemfile
```

The `bundle` command (from the bundler gem) will install Sinatra and the associated dependencies:

```
$ bundle
Using rack (1.5.2)
Using rack-protection (1.5.1)
Using tilt (1.4.1)
Using sinatra (1.4.4)
Using bundler (1.3.5)
Your bundle is complete!
Use `bundle show [gemname]` to see where a bundled gem is installed.
```

Why did we do things this way? Because now we can add the Gemfile to our repository locally, and then publish into our gist for sharing on the Web. Our repository now not only has the code, but a well-known manifest file that explains the necessary components when running the code.

Gists that Render Gists

Let's add to our application and use the Octokit Ruby gem to pull all public gists for any user we specify. The Octokit library is the the official Ruby library for accessing the GitHub API. Why would we want to make a gist that displays other gists? Self-referential meta code is all the rage, the modern-day response to René Magritte's famous work: "Ceci n'est pas une pipe."[1]

Add a view *index.erb* at the root of our directory:

```
<html>
<body>

User has <%= count %> public gists

</body>
</html>
```

Add the Octokit gem to our Gemfile:

```
gem "octokit"
```

Run bundle to install Octokit. Then, modify our *hi.rb* app to look like this:

```
require 'sinatra'
require 'octokit'

set :views, "."

get '/:username' do |username|
  user = Octokit.user username
  count = user.public_gists
  erb :index, locals: { :count => count }
end
```

Our filesystem should look like this, with three files:

```
$ ls -1
Gemfile
hi.rb
index.erb
```

Restart Sinatra by running Ctrl-C and then ruby hi.rb. If you visit *http://localhost:4567/xrd* in your browser, you will see the count of public gists for user xrd (Figure 2-2); modify the username in the URL to specify any GitHub username and you will see their last five gists displayed.

---

1 Explained best by Ben Zimmer (*http://bit.ly/1Ot2qOd*)

Figure 2-2. Displaying the gist count

Going Deeper into the Gist API

The GitHub API uses hypermedia instead of basic resource-driven APIs. If you use a client like Octokit, the hypermedia details are hidden behind an elegant Ruby client. But there is a benefit to understanding how hypermedia works when you need to retrieve deeper information from the GitHub API.

Most RESTful APIs come with a "sitemap," generally an API reference document that tells a user which endpoints to use. You view the resources available from that API and then apply some HTTP verb to do something to them. Hypermedia thinks of an API differently. Hypermedia APIs describe themselves inside their responses using "affordances." What this means is that the API might respond like this:

```
{
    "_links": {
        "self": {
            "href": "http://shop.oreilly.com/product/0636920030300.do"
        }
    }
    "id": "xrd",
    "name": "Chris Dawson"
}
```

In this payload, you can see that there is an id ("xrd") and a name ("Chris Dawson"). This particular payload was forked from the HAL explanation at the HAL Primer document (*http://bit.ly/1SGLDw3*), and you can find a more detailed explanation of these concepts there.

The important thing to note about hypermedia APIs is that payloads contain metadata about data itself and metadata about the possible options of operating on the data. RESTful APIs typically provide a mapping outside of the payload. You have to join the API sitemap with the data in an ad hoc way when using RESTful APIs; with hypermedia APIs your client can react to the payload itself correctly and intelligently without knowing anything about a sitemap stored in human-readable documentation.

This loose coupling makes APIs and their clients flexible. In theory, a hypermedia API works intuitively with a hypermedia-aware client. If you change the API, the client, as it understands hypermedia, can react and still work as expected. Using a RESTful API means that clients must be updated (a newer version of the client must be installed) or the client code must be upgraded. Hypermedia APIs can alter their backend, and then the client, as long as it is hypermedia-aware, can automatically and dynamically determine the right way to access information from the response itself. In other words, with a hypermedia client the API backend can change and your client code should not need to.

This is explained in great detail in the book *Building Hypermedia APIs with HTML5 and Node* (O'Reilly).

Using Hypermedia Data from Octokit

Now that you know a little about hypermedia, let's navigate it using Octokit:

- Start at a resource, with code like `user = Octokit.user "xrd"`. This begins the initialization of the client.
- `user` now is an object filled with the actual data of the resource. In this case, you could call a method like `user.followers` to see a meager follower count.
- `user` also has hypermedia references. You can see these by calling `user.rels`. This retrieves the relationships described in the hypermedia links.
- Relationships (found by calling `user.rels`) include avatar, self, followers, etc.
- Use a relationship by calling the `get.data` method to retrieve and access the data from the GitHub API (`followers = user.rels[:followers].get.data`).
- Calling `.get.data` populates an array of the followers (paged if it exceeds 100 items).

Let's extend our Sinatra app to retrieve actual data about the user's gists by using hypermedia references:

```
require 'sinatra'
require 'octokit'

set :views, "."

helpers do
  def h(text)
    Rack::Utils.escape_html(text)
  end
end

get '/:username' do |username|
  gists = Octokit.gists username, :per_page => 5
```

```
    erb :index, locals: { :gists => gists, username: username }
  end
```

The *index.erb* file contains code to iterate over each gist and pull the content. You can see that our response object is an array of gists, and each has an attribute called `fields`. This `fields` attribute specifies the filenames available in each gist. If you reference that filename against the files, the response includes a hypermedia `ref` attribute. Retrieve the `raw` content using the Octokit method `.get.data`:

```
<html>
<body>

<h2>User <%= username %>'s last five gists</h2>

<% gists.each do |g| %>
<% g[:files].fields.each do |f| %>
<b><%= f %></b>:

<%= h g[:files][f.to_sym].rels[:raw].get.data %>

<br/>
<br/>

<% end %>
<% end %>

</body>
</html>
```

Now we see the gists and the contents, as in Figure 2-3.

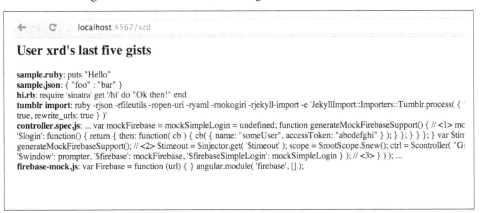

Figure 2-3. Last five gists, with details

Summary

In this chapter we looked at gists and learned how they can be used to share code snippets. We built a simple application and stored it as a gist. This application retrieves data from the GitHub API using our first higher-level language client library (the Octokit library for Ruby). We also went deeper into how hypermedia works and how a client library implements using hypermedia metadata.

In the next chapter we will look at Gollum, the GitHub wiki. This chapter provides an introduction to the Rugged Ruby library for accessing Git repositories and the Ruby library for accessing GitHub.

CHAPTER 3

GitHub Wikis with Gollum

Wikis have revolutionized the way we create and digest information. It turns out that they are a great complement to technical projects (code repositories) because they allow nontechnical users to contribute in ways other than adding code. Gollum is an open source wiki created by GitHub. Just as Git has revolutionized collaborative editing of code, Gollum wikis layer the benefits of Git onto the widely used wiki publishing workflow. Gollum wikis are themselves repositories that generally annotate other typically code-centric repositories. GitHub makes it easy to associate a wiki with any repository.

In this chapter we'll explore the basics of using Gollum, creating a wiki on GitHub and then learning how to edit it on GitHub and as a repository on our local machine. We will then create a Gollum wiki by hand from the command line, and show the bare minimum set of files to call something a Gollum repository. Finally, we will build a simple image organization tool that allows us to edit a Gollum wiki in an entirely different way, but still publishes information into GitHub as a regular Gollum wiki, exploring a little bit of the internals of Git along the way.

 This chapter demonstrates code that modifies a Git repository programmatically. You will be able to follow along without possessing a deep understanding of the internals of Git. And, a good supplement to this chapter (and later chapters as well) is the *Version Control with Git* book from O'Reilly.

"The Story of Smeagol..."

At its most basic form, a Gollum wiki is a Git repository with a single file, *Home.ext* (*ext* would be any of the supported wiki markup formats, which we will talk about later).

Repository Linked Wikis

Any repository on GitHub, public or private, can have an associated Gollum wiki. To create a wiki linked to your repository, visit the repository page and then look in the rightmost colum. You'll see an icon that looks like a book, next to which will be the word "Wiki," as in Figure 3-1.

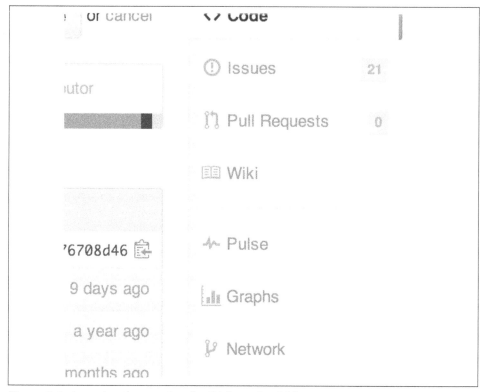

Figure 3-1. Accessing the associated wiki from the sidebar

Clicking this link will bring you to a page where you are asked to create a wiki for the first time. GitHub will ask you to create the "Home" page, which is the starting point in a Gollum wiki (Figure 3-2). GitHub will automatically create a page template with the project name; you can customize this information to suit your own needs. Clicking "Save Page" will save your first page and create the wiki for you.

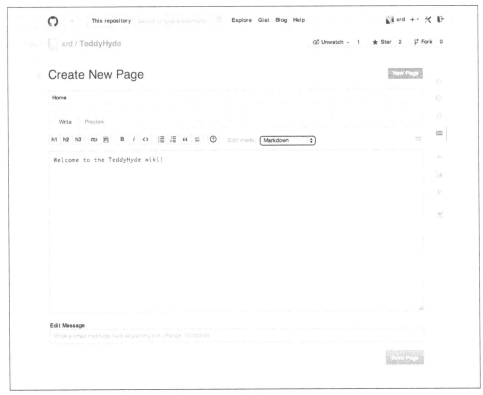

Figure 3-2. Genesis of a new wiki, creating the home page

Your wiki is now as public as your repository is public. Public repositories have public wikis, accessible to anyone. Private repositories have private wikis, accessible only to those users or organizations that have rights to edit the repository data.

Let's review the markup options for Gollum wikis now.

Markup and Structure

Gollum files can be written in any of the supported "Github Markup" formats, which include ASCIIdoc, Creole, Markdown, Org Mode, Pod, RDoc, ReStructuredText, Textile, and MediaWiki. The variety of markup languages brings flexibility but it can be difficult to know which one to use. Markdown (and its variant cousins) is the most popular markup language on GitHub, and is well liked on other popular sites like Stack Overflow. If you are unsure about which language to use, Markdown is a safe bet because it is ubiquitous across GitHub. Chapter 6 has a much deeper overview of Markdown.

If you do choose Markdown, in addition to the standard vanilla Markdown language tags, Gollum adds its own set of wiki-specific tags. There are often subtle (or conflicting) differences from other wiki markup so it is worth reviewing the Gollum repository documentation page (*https://github.com/gollum/gollum/wiki*). We'll go over the most important ones here.

Links

Links obviously convert into the <a> HTML tag. Each format has its own linking format: in Markdown you use [text](URL). Gollum adds its own link tag: [[Link]].

In addition:

- You can add a link title using the bar character: [[http://foobar.com|A link to foobar]].
- Links can be either external or internal links.
- A link like [[Review Images]] will be converted to a relative link to the page *review-images.ext* (where *.ext* is the preferred extension you are using with your wiki, most likely Markdown).

Wikis are generally a collection of pages linked together in myriad ways, and this assumption about the structure of links makes writing pages easier.

 As we mentioned, there are differences between Gollum wiki tags and other wikis, despite their having similar syntax. One such example is MediaWiki, where links with titles use the opposite ordering [[A link to foobar|http://foobar.com]], so caveat emptor.

Code snippets

Gollum (the wiki) was invented at GitHub, a company dedicated to improving the lives of software developers, so it stands to reason Gollum wikis would support insertion of code snippets. To include a snippet of code, use three backticks, followed by an optional language name, and close the block of code using three more backticks. If you use the language name, Gollum will do proper syntax highlighting for most languages:

```ruby
def hello
  puts "hello"
end
```

Gollum at one point (*http://bit.ly/1JMzd4m*) supported inclusion of files from any GitHub repository (and any branch!) using a syntax like this:

```
```ruby:github:xrd/TeddyHyde/blob/master/Gemfile```
```

Unfortunately, this no longer works. According to current documentation for Gollum, this tag allows inclusion of files from the parent repository:

```
```ruby:/lib/gollum/app.rb```
```

But I found this to be broken as well. At the time of writing, it tragically appears that there is no way to insert code from the parent repository (or any other repository) into your wiki content.

Structural components

Gollum includes capabilities to add sidebars, headers, and footers. If you include a file called *_Sidebar.ext* inside your repository, you'll see it as a sidebar for every file rendered. Sidebars are automatically added to any file and any file from subdirectories that do not have their own sidebar files. If you wanted to add sidebars specific to a subdirectory, add another sidebar file in the subdirectory and this file will override the top-level sidebar file.

No styling or JavaScript

For security reasons, Gollum strips out all CSS and JavaScript from raw markup files. You can include your own JavaScript or CSS file when running Gollum from the command line (discussed momentarily) using the `--custom-css` or `--custom-js` switches, but there is no way to include these files on a wiki when your Gollum wiki is hosted on GitHub.

Inserting images

Images are inserted into your document using the same tag format `[[ceo.png]]`: this adds the correct HTML tags to include an image named *ceo.png* inside your page. This basic syntax is often extended for additional funtionality. For example, to add a frame and an `alt` tag, you could use syntax like `[[ceo.png|frame|alt=Our CEO relaxing on the beach]]`. This creates the proper HTML tags for the same image, and also adds a frame and alt text (helpful for better context and the extra information is used by screenreaders for visually impaired users as well). Review the documentation on the Gollum repository for more details about the breadth of the image options.

You can also add images using the editor on GitHub. But you'll notice that either way you are adding a link to an image and that there is no way to upload images into GitHub from the editor (Figure 3-3).

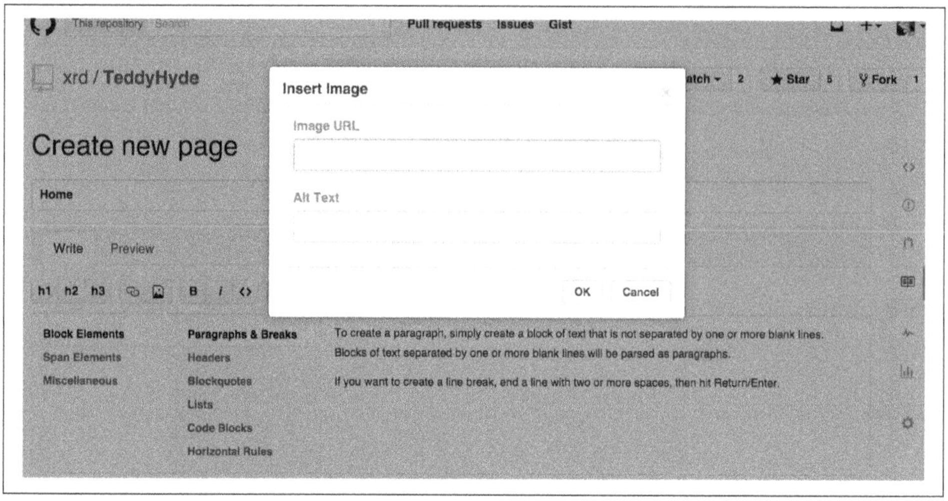

Figure 3-3. No image upload, only image URLs

For nontechnical users, this makes Gollum wikis on GitHub almost unusable if they need to add images. Let's address this problem by building our own customized image-centric Gollum editor that still interoperates with regular Gollum wikis. We can put this editor in front of nontechnical users, allowing them to add images, and then publish the wiki into GitHub as is.

Hacking Gollum

Would an image editor based on Gollum be of general use? On many software teams there is tension between the design team and the software team stemming from the fact that designers generally don't like using source-code tools to manage images. This causes issues when software developers rely on designs that are rapidly changing: coders quickly get out of sync with the latest designs. As a wiki, Gollum is the perfect tool to bridge this gap between designers and coders: wikis are easy to read and modify by nontechnical users. Since Gollum is a hackable wiki, we can build our own workflow tool that allows designers to manage images and coders to easily see those changes in a source-code repository.

This will be a dual-purpose repository. We can use the repository with Gollum as a standard wiki, and we can use it with our application to enter data in a more powerful way than Gollum permits from its default interface. The data will still be compatible with Gollum and will be hosted on GitHub.

To begin, install the Gollum Ruby gem and then initialize our repository:

```
$ gem install gollum
$ mkdir images
$ cd images
```

```
$ git init .
$ printf "### Our home" > Home.md
$ git add Home.md
$ git commit -m "Initial commit"
```

We've just created a wiki compatible with Gollum. Let's see what it looks like inside Gollum. Run the `gollum` command then open *http://localhost:4567/* in your browser, as shown in Figure 3-4.

Figure 3-4. Viewing the wiki home page running on our laptop

As you can see, this tiny set of commands was enough to create the basics of the Gollum wiki structure.

 If you edit a Gollum wiki from the command line, be aware that Gollum only looks inside the repository data for files. If you have added something to the working directory or have not yet commited files in your index, they will not be visible to Gollum.

Now let's begin creating the web app that will help us store images inside a Gollum wiki.

The Starting Point of a Gollum Editor

Now we will create our custom editor. We'll use Sinatra, a Ruby library that provides a simple DSL (domain-specific language) for building web applications. First, create a file called *image.rb* and put the following contents inside it:

```
require 'sinatra'
require 'gollum-lib'
wiki = Gollum::Wiki.new(".")
get '/pages' do
```

```
    "All pages: \n" + wiki.pages.collect { |p| p.path }.join( "\n" )
  end
```

Then, create the Gemfile, install the dependencies, and run the web application:

```
$ echo "source 'https://rubygems.org'
gem 'sinatra', '1.4.5'
gem 'gollum-lib', '4.1.0'" >> Gemfile
$ bundle install
Fetching gem metadata from https://rubygems.org/..........
Resolving dependencies...
Installing charlock_holmes (0.7.3)
Using diff-lcs (1.2.5)
Installing github-markup (1.3.3)
Using mime-types (1.25.1)
...
$ bundle exec ruby image.rb
$ open http://localhost:4567/pages
```

We specify at least the minimum 4.1.0 for gollum-lib as the interface and list of supporting libraries has changed. We then run within the bundler context (using gems installed from this Gemfile rather than system gems) using the bundle exec ruby image.rb command.

You'll see a report of the files that exist in our Gollum wiki right now. We've only added one file, the *Home.md* file.

Programmatically Handling Images

Let's add to our server. We want to support uploading ZIP files into our system that we will then unpack and add to our repository, as well as add a list of these files to our wiki. Modify our *image.rb* script to look like this:

```
require 'sinatra'
require 'gollum-lib'
require 'tempfile'
require 'zip'
require 'rugged'

def index( message=nil )
  response = File.read(File.join('.', 'index.html'))
  response.gsub!( "<!-- message -->\n",
  "<h2>Received and unpacked #{message}</h2>" ) if message
  response
end

wiki = Gollum::Wiki.new(".")
get '/' do
  index()
end
```

```ruby
post '/unpack' do
  @repo = Rugged::Repository.new('.')
  @index = Rugged::Index.new

  zip = params[:zip][:tempfile]
  Zip::Zip.open( zip ) { |zipfile|
    zipfile.each do |f|
      contents = zipfile.read( f.name )
      filename = f.name.split( File::SEPARATOR ).pop
      if contents and filename and filename =~ /(png|jp?g|gif)$/i
        puts "Writing out: #{filename}"
      end
    end
  }
  index( params[:zip][:filename] )
end
```

We'll need an *index.html* file as well, so add that:

```html
<html>
<body>
<!-- message -->
<form method='POST' enctype='multipart/form-data' action='/unpack'>
Choose a zip file:
<input type='file' name='zip'/>
<input type='submit' name='submit'>
</form>
</body>
</html>
```

This server script receives a POST request at the /unpack mount point and retrieves a ZIP file from the parameters passed into the script. It then opens the ZIP file (stored as a temp file on the server side), iterates over each file in the ZIP, strips the full path from the filename, and then prints out that filename (if it looks like an image) to our console. Regardless of whether we are accessing the root of our server, or have just posted to the /unpack mount point, we always need to render our index page. When we do render it after unzipping, we replace a comment stored in the index file with a status message indicating the script received the correct file we posted.

We need to add the new Ruby libraries (RubyZip and Rugged) to our Gemfile: update the required gems using the following commands, and then rerun our Sinatra server script:

```
$ echo "gem 'rubyzip', '1.1.7'
gem 'rugged', '0.23.2'" >> Gemfile
$ bundle install
$ bundle exec ruby image.rb
```

Rugged requires the libgit2 libraries (the pure C libraries for accessing Git repositories). Rugged gives you access to modification of Git repositories in the elegance of the Ruby language but with the speed of C. However, as this library is based on libgit2, and libgit2 requires a C compiler, you will need to install this toolset first to install Rugged. On OS X this can look like `brew install cmake` or `apt-get install cmake` for Linux.

Then, we can open *http://localhost:4567/* and test uploading a ZIP file full of images. You'll see output similar to this in your console after uploading a ZIP file:

```
...
[2014-05-07 10:08:49] INFO  WEBrick 1.3.1
[2014-05-07 10:08:49] INFO  ruby 2.0.0 (2013-05-14)
[x86_64-darwin13.0.0]
== Sinatra/1.4.5 has taken the stage on 4567 for development with
backup from WEBrick
[2014-05-07 10:08:49] INFO  WEBrick::HTTPServer#start: pid=46370
port=4567
Writing out: IMG1234.png
Writing out: IMG5678.png
Writing out: IMG5678.png
...
```

We are not doing anything beyond printing out the names of the images in the ZIP. We'll actually insert them into our Git repository in the next section.

Using the Rugged Library

Our end goal for this script is to add files to our Gollum wiki, which means adding files to the repository that backs our Gollum wiki. The Rugged library handles the grunt work of this type of task easily. Rugged is the successor to the original Ruby library for Git (called Grit). Gollum, at the time of writing, uses the Grit libraries, which also provide a binding to the libgit2 library, a "portable, pure C implementation of the Git core methods." Grit has been abandoned (though there are unofficial maintainers) and the Gollum team intends to use Rugged as the long-term library backing Gollum. Rugged is written in Ruby and (provided you like Ruby) is a more elegant way to interface with a Git repository than raw Git commands. As you might expect, Rugged is maintained by several employees of GitHub.

To change our script to modify our Git repository, let's change our script to no longer print the filename (using the `puts` method inside the ZIP decode block) and instead call a new method called `write_file_to_repo`. And, at the end of the ZIP block, add a method called `build_commit`, which builds the commit from our new files. Our new file (omitting the unchanged code at the head of the file) looks like this:

```
post '/unpack' do
  @repo = Rugged::Repository.new('.')
  @index = Rugged::Index.new

  zip = params[:zip][:tempfile]
  Zip::Zip.open( zip ) { |zipfile|
    zipfile.each do |f|
      contents = zipfile.read( f.name )
      filename = f.name.split( File::SEPARATOR ).pop
      if contents and filename and filename =~ /(png|jp?g|gif)$/i
        write_file_to_repo contents, filename # Write the file
      end
    end
    build_commit() # Build a commit from the new files
  }
  index( params[:zip][:filename] )
end

def get_credentials
  contents = File.read File.join( ENV['HOME'], ".gitconfig" )
  @email = $1 if contents =~ /email = (.+)$/
  @name = $1 if contents =~ /name = (.+)$/
end

def build_commit
  get_credentials()
  options = {}
  options[:tree] = @index.write_tree(@repo)
  options[:author] = { :email => @email, :name => @name, :time => Time.now }
  options[:committer] = { :email => @email, :name => @name, :time => Time.now }
  options[:message] ||= "Adding new images"
  options[:parents] = @repo.empty? ? [] : [ @repo.head.target ].compact
  options[:update_ref] = 'HEAD'

  Rugged::Commit.create(@repo, options)

end

def write_file_to_repo( contents, filename )
  oid = @repo.write( contents, :blob )
  @index.add(:path => filename, :oid => oid, :mode => 0100644)
end
```

As you can see from the code, Rugged handles a lot of the grunt work required when creating a commit inside a Git repository. Rugged has a simple interface to creating a blob inside your Git repository (write), and adding files to the index (the add method), and also has a simple and clean interface to build the tree object (write_tree) and then build the commit (Rugged::Commit.create).

To ease the burden of hardcoding our commit credentials, we implement a method called get_credentials that loads up your credentials from a file called *.gitconfig* located in your home directory. You probably have this if you have used Git for anything at all on your machine, but if this file is missing, this method will fail. On my machine this file looks like the following code snippet. The `get_credentials` method simply loads up this file and parses it for the name and email address. If you wanted to load the credentials using another method, or even hardcode them, you can just modify this method to suit your needs. The instance variables `@email` and `@name` are then used in the `build_commit()` method:

```
[user]
        name = Chris Dawson
        email = xrdawson@gmail.com
[credential]
        helper = cache --timeout=3600
...
```

Let's verify that things are working correctly after uploading a ZIP file. Jumping into a terminal window after uploading a new file, imagine running these commands:

```
$ git status
```

To our surprise, we will see something like this:

```
$ git status
On branch master
Changes to be committed:
  (use "git reset HEAD <file>..." to unstage)

    deleted:    images/3190a7759f7f668.../IMG_20120825_164703.jpg
    deleted:    images/3190a7759f7f668.../IMG_20130704_151522.jpg
    deleted:    images/3190a7759f7f668.../IMG_20130704_174217.jpg
```

We just added those files; why is Git reporting them as deleted?

To understand why this happens, remember that in Git there are three places files can reside: the working directory, the staging area or index, and the repository itself. Your working directory is the set of local files you are working on. The `git status` command describes itself as "show the working tree status." Rugged operates on the repository itself, and the Rugged calls in the preceding code operated on the index and then built a commit. This is important to note because our files will not exist in our working directory if we only write them using the Rugged calls, and if we do this, we cannot reference them inside our wiki page when we are running Gollum locally. We'll fix this in the next section.

We've now added the files to our repository, but we have not exposed these files inside our wiki. Let's modify our server script to write out each file to a wiki page for review. As we mentioned in the previous section, we need to make sure we write the files to both the working index and the repository (using the Rugged library `write` call). Then we can generate a Review file that details all the images uploaded.

Adding Images to a Review File

Now that we have successfully unzipped and processed the images, we can add them to a file for review. We will call this file Review.md. The code to write the review file looks like this:

```
def write_review_file( files, dir )
    review_filename = "Review.md"
    contents = "## Review Images\n\n"
    files.each do |f|
        contents += "### #{f} \n[[#{dir}/#{f}]]\n\n"
    end

    File.write review_filename, contents
    oid = @repo.write( contents, :blob )
    @index.add(:path => review_filename, :oid => oid, :mode => 0100644)
end
```

The method is straightforward: we pass in the list of files and a subdirectory where we wrote out the image files to disk. Then, we generate a Markdown file with a header (using the two hash formatting characters) stating "Review Images," and then iterate over the list of images, entering the filename as a subheader. We then use the Gollum image markup tag (two braces, then the image filename, then closing with two more braces). We write out the file to disk. Finally, we add the file to the repository and then to the index. The commit that we built for the images will include this review file as well, since it is added to the index before the images are processed—as long as we place the call to write_review_file before the call to build_commit like so:

```
...
write_review_file files, dir # write out a review file
build_commit() # Build a commit from the new files
...
```

Now, let's take a look at how images are stored inside our repository, particularly if the same image is uploaded twice.

Optimizing for Image Storage

If a designer uploads the same image twice, what happens? Our code writes the uploaded image to a path on disk that is based on the parent SHA hash of the repository (and this means we will always write the file to a different path, even when the file is the same as a previous uploaded file). It would look to an untrained eye like we are adding the file multiple times. However, the nature of Git permits us to add the same file multiple times without incurring any additional storage cost beyond the first addition (and the minimal cost of a tree structure). When a file is added to a Git repository, an SHA hash is generated from the file contents. For example, generating the SHA hash from an empty file will always return the same SHA hash:[1]

```
$ echo -en "blob 0\0" | shasum
e69de29bb2d1d6434b8b29ae775ad8c2e48c5391
$ printf '' | git hash-object -w --stdin
e69de29bb2d1d6434b8b29ae775ad8c2e48c5391
```

Adding a ZIP file with a bunch of files where only one or two differs from the prior ZIP file means that Git will properly reference the same file multiple times. Unfortunately, GitHub does not provide an interface for reviewing the statistics of wikis in the same way they do for regular repositories. We can, however, review our repository size from within the local repository by running the `count-objects` Git subcommand. As an example, I uploaded a ZIP file with two images inside of it. I then use the `count-objects` command and see this:

```
$ git gc
...
$ git count-objects -v
count: 0
size: 0
in-pack: 11
packs: 1
size-pack: 2029
prune-packable: 0
garbage: 0
size-garbage: 0
```

Inspecting the first ZIP file, I see these statistics about it:

```
$ unzip -l ~/Downloads/Photos\ \(4\).zip
Archive:  /Users/xrdawson/Downloads/Photos (4).zip
  Length      Date    Time    Name
---------  ---------- -----   ----
  1189130  01-01-12 00:00   IMG_20130704_151522.jpg
   889061  01-01-12 00:00   IMG_20130704_174217.jpg
---------                   -------
  2078191                   2 files
```

Now let's use another ZIP file with the same two files present but with an additional image file added:

```
unzip -l ~/Downloads/Photos\ \(5\).zip
Archive:  /Users/xrdawson/Downloads/Photos (5).zip
  Length      Date    Time    Name
---------  ---------- -----   ----
  1189130  01-01-12 00:00   IMG_20130704_151522.jpg
   566713  01-01-12 00:00   IMG_20120825_164703.jpg
   889061  01-01-12 00:00   IMG_20130704_174217.jpg
```

---

[1] This is explained beautifully in the blog *http://alblue.bandlem.com/2011/08/git-tip-of-week-objects.html*.

```
    --------                      -------
    2644904                       3 files
```

Then, I upload the second ZIP file. If I rerun the `count-objects` command (after running `git gc`, a command that packs files efficiently and makes our output more human readable), I see this:

```
$ git gc
...
$ git count-objects -v
count: 0
size: 0
in-pack: 17
packs: 1
size-pack: 2578
prune-packable: 0
garbage: 0
size-garbage: 0
```

Notice that our packed size has only changed by about half a MB, which is the compressed size of the additional third file, but more importantly, there was no impact from the other two files on our repository size, even though they were added at different paths.

If we upload the secondary file yet again, we will regenerate and commit a new version of the *Review.md* file, but no new files will need to be created inside our Git repository object store from the images directory (even though their paths have changed), so our impact on the repository will be minimal:

```
$ git gc
...
$ git count-objects -v
count: 0
size: 0
in-pack: 21
packs: 1
size-pack: 2578
prune-packable: 0
garbage: 0
size-garbage: 0
```

As you can see, our packed size has barely changed, an indication that the only changes were a new Git tree object and commit object. We still have the files located in our repository at a variety of paths so our review pages will work no matter what revision we are accessing:

```
$ find images
images
images/7507409915d00ad33d03c78af0a4004797eec4b4
images/7507409915d00ad33d03c78af0a4004797eec4b4/IMG_20120825_164703.jpg
images/7507409915d00ad33d03c78af0a4004797eec4b4/IMG_20130704_151522.jpg
images/7507409915d00ad33d03c78af0a4004797eec4b4/IMG_20130704_174217.jpg
```

```
images/7f9505a4bafe8c8f654e22ea3fd4dab8b4075f75
images/7f9505a4bafe8c8f654e22ea3fd4dab8b4075f75/IMG_20120825_164703.jpg
images/7f9505a4bafe8c8f654e22ea3fd4dab8b4075f75/IMG_20130704_151522.jpg
images/7f9505a4bafe8c8f654e22ea3fd4dab8b4075f75/IMG_20130704_174217.jpg
images/b4be28e5b24bfa46c4942d756a3a07efd24bc234
images/b4be28e5b24bfa46c4942d756a3a07efd24bc234/IMG_20130704_151522.jpg
images/b4be28e5b24bfa46c4942d756a3a07efd24bc234/IMG_20130704_174217.jpg
```

Git and Gollum can efficiently store the same file at different paths without overloading the repository.

Reviewing on GitHub

The raison d'être for this wiki is to annotate a development project. If you follow the instructions and create a new wiki for a repository, you'll then be able to push up the changes we've made using our `image.rb` script. Once you have created a new wiki, look for a box on the right that says "Clone this wiki locally," as seen in Figure 3-5.

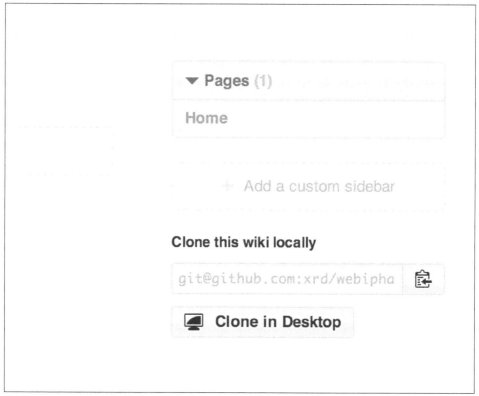

Figure 3-5. Getting the clone URL for our wiki

Copy that link, and then enter a terminal window where we can then add a remote URL to our local repository that allows us to synchronize our repositories and publish our images into GitHub. Gollum wikis have a simple URL structure based on the original clone URL: just add the word .wiki to the end of the clone URL (but before the final .git extension). So, if the original clone URL of the repository is git@git hub.com:xrd/webiphany.com.git our clone URL for the associated wiki will be git@github.com:xrd/webiphany.com.wiki.git. Once we have the URL, we can add it as a remote to our local repository using the following commands:

```
$ git remote add origin git@github.com:xrd/webiphany.com.wiki.git
$ git pull # This will require us to merge the changes...
$ git push
```

When we pull, we will be asked to merge our changes since GitHub created a *Home.md* file that did not exist in our local repository. We can just accept the merge as is. The git push publishes our changes. If we then visit the wiki, we'll see an additional file listed under the pages sidebar to the right. Clicking the Review page, as in Figure 3-6, we can see the images we've added most recently.

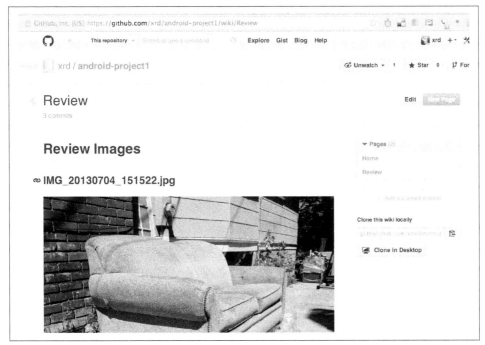

Figure 3-6. An image review page

Not sure why our designer is providing us with an image of a couch, but I am sure he has his reasons.

Once we have published the file, we can click the Review link in the sidebar to see the most current version of the Review page. We also can review the revisions of this file by clicking the "3 Commits" (or whatever number of commits have occurred with this file) link right underneath the page title. Jumping onto that page shows us the full history of this file, as shown in Figure 3-7.

Figure 3-7. Wiki history review via the Commit Log

Clicking any of the SHA hashes will display the page at that revision in our history and show us the state of the document at any given moment in history. Unfortunately, jumping back and forth between revisions requires two clicks, one from the Review page to the list of revisions, and then another click to jump into the revision we want, but this permits us to review changes between the comps provided from our designer.

It would be nice if GitHub provided a simple way to jump from a revision to the parent (older) revision, but it doesn't expose this in its site at this point. We can fix this, however, by generating our own special link inside the Review page itself, which will magically know how to navigate to a previous version of the page.

Improving Revision Navigation

In our example, we only have three revisions right now, and all share the same commit message ("Adding new images"). This is not very descriptive and makes it challenging to understand the differences between revisions, which is critical when we are trying to understand how things have changed between comps. We can improve this easily.

First, let's add a commit message field to our upload form:

```
<html>
<body>
<!-- message -->
<form method='POST' enctype='multipart/form-data' action='/unpack'>
Choose a zip file:
```

```
<input type='file' name='zip'/>
<input type='text' name='message' placeholder='Enter commit message'/>
<input type='submit' name='submit'>
</form>
</body>
</html>
```

Then, let's adjust the commit message inside our *image.rb* script, which is a one-line change to the options hash, setting the value of it to the parameter we are now passing in for commit:

```
...
options[:committer] = { :email => @email, :name => @name, :time => Time.now }
options[:message] = params[:message]
options[:parents] = @repo.empty? ? [] : [ @repo.head.target ].compact
...
```

Now, if our designer posts a new version of the UI comps, they can specify what changes were made, and we have a record of that in our change log, which is exposed on the revisions section of our wiki hosted on GitHub.

Fixing Linking Between Comp Pages

As noted, there is no quick way to jump between comps once we are inside a review revision. However, if you recall we used the parent SHA hash to build out our image links. We can use this to build out a navigation links inside our comp page when we are on a revision page while viewing the history.

Again, it is a simple change: one line within the `write_review_file` method. After the block that creates each link to the image files, add a line that builds a link to the parent document via its SHA hash using the parent SHA found in our Rugged object under `@repo.head.target`. This link will allow us to navigate to prior revisions in our history:

```
...
files.each do |f|
  contents += "### #{f} \n[[#{dir}/#{f}]]\n\n"
end
contents += "[Prior revision (only when viewing history)]" +
"(#{@repo.head.target})\n\n"

File.write review_filename, contents
oid = @repo.write( contents, :blob )
@index.add(:path => review_filename, :oid => oid, :mode => 0100644)
...
```

Now, when we view the Review file history, we see a link to each prior version. Is it possible to provide a link to the next version in our history? Unfortunately, we have no way to predict the SHA hash of the next commit made to the repository, so we cannot build this link inside our *Review.md* file with our Ruby script. However, we do get something just as good for free because we can simply use the back button to jump back to the prior page in the history stack of our browser. We might try to get clever and use a link with JavaScript to call `window.history.back()` but Gollum will foil this attempt by stripping JavaScript from rendered markup files. This is generally a good thing, as we don't want to permit rogue markup inside our wiki pages, but it does limit our options in this situation.

Unfortunately, these links do not work when you are viewing the review file itself (clicking them brings you to a page that asks you to create this as a new page). Gollum, unlike Jekyll, does not support Liquid tags, which would permit building a link using the username and repository. Right now we don't have access to these variables, so our link needs to be relative, which works when we are in history review, but not in the normal review. It does not affect viewing the files so this would require educating your stakeholders on the limitations of this link.

Summary

In this chapter we learned how to create a Gollum wiki from scratch, both on GitHub and as a fresh repository from the command line. We then looked at the different ways to use the Gollum command-line tool and learned why this is a nice option when we want to run our own Gollum server. Finally, we built a customized Gollum image-centric editor using the Rugged and Sinatra Ruby libraries.

In the next chapter we'll switch gears completely and build a GUI application for searching GitHub issues. And we'll do it in Python.

CHAPTER 4

Python and the Search API

Once you have enough data, no amount of organization will make everything easy to find. As Google has taught us, the only system that works at this scale is a search box. When you use GitHub, you're exposed to both sides of this phenomenon: the repositories you have direct access to—which are relatively small in number—are given a single level of hierarchy, so you can keep them straight in your head. For the rest, the uncountable millions of public repositories that belong to other people, there's a search box, with powerful features to help you find what you're looking for.

Helpfully, GitHub also exposes this capability as an API you can consume from your own applications. GitHub's Search API gives you access to the full power of the built-in search function. This includes the use of logical and scoping operators, like `"or"` and `"user"`. By integrating this feature with your application, you can provide your users a very powerful way of finding what they're looking for.

In this chapter we'll take a close look at this API, and try building a useful application with it. We'll see how the Search API is structured, what kind of results come back, and how it can help us create a feature for someone on our team.

Search API General Principles

The Search API is split into four separate parts: repositories, code, issues, and users. These APIs all have different subject matter, and have different formats for their results, but they all behave the same in a few key ways. We're covering these first, because they'll help you understand the results coming back from the specific API calls that we cover later. There are four major areas of commonality.

Authentication

Your identity as a user can determine the result set from a search query, so it's important to know about authentication. We cover GitHub authentication fully in "Authentication" on page 8, but this API is also available without logging in. However, there are a few limitations to this approach.

First, you'll only be able to search public repositories. This is probably fine if you're primarily working with open source software, but users of your application will probably expect to have access to their private code, as well as that of any organizations they belong to. Also, since *all* Enterprise repositories are private, anonymous search is completely useless there.

Secondly, authenticating opens up your rate limit. The limits on search are stricter than other APIs anyway, because search is computationally expensive, but anonymous searches are stricter still. As of this writing, and according to the documentation, anonymous searches are limited to 5 per minute, and you can do 20 authenticated queries per minute. Take a look at "GitHub API Rate Limits" on page 14 for more on how to work with rate limits.

Here's that same information in tabular form:

	Anonymous	Authenticated
Results include private repositories	No	Yes
Use with Enterprise	No	Yes
Rate limit	5/minute	20/minute

Result Format

No matter what you're searching for, the return value from the API follows a certain format. Here's a sample result from a query, which has been heavily edited to focus only on the parts you'll always see:

```
{
  "total_count": 824,
  "incomplete_results": false,
  "items": [
    {
      …
      "score": 3.357718
    }
  ]
}
```

Starting from the top: the `total_count` field represents the total number of search results that turned up from this query. It's not uncommon for a fairly specific search to turn up thousands of results—remember, there are millions of repositories on GitHub. By default, only the first 30 are returned, but you can customize this with `page` and `per_page` query parameters in the URL. For example, a GET request to this URL will return 45 items, starting with the 46th result:

```
search/repositories?q=foobar&page=2&page_size=45
```

Page sizes are generally limited to 100.

The `incomplete_results` field refers to a computational limit placed on the Search API. If your search takes too long, the GitHub API will stop it partway through executing, return the results that did complete, and set this flag to `true`. For most queries this won't be a problem, and the `total_count` will represent all the results from the search, but if your query is complicated, you might only get a partial result set.

Search results are returned in the `items` array, and each item always has a `score` field. This field is numeric, but it's only a relative measure of how well a result matches the query, and is used for the default sort order—highest score first. If you do pay attention to it, remember it only has meaning when compared to other results from the same query; a result with a score of 50 isn't necessarily ten times "better" than a result scored 5.

Here's a summary of the important fields:

Field	Meaning
`total_count`	Total search result count
`incomplete_results`	`true` if search was halted before finishing
`items`	List of search results
`(item).score`	Relevance of this item as a search result

Search Operators and Qualifiers

Of course, it's always better if you can avoid pagination altogether, or at least get the best results in the first page. Qualifiers and operators can help narrow your search results to fewer pages, hopefully allowing the right result to float to the top.

With the Search API, all searches are done through a search query, which is encoded and passed in the URL as the `q` parameter. Most of the query will be free text, but the API also supports some powerful syntax, such as these forms:

- x AND y, as well as OR and NOT
- user:*<name>*, where *name* is a user or organization
- repo:*<name>*
- language:*<name>*
- created:*<date(s)>*
- extension:*<pattern>* matches file extensions (like *py* or *ini*)

Numerical values and dates can have ranges:

- 2015-02-01 will match only the given date
- <2015-02-01 will match any date previous to the one given
- 2015-02-01..2015-03-01 will match dates within the given range, including the endpoints

For example, to find code written by the user tpope during July of 2012, you would write "user:tpope created:2012-07-01..2015-07-31" for the query parameter. That would be encoded in a URL like so:

```
search/repositories?q=user%3Atpope+created%3A2012-07-01..2015-07-31
```

To constrain this search to only Python code, we could add ` language=python`, URL encoded as +language%3Apython, to the end of the URL.

There are many other options. Check out *https://github.com/search/advanced* for a UI that can help you construct a query.

Sorting

If search query operators can't narrow down a result set to just the most important items, perhaps sorting them can. Search results are returned in a definite order, never at random. The default order is "best match," which sorts your results based on their search score, best score first. If you want to override this, you can pass stars, forks, or updated in the sort query parameter, as in search/repositories?q=foo bar&sort=stars.

You can also reverse the sort order using the order parameter, like search/reposito ries?q=foobar&sort=stars&order=desc. The default is desc ("descending"), but asc is also accepted, and will reverse the order.

Search APIs in Detail

Now that we've covered how all these APIs behave the same, let's discuss their specifics. The Search API is compartmentalized into four categories: repositories, code, issues, and users. The basic mechanism is the same for all four: send a GET request to the endpoint, and provide a URL-encoded search term as the q parameter. We'll show an abridged response from each of the four, along with some discussion of what to expect.

Repository Search

The search/repositories endpoint looks in the repository metadata to match your query. This includes the project's name and description by default, though you can also search the read me file by specifying in:readme in the query. Other qualifiers are documented at *https://developer.github.com/v3/search/#search-repositories*.

A query such as search/repositories?q=foobar might result in a response that looks something like this:

```
{
  "total_count": 824,
  "incomplete_results": false,
  "items": [
    {
      "id": 10869370,
      "name": "foobar",
      "full_name": "iwhitcomb/foobar",
      "owner": {
        "login": "iwhitcomb",
        "id": 887528,
        "avatar_url": "https://avatars.githubusercontent.com/u/887528?v=3",
        ...
      },
      "private": false,
      "html_url": "https://github.com/iwhitcomb/foobar",
      "description": "Drupal 8 Module Example",
      "fork": false,
      ...
      "score": 59.32314
    },
    ...
  ]
}
```

Each item in items is the description of a repository. All sorts of useful information is included, such as a URL to the UI for this repository (html_url), the owner's avatar (owner.avatar_url), and a URL suitable for cloning the repository using Git (git_url).

Code Search

The `search/code` endpoint is for searching the contents of a repository. You can try matching the contents of the files themselves, or their paths (using `in:path`). (For complete documentation on the other available qualifiers, check out *https://devel oper.github.com/v3/search/#search-code*.)

This API is subject to several limits that don't affect the other search endpoints, because of the sheer amount of data the server must sort through to find matches. First, it requires that you provide a general search term (a phrase to match); specifying a query with *only* operators (like `language:python`) is valid with other APIs, but not here. Second, any wildcard characters in the query will be ignored. Third, files above a certain size will not be searched. Fourth, it only searches the default branch of any given project, which is usually `master`. Fifth, and possibly most importantly, you *must* specify a repository owner using the `user:<name>` qualifier; you cannot search all repositories with one query.

The JSON returned looks something like this:

```
{
  "total_count": 9246,
  "incomplete_results": false,
  "items": [
    {
      "name": "migrated_0000.js",
      "path": "test/fixtures/ES6/class/migrated_0000.js",
      "sha": "37bdd2221a71b58576da9d3c2dc0ef0998263652",
      "url": "…",
      "git_url": "…",
      "html_url": "…",
      "repository": {
        "id": 2833537,
        "name": "esprima",
        "full_name": "jquery/esprima",
        "owner": {
          "login": "jquery",
          "id": 70142,
          "avatar_url": "https://avatars.githubusercontent.com/u/70142?v=3",
          …
        },
        "private": false,
        …
      },
      "score": 2.3529532
    },
    …
  ]
}
```

Each item has some data about the file that turned up, including its name and URLs for a couple of representations of it. Then there's the blob of data about its repository, followed by a score, which is used for the default "best match" sorting.

Issue Search

Repositories contain more than just code. The `search/issues` endpoint looks for matches in the issues and pull requests attached to a project. This endpoint responds to a wide variety of search qualifiers, such as:

type
> Either "pr" for pull requests, or "issue" for issues (the default is both).

team
> Match issues whose discussions mention a specific team (only works for organizations you belong to).

no
> Match issues that are missing a piece of data (as in "no:label").

There are many more; see *https://developer.github.com/v3/search/#search-issues* for complete documentation.

The result of a call to this endpoint looks like this:

```
{
  "total_count": 1278397,
  "incomplete_results": false,
  "items": [
    {
      "url": "…",
      "labels_url": "…",
      "comments_url": "…",
      "events_url": "…",
      "html_url": "…",
      "id": 69671218,
      "number": 1,
      "title": "Classes",
      "user": {
        "login": "reubeningber",
        "id": 2552792,
        "avatar_url": "…",
        …
      },
      "labels": [
        …
      ],
      "state": "open",
      "locked": false,
      "assignee": null,
```

```
        "milestone": null,
        "comments": 0,
        "created_at": "2015-04-20T20:18:56Z",
        "updated_at": "2015-04-20T20:18:56Z",
        "closed_at": null,
        "body": "There should be an option to add classes to the ul and li...",
        "score": 22.575937
    },
  ]
}
```

Again, each item in the list looks like the result of a call to the issued API. There are a lot of useful bits of data here, such as the issue's title (`title`), labels (`labels`), and links to information about the pull-request data (`pull_request.url`), which won't be present if the result isn't a pull request.

User Search

All the other Search APIs are centered around repositories, but this endpoint searches a different namespace: GitHub users. By default, only a user's login name and public email address are searched; the `in` qualifier can extend this to include the user's full name as well, with `in:fullname,login,email`. There are several other useful qualifiers available; see *https://developer.github.com/v3/search/#search-users* for complete documentation.

Querying the `search/users` endpoint gives you this kind of response:

```
{
  "total_count": 26873,
  "incomplete_results": false,
  "items": [
    {
      "login": "ben",
      "id": 39902,
      "avatar_url": "…",
      "gravatar_id": "",
      "url": "…",
      "html_url": "…",

      …
      "score": 98.24275
    },
    {
      "login": "bengottlieb",
      "id": 53162,
      "avatar_url": "…",
      "gravatar_id": "",
      "url": "…",
      "html_url": "…",

      …
      "score": 35.834213
```

```
        },
    ]
}
```

The list of items in this case look like the results from a query of the `users/<name>` endpoint. Useful items here are the user's avatar (`avatar_url`), several links to other API endpoints (`repos_url`, `url`), and the type of result (user or organization, in `type`).

Our Example Application

Now that we know a bit about how this API behaves, let's do something useful with it.

Imagine that your development team uses GitHub to store their Git repositories, and that there are lots of little repositories for parts of the application that work together at runtime. This kind of situation ends up being fairly difficult to work with for your nontechnical colleagues; if they want to report an issue, they don't know where to go, and they don't know how to find issues that already exist.

Search can make this possible, but doing a search across an entire organization's repositories involves using the `user:<organization>` operator, which is obtusely named, and kind of scary for nonprogrammers. Plus, the user would have to remember to add that option every single time they wanted to search for issues.

The Search API can make this a bit easier. Let's make a GUI application with just a single search box, which makes it dead simple for a nontechnical user to search all the issues in all the repositories in a single organization. It'll end up looking a bit like Figures 4-1, 4-2, and 4-3.

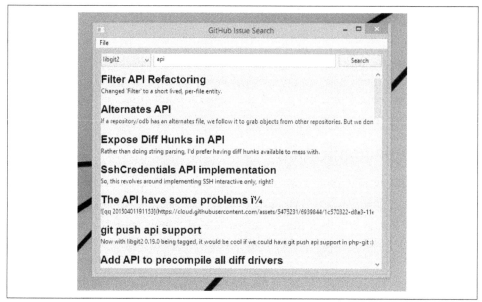

Figure 4-1. GitHub search application on Windows

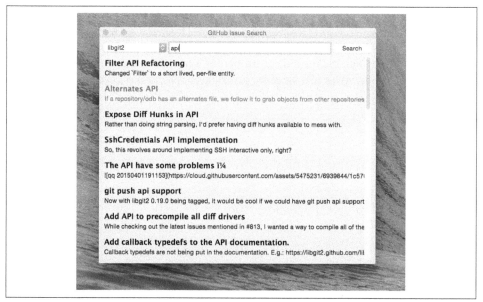

Figure 4-2. GitHub search application on Mac

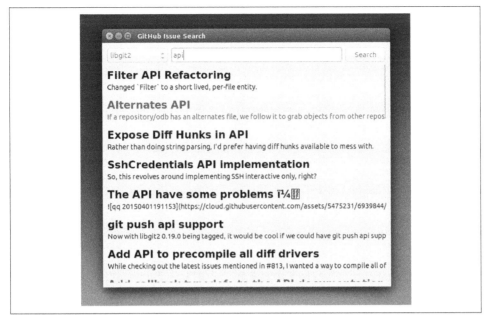

Figure 4-3. GitHub search application on Linux

User Flow

That's the overall goal, but let's dig in to more detail about how the user experiences the application.

The first thing we'll do is require the user to log in with GitHub credentials. Why? Partly because the Search API is throttled pretty aggressively, and the rate limits are higher with authenticated access. But also because our user is going to need the ability to search issues in private repositories. To make this easier, our program will try to get GitHub credentials from Git's credential store, but it'll fall back to a login form, which looks like Figure 4-4.

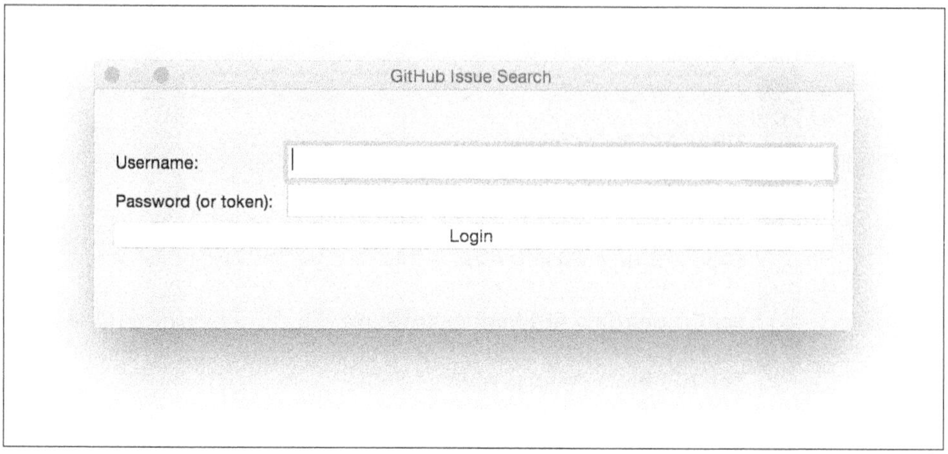

Figure 4-4. Login UI

Once the user logs in, they'll be shown a search box. Typing in a search query and hitting Enter will result in a scrollable list of search results, with titles and the first line of the description. Clicking a search result opens the issue in the user's browser.

That's about it. This application only has two main screens from the user's point of view. It's a simple, focused tool to solve a very tightly defined problem, so the code shouldn't be too hard.

Python

Now that we know how the program should act, let's decide how it should *work*.

We'll use Python for our implementation language, for several reasons. First, because we haven't yet seen it in this book, and we like to expose you to a wide variety of languages. One of our goals is to help the reader explore technologies they might not have seen before.

Secondly, there's a Python library for building GUI applications that run without modification on Mac OS X, Linux, and Windows. Surprisingly, this is a fairly unique feature among modern high-level programming languages. If you want this capability elsewhere, you usually have to use a high-complexity framework, a lower-level language like C++, or both.

Thirdly, this will help make it easy to distribute. There is a Python package that bundles an entire Python program and all of its dependencies into a single file (or *.app* bundle on OS X). So giving this program to a colleague is as easy as emailing her a ZIP file, which will help with our use case: a nontechnical user might not be totally comfortable clicking through an installer (or even have permissions to do so on their machine).

Let's take a quick look at the libraries we'll be using in our application's code. We'll see them in action later on, but a quick overview will help you understand what each one is trying to do. As is unfortunately typical with Python development, installation methods vary from package to package, so we'll also tell you how to get each one onto your machine.

AGitHub

The first thing we should mention is the library we'll use to talk to the GitHub API, which is called `agithub`. `agithub` is a very thin layer that converts GitHub's REST API into method calls on objects, resulting in delightfully readable code.

`agithub` can be found at *https://github.com/jpaugh/agithub*, and the "installation" is simply to download a copy of the *agithub.py* source file and place it alongside your project files.

WxPython

WxPython is how we'll create the graphical interface for our application. It's an object-oriented Python layer over the top of a toolkit called WxWidgets, which is itself a common-code adapter for native UI toolkits. WxWidgets supports Linux, Mac, and Windows operating systems with native controls, so you can access all of those platforms with the same Python code.

Information about the WxPython project can be found at *http://www.wxpython.org*, and you'll find a download link for your platform on the lefthand side of the page. The next version of WxPython (code-named "Phoenix") will be installable via PIP, but at the time of this writing Phoenix is still prerelease software, so it's probably safer to use the stable version.

 A bit of background on Python: it's undergoing a transition. Currently there are two actively used versions: Python 2.7 and Python 3 (3.5 at the time of this writing). Most of the details are unimportant, but in order to follow along with this example, you'll have to be running Python 2.7, because WxPython doesn't currently support Python 3. Support for Python 3 is planned for the upcoming Phoenix release, so most of the following code is written in a "polyglot" fashion, so you shouldn't run into any trouble running it under Python 3 if Phoenix has arrived by the time you read this.

PyInstaller

PyInstaller will be our distribution tool. Its main function is to read your Python code, analyze it to discover all its dependencies, then collect all these files (including the Python interpreter) and put them in one directory. It can even wrap all of that up in a single package that, when double-clicked, runs your program. It does all this without needing much input from you, and there are only a few configuration options. If you've written GUI applications before, you'll know how hard each of these problems are.

For information on this project, you can visit *http://pythonhosted.org/PyInstaller*. You can install it using Python's package manager by running pip install pyinstaller.

The Code

Alright, now you have an idea of which parts of the Python ecosystem will be helping us on our journey. Let's get started looking at the code that brings them all together. We'll start with this skeleton file:

```
#!/usr/bin/env python ❶

import os, subprocess
import wx
from agithub import Github ❷

class SearchFrame(wx.Frame): ❸
    pass

if __name__ == '__main__': ❹
    app = wx.App() ❺
    SearchFrame(None)
    app.MainLoop()
```

Let's take a look at a few key things:

❶ The "shebang" specifies that this is a Python 2.7 program.

❷ Here we import our handy libraries. We import WxPython (wx) whole cloth, but with agithub we only need the Github (note the capitalization) class. os and subprocess come from the Python standard library.

❸ This is the class for our main window. We'll walk through the particulars later on when we discuss the real implementation.

❹ In Python, you create the main entry point of an application using this syntax.

❺ And this is how you write a "main" function in WxPython. We instantiate an App instance, create an instance of our top-level frame, and run the app's main loop.

If you run this program right now, your command line will appear to hang, but it's actually waiting for GUI input. This is because the wx library won't create a "frame" window that has no contents. Let's correct that, but first a quick diversion into Git internals to make our experience a bit nicer.

Git Credential Helper

That's how most of the UI code is going to be structured, but before we go any further, we should define a function to help us get the user's GitHub credentials. We'll be cheating a bit, by asking Git if it has the user's login and password.

We'll leverage the `git credential fill` command. This is used internally by Git to avoid having to ask the user for their GitHub password every time they interact with a GitHub remote. The way it works is by accepting all the known facts about a connection as text lines through `stdin`, in the format `<key>=<value>`. Once the caller has supplied all the facts it knows, it can close the `stdin` stream (or supply an empty line), and Git will respond with all the facts *it* knows about this connection. With any luck, this will include the user's login and password. The whole interaction looks a bit like this:

```
$ echo "host=github.com" | git credential fill ❶
host=github.com
username=ben ❷
password=(redacted)
```

❶ This passes a single line to `git credential` and closes `stdin`, which Git will recognize as the end of input.

❷ Git responds with all the facts it knows about the connection. This includes the input values, as well as the username and password if Git knows them.

One other thing you should know about `git-credential` is that by default, if it doesn't know anything about the host, it'll ask the user at the terminal. That's bad for a GUI app, so we're going to be disabling that feature through the use of the GIT_ASK PASS environment variable.

Here's what our helper looks like:

```
GITHUB_HOST = 'github.com'
def git_credentials():
    os.environ['GIT_ASKPASS'] = 'true' ❶
    p = subprocess.Popen(['git', 'credential', 'fill'],
                         stdout=subprocess.PIPE,
                         stdin=subprocess.PIPE) ❷
    stdout,stderr = p.communicate('host={}\n\n'.format(GITHUB_HOST)) ❸

    creds = {}
    for line in stdout.split('\n')[:-1]: ❹
        k,v = line.split('=')
```

```
        creds[k] = v
    return creds ❺
```

❶ Here we set GIT_ASKPASS to the string 'true', which is a UNIX program that always succeeds, which will in turn cause git-credential to stop trying to get credentials when it gets to the "ask the user" stage.

❷ subprocess.Popen is the way you use a program with stdin and stdout in Python. The first argument is a list of arguments for the new program, and we also specify that we want stdin and stdout to be captured.

❸ p.communicate does the work of writing to stdin and returning the contents of stdout. It also returns the contents of stderr, which we ignore in this program.

❹ Here we process the stdout contents by splitting each line at the = character and slurping it into a dictionary.

❺ So the return value from this call should be a dictionary with 'username' and 'password' values. Handy!

Windowing and Interface

Okay, so now we have something that can help us skip a login screen, but we don't have a way of showing that login screen to the user. Let's get closer to that goal by filling in the main frame's implementation:

```
class SearchFrame(wx.Frame):
    def __init__(self, *args, **kwargs): ❶
        kwargs.setdefault('size', (600,500))
        wx.Frame.__init__(self, *args, **kwargs)

        self.credentials = {}
        self.orgs = []

        self.create_controls()
        self.do_layout()
        self.SetTitle('GitHub Issue Search')

        # Try to pre-load credentials from Git's cache
        self.credentials = git_credentials()
        if self.test_credentials():
            self.switch_to_search_panel()

        self.Show()
```

❶ There's a bit of syntax here that might be confusing. The *args and **kwargs entries here are ways of capturing multiple arguments into one parameter. For now, just know that we're only capturing them here so we can pass them to the parent class constructor two lines down.

The __init__ method is the constructor, so this is where we start when the main function calls SearchFrame(). Here's what's happening at a high level—we'll dig into the details in a bit:

1. Set up some layout dimensions and pass to the parent class's constructor

2. Create the UI controls

3. Retrieve the credentials from the user using the credential helper we described earlier

4. Change the title and display the application to the user

Before we get to *how* all those things are done, let's step back a bit and talk about this class's job. It's responsible for maintaining the top-level *frame* (a window with a title bar, a menu, and so on), and deciding what's displayed in that frame. In this case, we want to show a login UI first, and when we get valid credentials (either from Git or the user), we'll switch to a searching UI.

Alright, enough background. Let's walk through the code for getting and checking credentials:

```
def login_accepted(self, username, password):
    self.credentials['username'] = username
    self.credentials['password'] = password
    if self.test_credentials():
        self.switch_to_search_panel()

def test_credentials(self):
    if any(k not in self.credentials for k in ['username', 'password']):
        return False
    g = Github(self.credentials['username'], self.credentials['password'])
    status,data = g.user.orgs.get()  ❶
    if status != 200:
        print('bad credentials in store')
        return False
    self.orgs = [o['login'] for o in data]  ❷
    return True

def switch_to_search_panel(self):
    self.login_panel.Destroy()
    self.search_panel = SearchPanel(self,
                                    orgs=self.orgs,
                                    credentials=self.credentials)
    self.sizer.Add(self.search_panel, 1, flag=wx.EXPAND | wx.ALL, border=10)
    self.sizer.Layout()
```

❶ The `agithub` library always returns two values from every function call. Python lets us bind these directly to variables with this `a,b = <expr>` syntax.

❷ agithub decodes the JSON from the API call into a Python dictionary. Here we're only really interested in the names of the organization, so we use a *list comprehension*, where we tell Python to only keep the value of the `"login"` field from each dictionary in the `data` list.

Each of these three methods comes in at a different point during our program's execution. If our credentials are coming from Git, we proceed straight to `test_credentials`; if they're coming from the login panel (see "GitHub Login" on page 72), they go through the `login_accepted` callback first, which then calls `test_credentials`.

Either way, what we do is try to fetch a list of the user's organizations, to see if they work. Here you can see the usage pattern for `agithub`—the URL path is mapped to object-property notation on an instance of the `Github` class, and the HTTP verb is mapped to a method call. The return values are a status code and the data, which has been decoded into a dictionary object. If it fails—meaning the returned status is not `200`—we send the user to the login panel. If it succeeds, we call `switch_to_search_panel`.

 We're doing a synchronous network call on the UI thread. This is usually a bad idea, because the UI will become unresponsive until the network call completes. Ideally we'd move this out onto another thread, and get the return value with a message. However, this would add length and complexity to a chapter already rife with both, so we've decided not to include this advanced topic here. We hope you'll forgive us this small simplification; for this use case, the synchronous code will be just fine.

The last method handles the UI switch. The login panel is referenced by two things: the `SearchFrame` instance (the parent window), and the sizer that's controlling its layout. Fortunately, calling the `Destroy()` method cleans both of those up, so we can then create the `SearchPanel` instance and add it to our sizer. Doing this requires a specific call to the sizer's `Layout()` method; otherwise, the sizer won't know that it needs to adjust the position and size of the new panel:

```
def create_controls(self):
    # Set up a menu. This is mainly for "Cmd-Q" behavior on OSX
    filemenu = wx.Menu()
    filemenu.Append(wx.ID_EXIT, '&Exit')
    menuBar = wx.MenuBar()
    menuBar.Append(filemenu, '&File')
    self.SetMenuBar(menuBar)
```

```
        # Start with a login UI
        self.login_panel = LoginPanel(self, onlogin=self.login_accepted)

    def do_layout(self):
        self.sizer = wx.BoxSizer(wx.VERTICAL)
        self.sizer.Add(self.login_panel, 1, flag=wx.EXPAND | wx.ALL, border=10)
        self.SetSizer(self.sizer)
```

create_controls is fairly straightforward. It instantiates a menu that only contains File→Exit, and a login panel, whose implementation we'll cover a bit later on. Note that when we create a visible control, we pass self as the first parameter to the constructor. That's because the SearchFrame instance we're constructing is the parent window of that control.

do_layout uses a WxWidgets feature called *sizers* to do some automated layout. Sizers are a complex topic, but here's all you need to know about this snippet:

- A BoxSizer stacks widgets in a single direction, in this case vertically.

- The second parameter to sizer.Add is a scaling factor. If it's zero, the widget you're adding will always stay the same size if the parent window resizes; if it's anything else, all the things the sizer is controlling will adjust to fill their container. There's only one control in this sizer, but we still want it to take up the full area of the window, so we pass 1.

- The border parameter tells the sizer how much area to leave around the widget as padding.

- The wx.EXPAND flag tells the sizer that we want the widget to expand in the direction the sizer isn't stacking. In this case, we're stacking vertically, but we also want this widget to expand horizontally.

- The wx.ALL flag specifies which edges of the widget should have the border area.

Let's make sure we're following good practices, and write some tests. There isn't a lot here we can verify automatedly, but what there is should be covered:

```
from nose.tools import eq_, ok_, raises  ❶

class TestApp:
    def setUp(self):  ❷
        self.f = None
        self.app = wx.App()

    def tearDown(self):
        if self.f:
            self.f.Destroy()
        self.app.Destroy()
```

```
def test_switching_panels(self):  ❸
    self.f = SearchFrame(None, id=-1)
    # Sub-panels should exist, and be of the right type
    ok_(isinstance(self.f.login_panel, LoginPanel))
    ok_(isinstance(self.f.search_panel, SearchPanel))
    # Already destroyed
    raises(RuntimeError, lambda: self.f.login_panel.Destroy())
    # Not already destroyed
    ok_(self.f.search_panel.Destroy())
```

❶ Here we're using a testing tool called Nose. Install it with pip install nose, and invoke it at the command line by typing nosetests app.py. It uses naming conventions to identify tests and fixtures, and is generally nice to work with.

❷ Nose will automatically find these setUp and tearDown methods, and call them before and after each test method is run. In this case, we're just managing the frames we want to test, as well as an App instance for all of them to belong to.

❸ Here's a test method that Nose will find and run. We ensure the subpanels are the right type, and that we've auto-transitioned to the SearchPanel by finding credentials in Git's storage.

That's it! Aside from managing a couple of fields, most of this code is managing the UI, which is almost exactly what we'd want from a UI class. Let's write the first of the two panels we swap in and out.

GitHub Login

The LoginPanel class is similar in structure to the SearchFrame class, with a couple of key differences, which we'll describe after the wall of code:

```
class LoginPanel(wx.Panel):
    def __init__(self, *args, **kwargs):
        self.callback = kwargs.pop('onlogin', None)
        wx.Panel.__init__(self, *args, **kwargs)

        self.create_controls()
        self.do_layout()

    def create_controls(self):
        self.userLabel = wx.StaticText(self, label='Username:')
        self.userBox = wx.TextCtrl(self, style=wx.TE_PROCESS_ENTER)
        self.passLabel = wx.StaticText(self, label='Password (or token):')
        self.passBox = wx.TextCtrl(self, style=wx.TE_PROCESS_ENTER)
        self.login = wx.Button(self, label='Login')
        self.error = wx.StaticText(self, label='')
        self.error.SetForegroundColour((200,0,0))

        # Bind events
```

```
        self.login.Bind(wx.EVT_BUTTON, self.do_login)
        self.userBox.Bind(wx.EVT_TEXT_ENTER, self.do_login)
        self.passBox.Bind(wx.EVT_TEXT_ENTER, self.do_login)

    def do_layout(self):
        # Grid arrangement for controls
        grid = wx.GridBagSizer(3,3)
        grid.Add(self.userLabel, pos=(0,0),
                flag=wx.TOP | wx.LEFT | wx.BOTTOM, border=5)
        grid.Add(self.userBox, pos=(0,1),
                flag=wx.EXPAND | wx.LEFT | wx.RIGHT, border=5)
        grid.Add(self.passLabel, pos=(1,0),
                flag=wx.TOP | wx.LEFT | wx.BOTTOM, border=5)
        grid.Add(self.passBox, pos=(1,1),
                flag=wx.EXPAND | wx.LEFT | wx.RIGHT, border=5)
        grid.Add(self.login, pos=(2,0), span=(1,2),
                flag=wx.EXPAND | wx.LEFT | wx.RIGHT, border=5)
        grid.Add(self.error, pos=(3,0), span=(1,2),
                flag=wx.EXPAND | wx.LEFT | wx.RIGHT, border=5)
        grid.AddGrowableCol(1)

        # Center the grid vertically
        vbox = wx.BoxSizer(wx.VERTICAL)
        vbox.Add((0,0), 1)
        vbox.Add(grid, 0, wx.EXPAND)
        vbox.Add((0,0), 2)
        self.SetSizer(vbox)

    def do_login(self, _):
        u = self.userBox.GetValue()
        p = self.passBox.GetValue()
        g = Github(u, p)
        status,data = g.issues.get()
        if status != 200:
            self.error.SetLabel('ERROR: ' + data['message'])
        elif callable(self.callback):
            self.callback(u, p)
```

There's some structure that's similar to the preceding code. We'll start with the constructor.

Recall that this panel is created with a keyword argument in SearchFrame's create_controls method, like LoginPanel(self, onlogin=self.login_accepted). In the constructor definition, we pull that callback out and store it for later. Afterward, we just call the two other construction functions and return.

create_controls has more to it than SearchFrame's version, because this panel has more controls. Every static-text, text-input, and button control gets its own line of code. The wx.TE_PROCESS_ENTER style tells the library we want an event to be triggered if the user presses the Enter key while the cursor is inside that text box.

The next block binds control events to method calls. Every event in WxPython will call the handler with a single argument, an object that contains information about the event. That means we can use the same function to handle any number of different kinds of events, so we do—the ENTER handlers for both text boxes and the BUTTON handler for the button all go through self.do_login.

do_layout uses a different kind of sizer—a GridBagSizer. Again, the topic of sizers is *way* outside the scope of this chapter, but just know that this kind arranges things in a grid, and you can allow some of the rows or columns to stretch to fill the container. Here we drop all of the controls into their positions with the pos=(r,c) notation (here "rows" come first, which isn't like most coordinate systems), and cause one control to span two columns with the span parameter. The flags and border parameters mostly mean the same things as before, and the AddGrowableCol function tells the layout engine which parts of the grid should be allowed to stretch.

Then we do something curious: we put the GridBagSizer *into another sizer*. Sizer nesting is a powerful feature, and allows almost any window layout to be possible—although perhaps not easy or simple. The vertical box sizer also contains some bare tuples; this special form is called "adding a spacer." In this case, we sandwich the sizer with all the controls between two spacers with different weights, making it float about a third of the way down the window. The effect is like Figure 4-5.

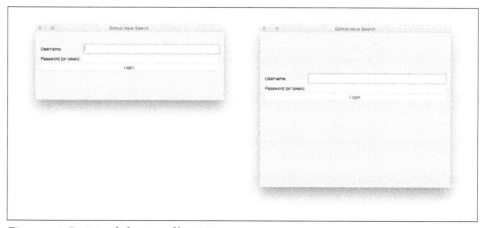

Figure 4-5. Resizing behavior of login UI

Then comes the do_login method, which tests out the given credentials, and if they work, passes them back through the callback set at construction time. If they don't work, it sets the text of a label, whose foreground color has been set to a nice, alarming shade of red.

Let's make sure this behavior is tested at least a little bit. Again, there's not much that it's doing other than setting up WxPython stuff, but we can validate that a login error is displayed by adding this method to the test class:

```python
def test_login_panel(self):
    self.f = wx.Frame(None)
    lp = LoginPanel(self.f)
    eq_(lp.error.GetLabelText(), '')
    lp.do_login(None)
    ok_(lp.error.GetLabelText().startswith('ERROR'))
```

GitHub Search

Once the user has successfully logged in, we destroy the `LoginPanel` instance and show the `SearchPanel`:

```python
class SearchPanel(wx.Panel):
    def __init__(self, *args, **kwargs):
        self.orgs = kwargs.pop('orgs', [])
        self.credentials = kwargs.pop('credentials', {})  ❶
        wx.Panel.__init__(self, *args, **kwargs)

        self.create_controls()
        self.do_layout()

    def create_controls(self):
        self.results_panel = None
        self.orgChoice = wx.Choice(self, choices=self.orgs, style=wx.CB_SORT)
        self.searchTerm = wx.TextCtrl(self, style=wx.TE_PROCESS_ENTER)
        self.searchTerm.SetFocus()
        self.searchButton = wx.Button(self, label="Search")

        # Bind events  ❷
        self.searchButton.Bind(wx.EVT_BUTTON, self.do_search)
        self.searchTerm.Bind(wx.EVT_TEXT_ENTER, self.do_search)

    def do_layout(self):
        # Arrange choice, query box, and button horizontally
        hbox = wx.BoxSizer(wx.HORIZONTAL)
        hbox.Add(self.orgChoice, 0, wx.EXPAND)
        hbox.Add(self.searchTerm, 1, wx.EXPAND | wx.LEFT, 5)
        hbox.Add(self.searchButton, 0, wx.EXPAND | wx.LEFT, 5)

        # Dock everything to the top, leaving room for the results
        self.vbox = wx.BoxSizer(wx.VERTICAL)
        self.vbox.Add(hbox, 0, wx.EXPAND)  ❸
        self.SetSizer(self.vbox)

    def do_search(self, event):
        term = self.searchTerm.GetValue()
        org = self.orgChoice.GetString(self.orgChoice.GetCurrentSelection())
        g = Github(self.credentials['username'], self.credentials['password'])
```

```
        code,data = g.search.issues.get(q="user:{} {}".format(org, term)) ❹
        if code != 200:
            self.display_error(code, data)
        else:
            self.display_results(data['items'])

    def display_results(self, results): ❺
        if self.results_panel:
            self.results_panel.Destroy()
        self.results_panel = SearchResultsPanel(self, -1, results=results)
        self.vbox.Add(self.results_panel, 1, wx.EXPAND | wx.TOP, 5)
        self.vbox.Layout()

    def display_error(self, code, data): ❻
        if self.results_panel:
            self.results_panel.Destroy()
        if 'errors' in data:
            str = ''.join('\n\n{}'.format(e['message']) for e in data['errors'])
        else:
            str = data['message']
        self.results_panel = wx.StaticText(self, label=str)
        self.results_panel.SetForegroundColour((200,0,0))
        self.vbox.Add(self.results_panel, 1, wx.EXPAND | wx.TOP, 5)
        self.vbox.Layout()
        width = self.results_panel.GetSize().x
        self.results_panel.Wrap(width)
```

There's quite a bit here, but some of it is familiar. We'll skip the usual walkthrough to point out a couple of interesting features:

❶ When creating the panel, we pass in the user's credentials and list of organizations as keyword arguments, so they show up in the kwargs dictionary. Here we use pop to make sure the parent class's constructor doesn't get confused by them.

❷ Here we capture both the search button's "click" event, as well as the text box's "enter key" event. Both should cause the search to be performed.

❸ When we add the search bar to the sizer, we use 0 as a scale factor. This means it shouldn't expand to fit the available size, but keep its own size instead, to leave room to add a results panel later on.

❹ Here's where the actual search is being done. We get the search term and organization, and send them to the agithub instance, which returns our results and an HTTP result code.

❺ We pass the search results into another class, then add it to the main sizer with parameters to fill the remaining available space.

❻ If an error is returned from the search call instead, we display it here. There's some code to adjust the wrap width of the text, based on the laid-out width of the control. This isn't a great approach, but doing it better is left as an exercise for the reader.

Again, there's a fair amount of code here, but most of it should look familiar. Here's the test code that covers the previous code:

```
def test_search_panel(self):
    self.f = wx.Frame(None)
    sp = SearchPanel(self.f, orgs=['a', 'b', 'c'])
    eq_(0, sp.orgChoice.GetCurrentSelection())
    eq_('a', sp.orgChoice.GetString(0))
    sp.display_error(400, {'errors': [{'message': 'xyz'}]})
    ok_(isinstance(sp.results_panel, wx.StaticText))
    eq_('xyz', sp.results_panel.GetLabelText().strip())
```

Displaying Results

So now we have our login panel, and a way for the user to enter a search query, but no way to display results. Let's fix that.

Whenever search results are retrieved, we create a new instance of SearchResultsPanel, which then creates a series of SearchResult instances. Let's look at both of them together:

```
class SearchResultsPanel(wx.ScrolledWindow): ❶
    def __init__(self, *args, **kwargs):
        results = kwargs.pop('results', [])
        wx.PyScrolledWindow.__init__(self, *args, **kwargs)

        # Layout search result controls inside scrollable area
        vbox = wx.BoxSizer(wx.VERTICAL)
        if not results:
            vbox.Add(wx.StaticText(self, label="(no results)"), 0, wx.EXPAND)
        for r in results:
            vbox.Add(SearchResult(self, result=r),
                     flag=wx.TOP | wx.BOTTOM, border=8)
        self.SetSizer(vbox)
        self.SetScrollbars(0, 4, 0, 0)

class SearchResult(wx.Panel):
    def __init__(self, *args, **kwargs):
        self.result = kwargs.pop('result', {})
        wx.Panel.__init__(self, *args, **kwargs)

        self.create_controls()
        self.do_layout()

    def create_controls(self): ❷
        titlestr = self.result['title']
```

```
            if self.result['state'] != 'open':
                titlestr += ' ({})'.format(self.result['state'])
            textstr = self.first_line(self.result['body'])
            self.title = wx.StaticText(self, label=titlestr)
            self.text = wx.StaticText(self, label=textstr)

            # Adjust the title font
            titleFont = wx.Font(16, wx.FONTFAMILY_DEFAULT,
                                wx.FONTSTYLE_NORMAL, wx.FONTWEIGHT_BOLD)
            self.title.SetFont(titleFont)

            # Bind click and hover events on this whole control ❸
            self.Bind(wx.EVT_LEFT_UP, self.on_click)
            self.Bind(wx.EVT_ENTER_WINDOW, self.enter)
            self.Bind(wx.EVT_LEAVE_WINDOW, self.leave)

        def do_layout(self):
            vbox = wx.BoxSizer(wx.VERTICAL)
            vbox.Add(self.title, flag=wx.EXPAND | wx.BOTTOM, border=2)
            vbox.Add(self.text, flag=wx.EXPAND)
            self.SetSizer(vbox)

        def enter(self, _):
            self.title.SetForegroundColour(wx.BLUE)
            self.text.SetForegroundColour(wx.BLUE)

        def leave(self, _):
            self.title.SetForegroundColour(wx.BLACK)
            self.text.SetForegroundColour(wx.BLACK)

        def on_click(self, event): ❹
            import webbrowser
            webbrowser.open(self.result['html_url'])

        def first_line(self, body):
            return body.split('\n')[0].strip() or '(no body)'
```

❶ The containing panel is simple enough that it only consists of a constructor. This class's job is to contain the results and present them in a scroll window.

❷ A SearchResult is comprised of two static text controls, which contain the issue's title and the first line of its body.

❸ We're not only binding the click handler for this entire panel, but also the mouse-enter and mouse-leave events, so we can make it behave more like a link in a browser.

❹ Here's how you open the default browser to a URL in Python.

So now you've seen the code for a simple WxPython application. Using this library tends to produce code of a certain style, which is kind of verbose. The positive side of this is that nothing is hidden; all the layout for your app is done right in the code, with no "magic," and the fact that it can run without modification on just about anybody's computer is a huge plus. WxPython may lack some facilities of newer frameworks, but there's nothing better for getting a basic cross-platform UI out the door quickly.

That's all of the code! If you've been following along and typing all this code into a file, you can run that file and do issue searches. However, our use case has a nontechnical user running this; let's see what can be done to make it easier for them to get started.

Packaging

What we're not going to do is require anyone to install Python 2.7 and a bunch of packages. We'll use PyInstaller to bundle our application into something that's easy to distribute and run.

Let's assume you wrote all the preceding code into a file called *search.py*, and *agithub.py* is sitting in the same directory. Here's how to tell PyInstaller to generate a single application for you:

```
$ pyinstaller -w search.py
```

That's it! The -w flag tells PyInstaller to create a "windowed" build of your application, rather than the default console build. On OS X, this generates a *search.app* application bundle, and on Windows this generates a *search.exe* file. You can take either of these to a computer with no Python installed, and they'll run perfectly.

That's because PyInstaller has copied everything necessary for your program to run, from the Python interpreter on up, inside that file. The one I just generated is 67 MB, which seems large for such a simple program, but that number is more reasonable when you consider what's inside the package.

Summary

Whew! This chapter was quite a journey. Let's take a breath, and look at what we've learned.

The main bulk of the code in this chapter had to do with defining a graphical interface. Code for this task is always pretty verbose, because of the sheer complexity of the task. With WxPython in your tool belt, however, you can now write GUI applications using Python, with code that's no harder to write than with other toolkits, and get the ability to run on every major platform for free.

We saw how to ask Git for credentials to a Git server using `git credential`. This feature is quite capable, and includes the ability to write a custom credential storage backend, but we at least saw a peek into how it works. Using this knowledge, you can piggyback on your users' existing habits to avoid having to ask them for the same things over and over again.

We also saw a rather nice HTTP API abstraction with `agithub`. We authenticated and queried the issue search API endpoint using what looked like object-method notation. `agithub` is a great example of how a library package can be both future-proof and idiomatic—the library constructs a query URL by looking at the chain of properties and methods used in the call. This is a great jumping-off point for querying other REST APIs using the same pattern.

Finally, the main thrust of this chapter was using the GitHub Search API. You've learned about its general behavior, the different categories of search, how to interpret and sort results, and ways of focusing a search to reduce the number of uninteresting results. Using this knowledge you should be able to find anything you're looking for on GitHub or GitHub Enterprise. You also know that the search UI on GitHub is just a thin layer over the Search API, so the same tricks and techniques will serve you whether you're writing code or using a browser.

Time to switch gears a bit. The next chapter introduces the Commit Status API, which is a way of annotating individual commits in a Git repository with a "good" or "bad" flag. We'll be using what only a few years ago would have been a polarizing choice: C# and the CLR.

CHAPTER 5

.NET and the Commit Status API

At the risk of oversimplifying things too much, one way to look at a Git repository is as just a long series of commits. Each commit contains quite a bit of information: the contents of the source files, who created the commit and when, the author's comments on what changes the commit introduces, and so on. This is all good stuff, and works very well for Git's main use case: controlling the history of a software project.

GitHub's Commit Status API adds another layer of metadata to a commit: what various services *say* about that commit. This capability primarily shows itself in the pull request UI, as shown in Figure 5-1. Each commit in the pull request is annotated with a symbol indicating its status—a red "×" for failure or error, a green "✓" for success, or an amber "•" to indicate that a decision is in the process of being made. This feature also surfaces at the bottom of the pull request; if the last commit in the branch is not marked as successful, you get a warning about merging the request.

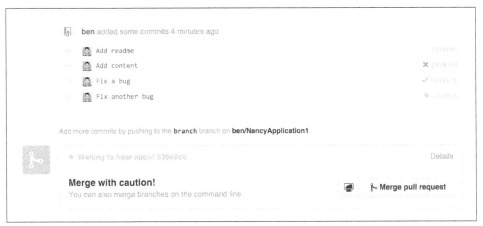

Figure 5-1. Commit status in the pull request UI

The most obvious application for this feature is a continuous-integration service. A program like Jenkins will get a notification when new commits are pushed to a branch, run a build/test cycle using the new code, and post the results through the Commit Status API. An application like this can even include a link back to the build results, so the user can find out which tests failed. This is a great way to bring together everything needed to make a decision about a proposal: what code has changed, what do people think about it, and does this change break anything? The answer to all of these questions is available on the same page: the pull-request conversation view.

But building and testing is only the beginning; the status of a commit can be used for other purposes as well. For example, open source projects often have a license agreement you must sign in order to submit a contribution. These are called "contributor license agreements," and usually contain language about licensing the contribution to the maintainers of the project. But it's tedious to manually check every incoming pull request to see if the author has signed the CLA, so a continuous-integration-style service can be used for this. CLAHub is one such example: it checks to see if all of the authors of the contained commits have signed the CLA, and marks the latest commit as "error" if not.

So now that we know what the feature is, and what its intended use is, let's take a look at how a program can interact with it.

The API

First, let's talk about access control. The Commit Status API exposes the need for OAuth as few others do. Making a repository private means you want complete control of what people or applications can access it. Naturally you trust GitHub's internal code to do the right thing with your data, but what about some random application from the Internet? OAuth gives you a way to grant private-repository access to an application *with limits*—the use of OAuth scopes allows an application to ask for a specific set of permissions, but it won't be able to do just any old thing with your data. Plus, this way you're always in control of these permissions; you can revoke an application's access at any time.

The OAuth system includes the concept of scopes, which can be requested by and granted to an application, each of which allows a certain set of actions. The Commit Status API requires the `repo:status` OAuth scope, which allows an application read and write access to *just* commit statuses; there is no access granted to the actual contents of the repository. This might seem strange: how can you judge the status of a commit without being able to inspect its contents? Just remember that this feature has use cases beyond continuous integration, and an application may not need full access to make a decision. For services that do need to be able to look at the repository contents, you can request the `repo` scope, which grants read *and* write access to the entire contents of a repository, including commit statuses. As of this writing, there's no way to request read-only access to repositories, so if a service needs access to your data, you have to trust it with write access.

You can also use this API in anonymous mode, without using OAuth at all. However, in that case you're limited to reading statuses from public repositories; there is no writing, and private repositories are off-limits.

Just to summarize:

OAuth scope	Access to statuses	Access to repo data
None (anonymous)	Read-only on public repos	Read-only on public repos
repo:status	Read/write	None
repo	Read/write	Read/write

Raw Statuses

Now that we know how we get access to commit statuses, let's see what they look like. Commit statuses exist as atomic entities, and each commit can have a practically unlimited number of them (the actual number is in the thousands). You can query for existing statuses by doing a GET request to the API server at /repos/*<user>*/*<repo>*/*<ref>*/statuses, and it will return a list of them that looks like this:

```
[
  {
    "url": "https://api.github.com/repos/…",
    "id": 224503786,
    "state": "success",
    "description": "The Travis CI build passed",
    "target_url": "https://travis-ci.org/libgit2/libgit2/builds/63428108",
    "context": "continuous-integration/travis-ci/push",
    "created_at": "2015-05-21T03:11:02Z",
    "updated_at": "2015-05-21T03:11:02Z"
  },
  …
]
```

Most of this is self-explanatory, but a couple of fields need explaining:

Field	Description
state	One of success, failure, error, or pending.
target_url	A URL for the specific decision made for this commit (in this case a build/test log), which helps the user figure out why a particular decision was reached.

Field	Description
context	Used for correlating multiple status updates to a single service; each application sets this according to its own rules, but any process that creates statuses should post the pending status and the result status using the same context value.

This API is useful for getting the raw data involved, but it gets complicated quickly. How do you decide if a given commit is "good?" What if there are three pending statuses, one success, another pending, two failures, and another success, in that order? The context field can help you correlate a single service's updates, and you can order them by created_at to see how each one turned out, but that's a lot of work. Fortunately, the API server can do it for you.

Combined Status

If you instead do a GET to /repos/<user>/<repo>/<ref>/status (note that the last word is singular), you'll instead get a response that looks like this:

```
{
  "state": "success",
  "statuses": [
    {
      "url": "https://api.github.com/repos/…",
      …
    },
    { … }
  ],
  "sha": "6675aaba883952a1c1b28390866301ee5c281d37",
  "total_count": 2,
  "repository": { … },
  "commit_url": "https://api.github.com/repos/…",
  "url": "https://api.github.com/repos/…"
}
```

The statuses array is the result of the logic you'd probably write if you had to: it collapses the statuses by context, keeping only the last one. The state field contains an overall status that takes into account all of the contexts, providing a final value based on these rules:

Status	Cause
failure	Any of the contexts posted a failure or error state
pending	Any of the contexts' latest state is pending, or there are no statuses
success	Latest status for every context is success

This is probably exactly what you want, but if you find that your use case calls for different rules, you can always use the `statuses` endpoint to get the raw data and calculate your own combined status.

Creating a Status

Now obviously these statuses have to come from somewhere. This API also includes a facility for creating them. To do this, you simply make a POST request to `/repos/<user>/<repo>/statuses/<sha>`, and supply a JSON object for the fields you want to include with your status:

Field	Description
state	Must be one of `pending`, `success`, `error`, or `failure` (required).
target_url	A link to detailed information on the process of deciding what the state is or will be.
description	A short string describing what the service is doing to make a decision.
context	An application-specific string to allow the API to manage multiple services contributing to a single commit's status.

Notice how the last component in that URL is `<sha>`. While you can query for statuses or a combined status using a ref name (like `master`), creating a status requires you to know the full SHA-1 hash of the commit you want to annotate. This is to avoid race conditions: if you were targeting a ref, it may have moved between when your process started and when it finished, but the SHA of a commit will never change.

Let's Write an App

Alright, now that we know how to read and write statuses, let's put this API to work. In this chapter, we'll build a simple HTTP service that lets you create commit statuses for repositories you have access to using the OAuth web flow for authorization. The system we'll build will be fairly limited in scope, but it's a great starting point to customize for your specific needs.

The language this time is C#, running on the CLR (Common Language Runtime). At one point in the history of computing this wouldn't have been a good choice for a book like this, since it was only available on Windows, the development tools cost quite a bit of money, and the language and libraries were fairly limited. However, with the advent of Mono (an open source implementation of the .NET runtime), the open sourcing of the CLR core, and the availability of free tools, C# is now a completely valid and rather nice option for open source or hobby developers. Plus, it has a vibrant ecosystem of packages we can leverage to make our jobs easier.

Libraries

You'll be happy to know we won't be writing an entire HTTP server from scratch in this chapter. There are a number of open source packages that do this work for us, and in this project we'll be using Nancy. Nancy is a project that started as a CLR port of the Sinatra framework for Ruby (it takes its name from Frank Sinatra's daughter, Nancy). It's very capable, but also very succinct, as you'll see.

We also won't be directly implementing access to the GitHub API, because GitHub provides a CLR library for that. It's called octokit.net, and it does all the right things with regard to asynchrony and type safety. This is the same library used by the Git-Hub client for Windows, so it'll definitely do the job for our little application. It is, however, the source of a constraint on how we set up our example project: it requires a rather new version of the CLR (4.5) in order to function. If you want some guidance on how to avoid this pitfall and follow along, continue reading the next section. If you've worked with Nancy before, and have installed NuGet packages in the past, you might be able to skip to the section labeled "Sending the Request" on page 89.

Development Environment

If you'd like to follow along with the code examples, here's how to set up a development environment with all the necessary elements. The process is different on Windows (using Visual Studio) and any other platforms (using Xamarin tools).

Visual Studio

If you're running Windows, you'll want to visit *https://www.visualstudio.com/* and download the Community edition of Visual Studio. The installer will present you with lots of options; for this example, we'll only need the "web developer" components, but feel free to check all the boxes that look interesting to you. (If you have access to a higher tier of Visual Studio, or already have it installed with the web-development packages, you're all set.)

In order to make things just a little smoother, you'll want to install a plug-in: the Nancy project templates. Visit *https://visualstudiogallery.msdn.microsoft.com/* and search for "nancy.templates." Choose the search result "Nancy.Templates," which belongs to the NancyFx organization, and click "Get Now." This should download a *.vsix* file that you can double-click to install the templates into Visual Studio.

The next step is to create a new project using one of the newly installed templates. Go to "File→New Project" and select "Visual C#→Web→Nancy Application with ASP.NET Hosting" from the template list (as shown in Figure 5-2). Make sure the path and name settings at the bottom are to your liking, and click OK.

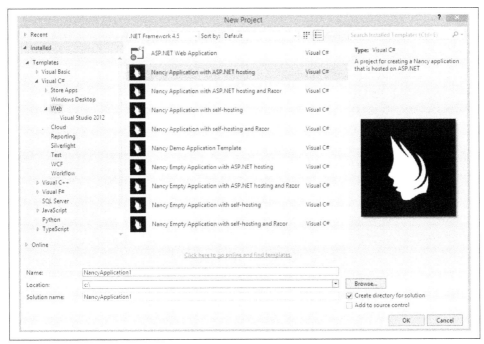

Figure 5-2. Creating a Nancy application in Visual Studio

Next, change the target CLR framework version to something that will work with Octokit. Right-click the project's node in the Solution Explorer, and select "Properties." In the Application section, set Target Framework to be .NET 4.5 (or later), and save. You may be prompted to reload the solution.

The very last step is to add NuGet packages for Octokit and Nancy. Right-click the project node in Solution Explorer, and select "Manage NuGet Packages." Do a search for "Nancy," and upgrade it if necessary—there's a chance the Nancy project template specifies an out-of-date version. Then do a search for "Octokit," and install that. At this point, you should have an empty solution, configured and ready for our example code. To run it with debugging, go to "Debug→Start Debugging," or hit F5. Visual Studio will start the server under a debugger, and open an IE instance on *http://local host:12008/* (the port might be different), which should serve you the default Nancy "404 Not Found" page.

Xamarin Studio

On OS X and Linux, as of this writing the easiest way forward is to visit *http://www.monodevelop.com/* and install MonoDevelop. Mono is an open source implementation of Microsoft's CLR specification, and MonoDevelop is a development environment that works much like Visual Studio, but is built on Mono, and is completely open source. If you try to download MonoDevelop on a Windows or OS X machine, you'll be prompted to install Xamarin Studio instead; this is a newer version of MonoDevelop with more capabilities, and will work just as well for these examples.

There are no Nancy-specific project templates for these IDEs, so you'll just start with an empty web project. Go to "File→New→Solution," and choose "ASP.NET→Empty ASP.NET Project" from the template chooser, as shown in Figure 5-3.

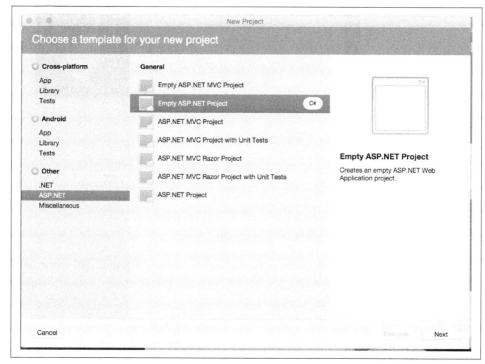

Figure 5-3. Creating an empty ASP.NET application in Xamarin Studio

The rest of the wizard steps are about the project name and location; feel free to name and locate this project however you like.

Next, update the target framework setting. Control- or right-click the node in the solution explorer that corresponds with your project (*not* your solution), and select Options from the menu. Under "Build→General," set the Target Framework to "Mono / .NET 4.5" (or later) and click OK.

Lastly, install the Nancy and Octokit NuGet packages. Go to "Project→Add NuGet Packages" in the menu to open the package manager. Search for Nancy, check the box next to it, search for Octokit, check its box, and click "Add Packages" at the bottom right. Once the process is complete, your project is ready for our example code. To run it under the debugger, go to "Run→Start Debugging," or type ⌘-Enter. Xamarin will start the server and open a browser window to *http://127.0.0.1:80080* (possibly with a different port), which at this point will just show the default "404 Not Found" page.

Sending the Request

Alright, now that we have a project ready for some code, let's get our Nancy application up and running. Let's be good engineers, and write our tests first. In order to do this, generate a new unit-test project alongside your existing application project, and add a NuGet reference to the Nancy.Testing package. You can then copy and paste the test examples over the top of the default test module that comes with that template.

The first thing we're going to write is an endpoint that reports how many followers a user has. In order to test it, we'll choose a well-known user and make sure their real name is fetched. Here's what the test code looks like:

```
using NUnit.Framework;
using Nancy;
using Nancy.Testing;
using Nancy.Bootstrapper;
using System.Collections.Generic;
using Nancy.Session;

namespace NancyApplication1.Tests
{
  [TestFixture ()]
  public class Test
  {
    private Browser browser;

    [SetUp]
    public void Setup(){
      this.bootstrapper =
        new ConfigurableBootstrapper(with => {
        with.Module<Handler>();
      });
      this.browser = new Browser (bootstrapper);
    }

    [Test ()]
    public void FetchesUserDetails ()
    {
      var result = this.browser.Get ("/mojombo", ❶
        with => with.HttpRequest ());
      Assert.AreEqual (HttpStatusCode.OK, result.StatusCode);
      Assert.IsTrue (result.Body.AsString()
        .Contains("Tom Preston-Werner")); ❷
    }
```

```
        }
    }
```

❶ Here we're using the `Browser` class provided by `Nancy.Testing` to make a request to `/mojombo`, which should give us the number of likes for that GitHub user.

❷ Here we're asserting that mojombo's real name is fetched by the endpoint.

Now that we have a failing test, let's write the code to implement that endpoint in Nancy. Here's what the initial version of that file will look like:

```
using Nancy;
using Octokit;
using System;
using System.Collections.Generic;
using System.Linq;

namespace NancyApp
{
    public class Handler : NancyModule ❶
    {
        private readonly GitHubClient client =
            new GitHubClient(new ProductHeaderValue("MyHello")); ❷

        public Handler()
        {
            Get["/{user}", true] = async (parms, ct) => ❸
            {
                var user = await client.User.Get(parms.user.ToString()); ❹
                return String.Format("{0} people love {1}!",
                                    user.Followers, user.Name); ❺
            };
        }
    }
}
```

❶ Here we derive a class from `NancyModule`, which is all you have to do to start receiving and processing HTTP requests in Nancy.

❷ The `GitHubClient` class is the entry point for Octokit. Here we create an instance we'll use later on, using a placeholder product name—this name will not be used for the APIs we'll be accessing.

❸ The module's constructor needs to set up route mappings. We map `/{user}` to a lambda function using the `Get` dictionary that comes with `NancyModule`. The second parameter to the index operator says that the handler will be asynchronous.

❹ Here we see how to get the `{user}` part of the request URL (it comes as a property on the `parms` parameter), and how to query the GitHub User API using

Octokit. Note that we have to `await` the result of the network query, since it may take some time.

❺ Nancy request handlers can simply return a text string, which will be marked as HTML for the viewing browser. Here we return a simple string with the user's name and number of followers.

 The `async` and `await` keywords bear special mention. These comprise a syntactic nicety that encapsulates a series of functions that are running on an event loop. The code looks like it runs in order, but really when the `await` keyword is reached, the system starts an asynchronous request, and returns control back to the main event loop. Once the request has finished, and the promise is fulfilled, the event loop will then call back into the code that's expecting the return value of the `await` keyword, with all the scope variables intact. This feature was introduced in .NET 4.0 (which was released in 2012), and it lets you write asynchronous code almost as though it were synchronous. This is but one of the features that make C# the favorite of many developers.

This example is a bit more complicated than "hello, world," but it's still fairly succinct and clear. This bodes well, because we're about to introduce some complexity, in the form of OAuth.

OAuth Flow

In order to post a status update for a commit, we're going to have to ask the user for permission. Apart from asking for their username and password (which gives way too much control, and if two-factor authentication is enabled may not even be enough), the only way to do this is OAuth, which isn't entirely straightforward.

Here's a simple outline of the OAuth process, from our little server's point of view:

1. We need an authorization token, either because we don't have one, or because the one we have is expired. This is just a string of characters, but we can't generate it ourselves, so we ask GitHub for one. This involves redirecting the user's browser to a GitHub API endpoint, with the kind of permission we're asking for and some other details as query parameters.

2. GitHub tells the user (through their browser) that an application is requesting some permissions, and they can either allow or deny them.

3. If the user allows this access, their browser is redirected to a URL we specified in step 1. A "code" is passed as a query parameter; this is not the access token we want, but a time-limited key to get one.

4. From inside the handler for this request, we can use a REST API to get the actual OAuth access token, which we can store somewhere safe. We do this because if we already have a token, we can skip all the way to the last step of this process.

5. Now we have permission, and we can use the GitHub API in authenticated mode.

This might seem overly complicated, but its design achieves several goals. First, permission can be scoped—an application is almost never given full access to the user's account and data. Second, the whole exchange is secure; at least one part of this has to go through the user, and cannot be automated. Third, the access token is never transmitted to the user's browser, which avoids an entire class of security vulnerabilities.

Let's walk through the code for our tiny little server's implementation of this flow. First, once we have a token, we should store it so we're not going through the entire redirect cycle for every user request. We're going to store it in a cookie (though since this goes back and forth to the user's browser, a production application would probably use a database). Nancy can help us with this, but first we have to enable it, and the way this is accomplished is by using a bootstrapper. We're going to add this class to our application:

```
using Nancy;
using Nancy.Bootstrapper;
using Nancy.Session;
using Nancy.TinyIoc;

namespace NancyApp
{
    public class Bootstrapper : DefaultNancyBootstrapper
    {
        protected override void ApplicationStartup(TinyIoCContainer container,
                                                    IPipelines pipelines)
        {
            CookieBasedSessions.Enable(pipelines);
        }
    }
}
```

Nancy will automatically detect a bootstrapper class, and use it to initialize our server. Now, from within a NancyModule, we can use the Session property to store and retrieve values that are transmitted as cookies.

Next, we have to include our application's ID and secret in some of the requests, so we embed them in the code by adding these fields to the Handler class. If you don't have an application, visit *https://github.com/settings/developers* to create one and use http://localhost:8080/authorize (depending in your environment, the port number might be slightly different) for the callback URL—we'll see why in a bit:

```
            private const string clientId = "<clientId>";
            private const string clientSecret = "<clientSecret>";
```

Obviously, you should use values from your own API application if you're following along.

After that, we'll need a helper method that kicks off the OAuth process:

```
private Response RedirectToOAuth()
{
    var csrf = Guid.NewGuid().ToString();
    Session["CSRF:State"] = csrf; ❶
    Session["OrigUrl"] = this.Request.Path; ❷

    var request = new OauthLoginRequest(clientId)
        {
            Scopes = { "repo:status" }, ❸
            State = csrf,
        };
    var oauthLoginUrl = client.Oauth.GetGitHubLoginUrl(request);
    return Response.AsRedirect(oauthLoginUrl.ToString()); ❹
}
```

❶ CSRF stands for *cross-site request forgery*. This is a mechanism by which we can be sure the OAuth request process really did originate from our site. The GitHub OAuth API will pass this value back to us when the user authorizes access, so we store it in the cookie for later reference.

❷ Storing the original URL in the session cookie is a UX feature; once the OAuth process has completed, we want to send the user back to what they were trying to do in the first place.

❸ repo:status is the permission set we're asking for. Note that we're also including our CSRF token in this object; this is so GitHub can give it back to us later for verification.

❹ Here we use Octokit to generate the redirect URL, and send the user's browser there.

RedirectToOAuth is a method that can be called from any route handler in our module, if it's discovered that the token is missing or invalid. We'll see how it's called a bit later, but for now let's follow the rest of the OAuth process.

In our GitHub application settings, we specified an authorization URL. In this case, we've specified http://localhost:8080/authorize, and that's where GitHub will redirect the user's browser if they decide to grant our application the permissions it's asking for. Here's the handler for that endpoint, which has been inserted into the module constructor:

```
Get["/authorize", true] = async (parms, ct) => ❶
    {
        var csrf = Session["CSRF:State"] as string;
        Session.Delete("CSRF:State");
        if (csrf != Request.Query["state"]) ❷
        {
            return HttpStatusCode.Unauthorized;
        }

        var queryCode = Request.Query["code"].ToString();
        var tokenReq =  new OauthTokenRequest(clientId, ❸
                                              clientSecret,
                                              queryCode);
        var token = await client.Oauth.CreateAccessToken(tokenReq);
        Session["accessToken"] = token.AccessToken; ❹

        var origUrl = Session["OrigUrl"].ToString();
        Session.Delete("OrigUrl");
        return Response.AsRedirect(origUrl); ❺
    };
```

❶ This is how you map paths to handler functions in Nancy. Any class that derives
   from NancyModule has an indexable object for every HTTP verb, and you can
   attach a synchronous or asynchronous handler to any one of them. There are
   also ways to include dynamic portions of URLs, which we'll see later on.

❷ Here we verify the CSRF token we generated before. If it doesn't match, something shady is happening, so we return a 401.

❸ This is the REST call that converts our OAuth code to an access token. In order
   to verify that this really is our application asking for the token, we pass in both
   the client ID and secret, as well as the code given to us by GitHub.

❹ This is where we store the resulting token in the session cookie. Again, this
   wouldn't be a good idea for a real application, but for our purposes it'll do.

❺ Here we redirect the user back to what they were originally trying to do, with as
   little disruption as possible.

This last endpoint is something we can test, but we'll need to be able to handle sessions. In order to do that, we'll add this snippet to our test project's namespace:

```
public static class BootstrapperExtensions
{
  public static void WithSession(this IPipelines pipeline,
                                      IDictionary<string, object> session)
  {
    pipeline.BeforeRequest.AddItemToEndOfPipeline(ctx =>
      {
```

```
            ctx.Request.Session = new Session(session);
            return null;
        });
    }
}
```

This is an *extension method* that allows us to provide a `Session` object for a request, something the CSRF handling uses. Now that that exists, we can add a test method to our test-suite class:

```
[Test]
public void HandlesAuthorization()
{
  // Mismatched CSRF token
  bootstrapper.WithSession(new Dictionary<string, object> {
    { "CSRF:State", "sometoken" },
  });
  var result = this.browser.Get ("/authorize", (with) => {
    with.HttpRequest();
    with.Query("state", "someothertoken");
  });
  Assert.AreEqual (HttpStatusCode.Unauthorized, result.StatusCode);

  // Matching CSRF token
  bootstrapper.WithSession(new Dictionary<string, object> {
    { "CSRF:State", "sometoken" },
                { "OrigUrl", "http://success" },
  });
  result = this.browser.Get ("/authorize", (with) => {
    with.HttpRequest();
    with.Query("state", "sometoken");
  });
  result.ShouldHaveRedirectedTo ("http://success");
}
```

The first part sets up a mismatched CSRF token; it's `"sometoken"` in the session (which is set before the API call is made), and `"someothertoken"` in the request (which should be sent from GitHub), so we assert that the status code is 401. The second part has matching tokens, so we assert that the response is a redirect to the URL we stored in the session.

Once all that is done, we've got our token and are able to continue on our merry way. All our handlers have to do to trigger an OAuth sequence is to call `Redirect ToOAuth()` if it's necessary, and we'll automatically return the user to where they were when the process completes.

Status Handler

Having gone through all that OAuth business, we should now have a token that grants us permission to create commit statuses. We're going to add this handler to our Nancy module constructor:

```
Get["/{user}/{repo}/{sha}/{status}", true] = async (parms, ct) => ❶
    {
        var accessToken = Session["accessToken"] as string;
        if (string.IsNullOrEmpty(accessToken))
            return RedirectToOAuth(); ❷
        client.Credentials = new Credentials(accessToken);

        CommitState newState = Enum.Parse(typeof(CommitState), ❸
                                        parms.status,
                                        true);
        try
        {
            var newStatus = new NewCommitStatus ❹
            {
                State = newState,
                Context = "example-api-app",
                TargetUrl = new Uri(Request.Url.SiteBase),
            };
            await client.Repository.CommitStatus.Create(parms.user, ❺
                                                parms.repo,
                                                parms.sha,
                                                newStatus);
        }
        catch (NotFoundException) ❻
        {
            return HttpStatusCode.NotFound;
        }

        var template = @"Done! Go to <a href=""https://" ❼
        + @"api.github.com/repos/{0}/{1}/commits/{2}/status"
        + @""">this API endpiont</a>";
        return String.Format(template,
                            parms.user, parms.repo, parms.sha);
    };
```

❶ Note the request path for this handler: a GET request to localhost:8080/user/
repo/<sha>/<status> will create a new status. This is easy to test with the browser, but also makes it easy for web crawlers to unknowingly trigger this API. For this example it's okay, but for a real application you'd probably want to require this to be a POST request.

❷ Here's where our OAuth helper comes in. We redirect through the OAuth flow if the session cookie doesn't have an authorization token. It's not shown here, but we'd also want to do this if we get an authorization exception from any of the Octokit APIs.

❸ Here we're trying to parse the last segment of the request URL into a member of the `CommitState` enumeration. Octokit tries to maintain type safety for all of its APIs, so we can't just use the raw string.

❹ The `NewCommitStatus` object encapsulates all the things you can set when creating a new status. Here we set the state we parsed earlier, a (hopefully) unique context value that identifies our service, and a not-very-useful target URL (which should really go to an explanation of how the result was derived).

❺ This is the REST call to create the new status. It's an `async` method, which means we have to `await` the result before we can do anything with it.

❻ There are a number of exceptions that could be thrown from the API, but the biggest one we want to handle is the `NotFoundException`, which has been translated from the HTTP 404 status. Here we translate it back to make for a nice(r) experience for the user.

❼ If we succeed, we render a snippet of HTML and return it from our handler. Nancy sets the response's `content-type` to `text/html` by default, so the user will get a nice clickable link.

That's it! If you've typed all this into a project of your own, you should be able to run it under the debugger, or host it in an ASP.NET server, and create commit statuses for your projects by opening URLs in your browser.

We noted this a bit earlier, but it bears repeating: this particular example responds to GET requests for ease of testing, but for a real service like this you'd probably want creation of statuses to use a POST request.

Summary

Even if you haven't written a lot of code during this chapter, you've learned a lot of concepts.

You've seen the Commit Status API, and you've seen how it's used by continuous integration software, but you know that it can be used for much more. You can read and write statuses, and you know how the API server coalesces many statuses into a single pass/fail value, and you also know how to write your own multistatus calculation if the default one doesn't meet your needs. You also know what's behind the green checkmarks and red Xs you see in your pull requests.

You've learned how the OAuth web flow works, and why it's designed the way it is. OAuth is the key to many other capabilities of the GitHub API, and it's the right thing to do with regards to trust and permissions. This will allow you to write truly world-class GitHub-interfacing applications, whether running on the Web or on a user's device.

You've gained a passing knowledge of C#, including its package system, at least one IDE, lambda functions, object initializers, and more. C# really is a nice language, and if you use it for a while, you'll probably miss some of its features if you write in anything else.

You've seen NuGet, the .NET package manager, and had a peek at the multitudes of packages in this ecosystem. The capability you have here is astounding; libraries exist for many common activities, and lots of uncommon ones too, so no matter what you need to do, you're likely to find a NuGet package to help you do it.

You've learned about Nancy, with which you can quickly build any HTTP service, from a REST API to an HTML-based interface, and all with a compact syntax and intuitive object model. If you've never been exposed to the Sinatra view of the world, this probably makes you think about web servers a bit differently, and if you have, you'll have a new appreciation for how this model can be idiomatically implemented.

And you've had an introduction to Octokit, a type-safe implementation of a REST API, with built-in asynchrony and OAuth helpers. This toolkit really does make working with the GitHub API as simple and straightforward as using any .NET library, including the ability to explore it using Intellisense.

Now it's time to switch back to Ruby. In our next chapter, we'll take a look at Jekyll (which is what really runs GitHub Pages), and how to use it to write a blog.

CHAPTER 6

Ruby and Jekyll

The Jekyll project calls itself a "blog-aware, static site generator in Ruby." At its core, Jekyll is a very simple set of technologies for building websites. Simplicity is what gives Jekyll its power: using Jekyll you will never have to learn about database backends, complicated server installations, or any of the myriad processes involved with most monolithic website technologies. Many prominent technical bloggers use Jekyll as their blogging platform.

Like many of the open source technologies in heavy usage at GitHub, Jekyll was originally developed by Tom Preson Warner, one of the cofounders of GitHub, and Nick Quaranto, of 37 Signals, though there are now thousands of contributors to the Jekyll codebase. Unsurprisingly, the strength of the Jekyll tool comes not from the brilliance of the original developers or the brilliance of the idea, but the way those original developers cultivated community and involvement among their users.

Learning and Building with Jekyll

In this chapter we will investigate the structure of a Jekyll blog, illustrating the few major technology pieces involved. Once we have familiarized ourselves with Jekyll, we will then create a Jekyll blog from scratch using the command-line tools. Then we will write a Ruby program that scrapes a blog-like website and converts the scraped information into a new Jekyll blog.

What Is Jekyll?

Jekyll specifies a file structure format: conform to this format and Jekyll will compile your files into HTML. Jekyll builds on top of two proven tools: Markdown, a markup language that is surprisingly readable and expressive, and Liquid Markup, a simple programming language that gives you just enough components to build modern web pages requiring conditionals and loops, but safe enough that you can run untrusted pages on public servers. With these two technologies and agreement on a layout structure, Jekyll can build very complicated websites paradoxically without requiring a complicated structure of files and technologies.

Jekyll works natively with GitHub because a Jekyll blog is stored as a Git repository. When you push files into GitHub from a repository GitHub recognizes as a Jekyll site, GitHub automatically rebuilds the site for you. Jekyll is an open source generator and defines a format for your source files, a format other tools can easily understand and operate upon. This means you can build your own tools to interact with a Jekyll blog. Combining an open source tool like Jekyll with a well-written API like the GitHub API makes for some powerful publishing tools.

Operating Jekyll Locally

To really use Jekyll, you'll need the `jekyll` gem. As we explain in Appendix B, we could install a ruby gem using this command:

```
$ gem install jekyll
```

There are two issues with installing this way. The first is that any commands we run inside the command line are lost to us and the world (other than in our private shell history file). The second is that if we are going to publish any of our sites to GitHub, we will want to make sure we are matching the exact versions of Jekyll and its dependencies so that a site that works on our local laptop also works when published into GitHub. If you don't take care of this, you'll occasionally get an email like this from GitHub:

```
The page build failed with the following error:

page build failed

For information on troubleshooting Jekyll see
https://help.github.com/articles/using-jekyll-with-pages#troubleshooting
If you have any questions please contact GitHub Support.
```

The fix for these two issues is a simple one. You've probably seen other chapters using a `Gemfile` to install Ruby libraries. Instead of using a manual command like `bundle` to install from the command line, let's put this dependency into the Gemfile. Then, anyone else using this repository can run the command `bundle install` and install the correct dependencies. And instead of using the `jekyll` gem directly, use the `github-pages` gem, which synchronizes your Jekyll gem versions with those on GitHub. If you do get the preceding email, run the command `bundle update` to make sure that everything is properly set up and synchronized and generally this will reproduce the issues on your local setup, which is a much faster place to fix them:

```
$ printf "gem 'github-pages' >> Gemfile
$ bundle install
```

Creating and managing your dependencies inside a Gemfile is the smart way to get your Jekyll tool synced with the version running on GitHub.

Now we are ready to create a Jekyll blog.

Jekyll Blog Quick Start

We have our required tools installed, so let's create a simple blog. Run these commands:

```
$ jekyll new myblog
$ cd myblog
```

The `jekyll new` command creates the necessary structure for a minimal Jekyll blog. Taking a look inside the directory, you'll see a few files that comprise the structure of a basic Jekyll blog.

The `jekyll new` command installs two CSS files: one for the blog (*main.css*) and one for syntax highlighting (*syntax.css*). Remember, you are in full control of this site; the *main.css* file is simply boilerplate, which you can completely throw away if it does not suit your needs. The syntax file helps when including code snippets and contains syntax highlighting CSS that prettifies many programming languages.

Installation of a new blog comes with a *.gitignore* file as well that contains one entry: *_site*. When you use the Jekyll library to build your site locally, all files are by default built into the *_site* directory. This *.gitignore* file prevents those files from being included inside your repository as they are overwritten by the Jekyll command on GitHub when your files are pushed up to GitHub.

> The `jekyll new` command does not create or initialize a new Git repository for you with your files. If you want to do this, you will need to use the `git init` command. The Jekyll initialization command does create the proper structure for you to easily add all files to a Git repository; just use `git add .`; `git commit` and your *.gitignore* file will be added and configure your repository to ignore unnecessary files like the *_site* directory.

All your blog posts are stored in the *_posts* directory. Jekyll sites are not required to have a *_posts* directory (you can use Jekyll with any kind of static site) but if you do include files in this directory Jekyll handles them in a special way. If you look in the *_posts* directory now, you see that the Jekyll initialization command has created your first post for you, something like *_posts/2014-03-03-welcome-to-jekyll.Markdown*. These posts have a special naming format: the title of the post (with any whitespace replaced with hyphens) trailed by the date and then an extension (either *.Markdown* or *.md* for Markdown files, or *.textile* for Textile).

Your new Jekyll blog also comes with a few HTML files: an *index.html* file, which is the starting point for your blog, and several layout files, which are used as wrappers when generating your content. If you look in the *_layouts* directory, notice there is a file named *default.html* and another named *post.html*. These files are the layout files, files that are wrapped around all generated content, like those from your Markdown-formatted blog posts. For example, the *post.html* file is wrapped around the generated content of each file stored inside the *_posts* directory. First, the markup content is turned into HTML and then the layout wrapper is applied. If you look inside each of the files inside the *_layouts* directory, you will see that each contains a placeholder with {{ content }}. This placeholder is replaced with the generated content from other files.

These placeholders are actually a markup language on their own: *Liquid Markup*. Liquid Markup was developed and open sourced by Shopify.com. Liquid Markup arose from a desire to have a safe way to host programmatic constructs (like loops and variables) inside a template, without exposing the rendering context to a full-fledged programming environment. Shopify wanted to create a way for untrusted users of its public-facing systems to upload dynamic content but not worry that the markup language would permit malicious activity; for example, given a full-fledged embedded programming language, Shopify would open itself to attack if a user wrote code to open network connections to sites on its internal networks. Templating languages like PHP or ERB (embedded Ruby templates, popular with the Ruby on Rails framework) allow fully embedded code snippets, and while this is very powerful when you have full control over your source documents, it can be dangerous to provide a mechanism where that embedded code could look like system("rm -rf /"). Liquid Markup provides many of the benefits of embedded programming templates, without the dangers. We will show several examples of Liquid Markup and how they work later in the chapter.

Lastly, your Jekyll directory has a special file called *_config.yml*. This is the Jekyll configuration file. Peering into it, you'll see it is very basic:

```
name: Your New Jekyll Site
markdown: redcarpet
highlighter: pygments
```

We only have three lines to contend with and they are simple to understand: the name of our site, the Markdown parser used by our Jekyll command, and whether to use pygments to do syntax highlighting.

To view this site locally run this command:

```
$ jekyll serve
```

This command builds the entirety of your Jekyll directory, and then starts a mini web server to serve the files up to you. If you then visit *http://localhost:4000* in your web browser, you will see something on the front page of your site and a single blog post listed in the index, as shown in Figure 6-1.

Figure 6-1. A bare Jekyll site

Clicking into the link inside the "Blog Posts" section, you will then see your first post, as in Figure 6-2.

Figure 6-2. A sample post

Our Jekyll initialization command created this new post for us. This page is backed by the Markdown file inside the _posts directory we saw earlier:

```
---
layout: post
title:  "Welcome to Jekyll!"
date:   2014-03-03 12:56:40
categories: jekyll update
---
```

You'll find this post in your _posts directory—edit this post and rebuild (or run with the -w switch) to see your changes! To add new posts, simply add a file in the _posts directory that follows the convention: YYYY-MM-DD-name-of-post.ext.

Jekyll also offers powerful support for code snippets:

```
{% highlight ruby %}
def print_hi(name)
  puts "Hi, #{name}"
end
print_hi('Tom')
#=> prints 'Hi, Tom' to STDOUT.
{% endhighlight %}
```

Check out the Jekyll docs (*http://jekyllrb.com*) for more info on how to get the most out of Jekyll. File all bugs/feature requests at Jekyll's GitHub repo (*https://github.com/mojombo/jekyll*).

Hopefully you agree that this is a fairly intuitive and readable alternative to raw HTML. This simplicity and readability is one of the major benefits of using Jekyll. Your source files maintain a readability that allows you to focus on the content itself, not on the technology that will eventually make them beautiful. Let's go over this file and investigate some of the important pieces.

YFM: YAML Front Matter

The first thing we see in a Jekyll file is the YAML Front Matter (YFM):

```
---
layout: post
title:  "Welcome to Jekyll!"
date:   2014-03-03 12:56:40
categories: jekyll update
---
```

YFM is a snippet of YAML ("YAML Aint Markup Language") delimited by three hyphens on both the top and bottom. YAML is a simple structured data serialization language used by many open source projects instead of XML. Many people find it more readable and editable by humans than XML. The YFM in this file shows a few configuration options: a layout, the title, the date, and a list of categories.

The layout specified references one of the files in our *_layouts* directory. If you don't specify a layout file in the YFM, then Jekyll assumes you want to use a file called *default.html* to wrap your content. You can easily imagine adding your own custom layout files to this directory and then overriding them in the YFM. If you look at this file, you see that it manually specifies the `post` layout.

The title is used to generate the `<title>` tag and can be used anywhere else you need it inside your template using the double-braces syntax from Liquid Markup: `{{ page.title }}`. Notice that any variable from the *_config.yml* file is prefixed with the `site.` namespace, while variables from your YFM are prefixed with `page.` Though the title matches the filename (after replacing spaces with hyphens), changing the title in the YFM does not affect the name of the URL generated by Jekyll. If you want to change the URL, you need to rename the file itself. This is a nice benefit if you need to slightly modify the title and don't want to damage preexisting URLs.

The date and categories are two other variables included in the YFM. They are completely optional and strangely unused by the structure and templates created by default using the Jekyll initializer. They do provide additional context to the post, but are only stored in the Markdown file and not included inside the generated content itself. The categories list is often used to generate an index file of categories with a list of each post included in a category. If you come from a Wordpress background, you'll likely have used categories. These are generated dynamically from the MySQL database each time you request a list of them, but in Jekyll this file is statically generated. If you wanted something more dynamic, you could imagine generating a JSON file with these categories and files, and then building a JavaScript widget that requests this file and then does something more interactive on the client side. Jekyll can take any template file and convert it to JSON (or any other format)—you are not limited to just generating HTML files.

YFM is completely optional. A post or page can be rendered into your Jekyll site without any YFM inside it. Without YFM, your page is rendered using the defaults for those variables, so make sure the default template, at the very least, is what you expect will wrap around all pages left with unspecified layouts.

One important default variable for YFM is the published variable. This variable is set to true by default. This means that if you create a file in your Jekyll repository and do not manually specify the published setting, it will be published automatically. If you set the variable to false, the post will not be published. With private repositories you can keep the contents of draft posts entirely private until writing has completed by making sure published is set to false. Unfortunately, not all tools that help you create Jekyll Markdown files remember to set the published variable explicitly inside of YFM, so make sure you check before committing the file to your repository if there is something you don't yet want published.

Jekyll Markup

Going past the YFM, we can start to see the structure of Markdown files. Markdown files can be, at their simplest, just textual information without any formatting characters. In fact, if your layout files are well done, you can definitely create great blog posts without any fancy formatting, just pure textual content.

But with a few small Markdown additions, you can really make posts shine. One of the first Markdown components we notice is the backtick character, which is used to wrap small spans of code (or code-ish information, like filenames in this case). As you use more and more Markdown, you'll find Markdown to be insidiously clever in the way it provides formatting characters without the onerous weight that HTML requires to offer the same explicit formatting.

Links can be specified using [format][link], where link is the fully qualified URL (like "*http://example.com*"), or a reference to a link at the bottom of the page. In our page we have two references, keyed as jekyll-gh and jekyll; we can then use these inside our page with syntax like [Jekyll's GitHub repo][jekyll-gh]. Using references has an additional benefit in that you can use the link more than once by its short name.

Though not offered in the sample, Markdown provides an easy way to generate headers of varying degrees. To add a header, use the # character, and repeat the # character to build smaller headers. These delimiters simply map to the H tag; two hash characters (##) turns into an <h2> tag. Building text enclosed by <h3> tags looks like ### Some Text. You can optionally match the same number of hash symbols at the end of the line if you find it more expressive (### Some Text ###), but you don't have to.

Markdown offers easy shortcuts for most HTML elements: numbered and unordered lists, emphasis, and more. And, if you cannot find a Markdown equivalent, you can embed normal HTML right next to Markdown formatting characters. The best way to write Markdown is to keep a Markdown cheat sheet (*https://github.com/adam-p/Markdown-here/wiki/Markdown-Cheatsheet*) near you when writing. John Gruber from Daring Fireball (*http://daringfireball.net*) invented Markdown, and his site has a more in-depth description of the how and why of Markdown.

Using the Jekyll Command

Running jekyll --help will show you the options for running Jekyll. You already saw the jekyll serve command, which builds the files into the *_site* directory and then starts a web server with its root at that directory. If you start to use this mechanism to build your Jekyll sites then there are a few other switches you'll want to learn about.

If you are authoring and adjusting a page often, and switching back into your browser to see what it looks like, you'll find utility in the -w switch ("watch"). This can be used to automatically regenerate the entire site if you make changes to any of the source files. If you edit a post file and save it, that file will be regenerated automatically. Without the -w switch you would need to kill the Jekyll server, and then restart it.

 The Jekyll watch switch does reload all HTML and markup files, but does not reload the _config.yml file. If you make changes to it, you will need to stop and restart the server.

If you are running multiple Jekyll sites on the same laptop, you'll quickly find that the second instance of `jekyll serve` fails because it cannot open port 4000. In this case, use `jekyll --port 4010` to open port 4010 (or whatever port you wish to use instead).

Privacy Levels with Jekyll

Jekyll repositories on GitHub can be either public or private repositories. If your repository is public you can host public content generated from the Jekyll source files without publishing the source files themselves. Remember, as noted previously, that any file without `publishing: false` inside the YFM will be made public the moment you push it into your repository.

Themes

Jekyll does not support theming internally, but it is trivial to add any CSS files or entire CSS frameworks. You can also fork an existing Jekyll blog that has the theming you like. We will show how and where to add your own customized CSS later in the chapter.

Publishing on GitHub

Once you have your blog created, you can easily publish it to GitHub. There are two ways you can publish Jekyll blogs:

- As a github.io site
- On a domain you own

GitHub offers free personal blogs that are hosted on the github.io domain. And you can host any site with your own domain name with a little bit of configuration.

Using a GitHub.io Jekyll blog

To create a github.io personal blog site, your Jekyll blog should be on the master branch of your Git repository. The repository should be named `username.github.io` on GitHub. If everything is set up correctly you can then publish your Jekyll blog by adding a remote for GitHub and pushing your files up. If you use the hub tool (a command for interacting with Git and GitHub), you can go from start to finish with a few simple commands. Make sure to change the first line to reflect your username.

 The hub tool was originally written in Ruby and as such could be easily installed using only `gem install hub`, but hub was recently rewritten in Go. Go has a somewhat more complicated installation process, so we won't document it here. If you have the `brew` command installed for OS X, you can install hub with the `brew install hub` command. Other platforms vary, so check *http://github.com/github/hub* to determine the best way for your system.

Use these commands to install your github.io hosted Jekyll blog:

```
$ export USERNAME=xrd
$ jekyll new $USERNAME.github.io
$ cd $USERNAME.github.io
$ git init
$ git commit -m "Initial checkin" -a
$ hub create  # You'll need to login here...
$ sleep $((10*60)) && open $USERNAME.github.io
```

The second to the last line creates a repository on GitHub for you with the same name as the directory. That last line sleeps for 10 minutes while your github.io site is provisioned on GitHub, and then opens the site in your browser for you. It can take ten minutes for GitHub to configure your site the first time, but subsequent content pushes will be reflected immediately.

Hosting On Your Own Domain

To host a blog on your own domain name, you need to use the `gh-pages` branch inside your repository. You need to create a CNAME file in your repository, and then finally establish DNS settings to point your domain to the GitHub servers.

The gh-pages branch

To work on the `gh-pages` branch, check it out and create the branch inside your repository:

```
$ git checkout -b gh-pages
$ rake post title="My next big blog post"
$ git add _posts
```

```
$ git commit -m "Added my next big blog post"
$ git push -u origin gh-pages
```

You will need to always remember to work on the gh-pages branch; if this repository is only used as a blog, then this probably is not an issue. Adding the -u switch will make sure that Git always pushes up the gh-pages branch whenever you do a push.

The CNAME file

The CNAME file is a simple text file with the domain name inside of it:

```
$ echo 'mydomain.com' > CNAME
$ git add CNAME
$ git commit -m "Added CNAME"
$ git push
```

Once you have pushed the CNAME file to your repository, you can verify that Git-Hub thinks the blog is established correctly by visiting the admin page of your repository. An easy way to get there is using the github gem, which is no longer actively maintained but is still a useful command-line tool:

```
$ gem install github
$ github admin # Opens up https://github.com/username/repo/settings
```

The github gem is a useful command-line tool, but unfortunately it is tied to an older version of the GitHub API, which means the documented functionality is often incorrect.

If your blog is correctly set up, you will see something like Figure 6-3 in the middle of your settings page.

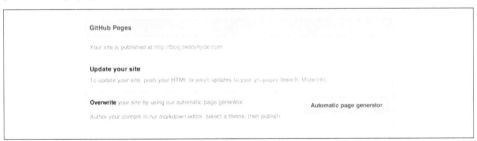

Figure 6-3. Settings for a Jekyll blog

GitHub has properly recognized the CNAME file and will accept requests made to that host on its servers. We are still not yet complete, however, in that we need to make sure the DNS is established for our site.

DNS settings

Generally, establishing DNS settings for your site is straightforward. It is easiest if you are setting up DNS with a *subdomain* as opposed to an *apex domain*. To be more concrete, an apex domain is a site like *mypersonaldomain.com*, while a subdomain would be *blog.mypersonaldomain.com*.

Setting up a blog on a subdomain is simple: create a CNAME record in DNS that points to *username.github.io*.

For an apex domain, things are slightly more complicated. You must create DNS A records to point to these IP addresses: `192.30.252.153` and `192.30.252.154`. These are the IP addresses right now; there is always the possibility that GitHub could change these at some point in the future. For this reason, hosting on apex domains is risky. If GitHub needed to change its IP addresses (say during a denial-of-service attack), you would need to respond to this, and deal with the DNS propagation issues. If you instead use a subdomain, the CNAME record will automatically redirect to the correct IP even if it is changed by GitHub.[1]

Importing from Other Blogs

There are many tools that can be used to import an existing blog into Jekyll. As Jekyll is really nothing more than a file-layout convention, you just need to pull the relevant pieces (the post itself, and associated metadata like the post title, publishing date, etc.) and then write out a file with those contents. Jekyll blogs prefer Markdown, but they work fine with HTML content, so you can often convert a blog with minimal effort, and there are good tools that automate things for you.

From Wordpress

The most popular importer is the Wordpress importer. You will need the *jekyll-import* gem. This gem is distributed separately from the core Jekyll gem, but will be installed if you use the `github-pages` gem inside your Gemfile and use the `bundle` command.

Importing with direct database access

Once you have the `jekyll-import` gem, you can convert a Wordpress blog using a command like this:

```
$ ruby -rubygems -e 'require "jekyll-import";
    JekyllImport::Importers::WordPress.run({
       "dbname"   => "wordpress",
       "user"     => "hastie",
       "password" => "lanyon",
       "host"     => "localhost",
       "status"          => ["publish"]
    })'
```

---

1 This is all well documented on the GitHub blog. (*https://help.github.com/articles/setting-up-a-custom-domain-with-github-pages*)

This command will import from an existing Wordpress installation, provided that your Ruby code can access your database. This will work if you can log in to the server itself and run the command on the server, or if the database is accessible across the network (which is generally bad practice when hosting Wordpress!).

Note the status option: this specifies that imported pages and posts are published automatically. More specifically, the YAML for each file will specify `published: true`, which will publish the page or post into your blog. If you want to review each item individually, you can specify a status of `private`, which will export the pages into Jekyll but leave them unpublished. Remember that if your repository is public, posts marked as unpublished will not be displayed in the blog but can still be seen if someone visits your the repository for your blog on GitHub.

There are many more options than listed here. For example, by default, the Wordpress-Jekyll importer imports categories from your Wordpress database, but you can turn this off by specifying `"categories" => false`.

Importing from the Wordpress XML

Another alternative is to export the entire database as an XML file. Then, you can run the importer on that file:

```
ruby -rubygems -e 'require "jekyll-import";
    JekyllImport::Importers::WordpressDotCom.run({
      "source" => "wordpress.xml",
      "no_fetch_images" => false,
      "assets_folder" => "assets"
    })'
```

This can be used to export files from a server you don't maintain, but works with sites you do maintain and might be a more plausible option than running against a database.

To export the XML file, visit the export page on your Wordpress site. This is usually mapped to */wp-admin/export.php*, so it will be something like *https://blogname.com/wp-admin/export.php* (replacing "blogname.com" with your blog's name).

Like many free tools, there are definitely limitations to using this method of export. If your Wordpress site is anything beyond the simplest of Wordpress sites, then using this tool to import from Wordpress means you will lose much of the metadata stored inside your blog. This metadata can include pages, tags, custom fields, and image attachments.

If you want to keep this metadata, then you might consider another import option like Exitwp. Exitwp is a Python tool that provides a much higher level of fidelity between the original Wordpress site and the final Jekyll site, but has a longer learning curve and option set.

Exporting from Wordpress Alternatives

If you use another blog format other than Wordpress, chances are there is a Jekyll importer for it. Jekyll has dozens of importers, well documented on the Jekyll importer site (*http://import.jekyllrb.com*).

For example, this command-line example from the importer site exports from Tumblr blogs:

```
$ ruby -rubygems -e 'require "jekyll-import";
    JekyllImport::Importers::Tumblr.run({
      "url"           => "http://myblog.tumblr.com",
      "format"        => "html", ❶
      "grab_images"   => false, ❷
      "add_highlights" => false, ❸
      "rewrite_urls"  => false ❹
    })'
```

The Tumblr import plug-in has a few interesting options.

❶ Write out HTML; if you prefer to use Markdown use md.

❷ This importer will grab images if you provide a true value.

❸ Wrap code blocks (indented four spaces) in a Liquid Markup "highlight" tag if this is set to true.

❹ Write pages that redirect from the old Tumblr paths to the new Jekyll paths using this configuration option.

Exporting from Tumblr is considerably easier than Wordpress. The Tumblr exporter scrapes all public posts from the blog, and then converts to a Jekyll-compatible post format.

We've seen how we can use the importers available on *import.jekyllrb.com* to import. What if we have a nonstandard site we need to import?

Scraping Sites into Jekyll

Jekyll provides various importers that make it easy to convert an existing blog into a Jekyll blog. But if you have a nonstandard blog, or a site that is not a blog, you still have options for migrating it to Jekyll. The first option is to write your own importer by perusing the source of the Jekyll importers on GitHub (*http://github.com/jekyll/jekyll-import*). This is probably the right way to build an importer if you plan on letting others use it, as it will extend several Jekyll importer classes already available to make importing standard for other contributors.

Another option is to simply write out files in the simple format that is a Jekyll blog. This is much lazier than reading through the Jekyll tools and their libraries, of course. I started as a Perl programmer and always loved this quote from Larry Wall, the creator of Perl: "We will encourage you to develop the three great virtues of a programmer: laziness, impatience, and hubris." Let's accept our inherent laziness and choose the second route. We'll write some code to scrape a site and make a new Jekyll site from scratch, learning about the structure of a Jekyll blog through trial and error.

While living in Brazil in 2000 I built a site called ByTravelers.com, an early travel blog. At some point, I sadly lost the database and thought the site contents were completely gone. Almost by accident, I happened upon ByTravelers on Archive.org, the Internet Archive. I found that almost all of the articles were listed there and available. Though the actual database is long gone, could we recover the data from the site using Archive.org?

Jekyll Scraping Tactics

We can start by looking at the structure of the archive presented on Archive.org. Go to Archive.org, enter "bytravelers.com" into the search box in the middle of the page, and then click "BROWSE HISTORY." You will see a calendar view that shows all the pages scraped by the Internet Archive for this site as shown in Figure 6-4.

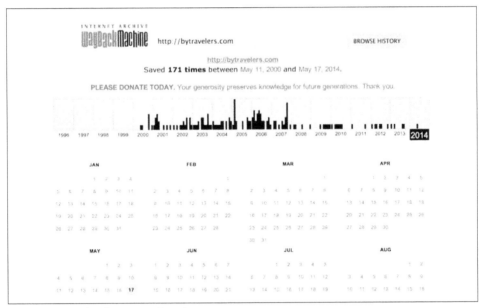

Figure 6-4. Calendar view of Archive.org

In the middle of 2003 I took down the server, intending to upgrade it to another set of technologies, and never got around to completing this migration, and then lost the data. If we click the calendar item on June 6th, 2003, we will see a view of the data that was more or less complete at the height of the site's functionality and data. There are a few broken links to images, but otherwise the site is functionally archived inside Archive.org (Figure 6-5).

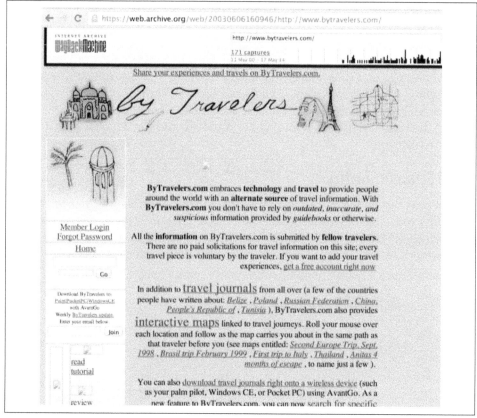

Figure 6-5. Archive of ByTravelers.com on Archive.org

Taking the URL from our browser, we can use this as our starting point for scraping. Clicking around throughout the site, it becomes evident that each URL to a journal entry uses a standard format; in other words, *http://www.bytravelers.com/journal/entry/56* indicates the 56th journal item stored on the site. With this knowledge in hand, we can iterate over the first hundred or so URLs easily.

Setting Up

A naive implementation of a scraper would be a single Ruby file in which the execution and functionality were contained all in one. However, if we expose the functionality as a class, and then instantiate the class in a separate file, we can also write tests that utilize and validate the same steps as the runner script. So, let's take this smarter approach and create three files: the scraper class, the runner class (which instantiates and "runs" our scraper), and the test file (which instantiates and validates the functionality of our scraper).

First, the runner script:

```
#!/usr/bin/env ruby

require './scraper'

scraper = Scraper.new()
scraper.run()
```

Our barebones scraper class just looks like this:

```
class Scraper
  def run

  end
end
```

We also need to have a manifest file, the Gemfile, where we will document our library dependencies:

```
source "https://rubygems.org"

gem "github-pages"
gem "rspec"
```

Then, install our gems using the command `bundle`. That installs the `rspec` tool, the Jekyll tool, and associated libraries.

Finally, we can create our test harness:

```
require './scraper'

describe "#run" do
  it "should run" do
    scraper = Scraper.new
    scraper.run()
  end
end
```

Remember to run using the `bundle exec rspec scraper_spec.rb` command, which makes everything run inside the bundler context (and load our libraries from the Gemfile, instead of the default system gems):

```
$ bundle exec rspec scraper_spec.rb
.

Finished in 0.00125 seconds (files took 0.12399 seconds to load)
1 example, 0 failures
```

There is nothing we are explicitly testing yet, but our test harness displays that our code inside our tests will match closely the code we write inside our runner wrapper.

Scraping Titles

Let's start with something simple: scraping the titles from the site. We'll use Ruby to scrape the site; Ruby has some intuitive gems like mechanize that simplify building web clients. There is an API for the Internet archive, but I found it flakey and unreliable, so we'll just scrape the site. Add these additional lines to the Gemfile using this command and then install the libraries:

```
$ echo "gem 'mechanize'" >> Gemfile
$ bundle
```

Now we can modify our scraper to use the mechanize gem and retrieve content from Archive.org:

```
require 'mechanize' # ❶

class Scraper

  attr_accessor :root # ❷
  attr_accessor :agent

  def initialize # ❸
    @root = "http://web.archive.org/web/20030820233527/" +
    "http://bytravelers.com/journal/entry/" # ❹
    @agent = Mechanize.new
  end

  def run
    100.times do |i| # ❺
      url = "#{@root}#{i}" # ❻
      @agent.get( url ) do |page|
        puts "#{i} #{page.title}"
      end
    end
  end

end
```

❶ Require the mechanize library.

❷ We use a Ruby method called attr_accessor, which creates a public instance variable. We can use variables created using attr_accessor by prefixing the variable name with an @ character. Instance variables are accessible outside the class as well.

❸ When a method named `initialize` is defined for a class, this method is called right after object creation, so this is the appropriate place for us to initialize the member variables.

❹ Initialize the variables to default values. We store the root of the URL to the cached copy of ByTravelers.com here.

❺ Our run method runs the block inside 100 times.

❻ Our block starts by generating a URL to the specific page, retrieves the page, and then prints out the index in our loop plus the title of the page object.

Let's run our scraper and see what happens now:

```
$ bundle exec ./run.rb
...
53 Read Journal Entries
54 Read Journal Entries
55 Read Journal Entries
56 Read Journal Entries
57 Internet Archive Wayback Machine
58 Internet Archive Wayback Machine
...
```

You can see that some of the entries have a generic "Internet Archive Wayback Machine" while some have "Read Journal Entries." Archive.org will respond with a placeholder title when it does not have content from the site (as is the case with item #58, for example). We should ignore those pages that don't have the string "Read Journal Entries" as the title (which tells us Archive.org does have cached content from our site).

Now that we have all the content, we can start finding the important pieces inside and putting them into our Jekyll posts.

Refinining with Interactive Ruby

There are two things that make Mechanize immensely powerful as the foundation for a scraping tool: easy access to making HTTP calls, and a powerful searching syntax once you have a remote document. You've seen how Mechanize makes it simple to make a GET request. Let's explore sifting through a massive document to get the important pieces of textual content. We can manually explore scraping using the Ruby IRB (interactive Ruby shell):

```
$ irb -r./scraper
2.0.0-p481 :001 > scraper = Scraper.new
 => #<Scraper:0x00000001e37ca8...>
2.0.0-p481 :002 > page = scraper.agent.get "#{scraper.root}#{56}"
 => #<Mechanize::Page {url #<URI::HTTP:0x00000001a85218...>
```

The first line invokes IRB and uses the -r switch to load the scraper library in the current directory. If you have not used IRB before, there are a few things to know that will make life easier. The IRB has a prompt, which indicates the version of Ruby you are using, and the index of the command you are running. IRB has a lot of features beyond what we will discuss here, but those indexes can be used to replay history and for job control, like many other types of shells. At the IRB prompt you can enter Ruby and IRB executes the command immediately. Once the command executes, IRB prints the result; the characters => indicate the return value. When you are playing with Ruby, return values will often be complex objects: the return value when you use `scraper.agent.get` is a Mechanize Ruby object. This is a very large object, so printing it out takes a lot of real estate. We've abbreviated the majority of it here, and will do that for many complex objects to save space when discussing IRB.

The last command in IRB saves the HTTP GET request as a page object. Once we have the page, how do we extract information from it? Mechanize has a nice piece of syntactic sugar that makes it easy to search the DOM structure: the "/" operator. Let's try it:

```
2.0.0-p481 :003 > page / "tr"
 => []
```

If our query path had found anything, we would have seen a return value with an array of Mechanize objects, but in this case we got back an empty array (which indicates nothing was found). Unfortunately, the paths vary when the document is loaded into a browser (the browser can customize the DOM or the server can send slightly different data to the client). But if we experiment with similar paths inside IRB, we will find what we need. It helps to jump back and forth between Chrome and IRB, examining the structure of the HTML inside Chrome and then testing a search path using IRB. Eventually, we come across this search path:

```
2.0.0-p481 :004 > items = page / "table[valign=top] tr"
 => [#<Nokogiri::XML::Element:0xc05670 name="font"
      attributes=[#<Nokogiri::XML::Attr:0xc05328 name="size"
      value="-2">]...
2.0.0-p481 :005 > items.length
 => 5
2.0.0-p481 :006 > items[0].text()
 => "\n\n\n\n\n\n\n\n\nBeautiful Belize\n\n\n\n\n\n\n"
2.0.0-p481 :005 > items[0].text().strip
 => "Beautiful Belize"
```

Eureka, we found the pattern that gives us our title. We had to jump around inside the results from the query, but we can correlate the text on the page inside the browser with different structures found using the query inside IRB. It is important to note that we have to strip whitespace from the title to make it presentable. We can incorporate this into our scraper code, but this is a good moment to think about how we can write tests to verify this works properly. And when we start writing tests, we open the door for another opportunity: caching to our HTTP requests.

Writing Tests and Caching

Were we to run our run.rb script again, we would notice that it prints the document title, then halts as it retrieves the content from the server, and then prints again, stopping and starting until complete. The content from Archive.org does not change at all since the original site was scraped years ago, so there is no reason we need to get the latest content; content even several months stale will be the same as content retrieved a few moments ago. It seems like a good opportunity to put a caching layer between us and the code, reducing impact on Archive.org and making our script run faster. In addition, if we structure our code to make retrieval and processing happen independently, we can write tests to verify the processing:

```ruby
require 'mechanize'
require 'vcr' # ❶
VCR.configure do |c| # ❷
  c.cassette_library_dir = 'cached'
  c.hook_into :webmock
end

class Scraper

  attr_accessor :root
  attr_accessor :agent
  attr_accessor :pages # ❸

  def initialize
    @root = "http://web.archive.org/web/20030820233527/" +
    "http://bytravelers.com/journal/entry/"
    @agent = Mechanize.new
    @pages = [] # ❹
  end

  def scrape
    100.times do |i|
      begin
        VCR.use_cassette("bt_#{i}") do # ❺
          url = "#{@root}#{i}"
          @agent.get( url ) do |page|
            if page.title.eql? "Read Journal Entries" # ❻
              pages << page
            end
          end
        end
      rescue Exception => e
        STDERR.puts "Unable to scrape this file (#{i})"
      end
    end
```

```
      end

      def process_title( row )
        row.strip  # ❼
      end

      def run
        scrape()
        @pages.each do |page|  # ❽
          rows = ( page / "table[valign=top] tr" )
          puts process_title( rows[0].text() )
        end
      end

    end
```

❶ We require the VCR gem: this gem intercepts HTTP requests, sending them out normally the first time, and caching all successive calls, completely transparent to the user.

❷ VCR must be configured when you use it: in this case we specify a directory where results will be cached, and tell it what mocking library we should use to store the cached results.

❸ We establish a new variable called pages. We will scrape all the pages into this array (and get them for free once the information is cached).

❹ Initialize the pages array here.

❺ To use the VCR recording feature, we wrap any code that makes HTTP requests inside a VCR block with a name specifying the cassette to save it under. In this case, we use a cassette named bt (for ByTravelers) with the index of the page. The first time we use the scraper to request the page, it is retrieved and stored inside the cache. Successive calls to the scraper get method are retrieved from the cached responses.

❻ We then look for any titles that look like pages archived into Archive.org (using the title to differentiate) and if we find one, store that page into our pages array for later processing.

❼ We move the title processing into its own method called process_title. Here we use the information and remove any whitespace.

❽ Inside of run we now call scrape to load the pages, and then iterate over each page, searching inside them and processing the titles.

We need to install the VCR and webmock libraries, so add them to the Gemfile:

```
$ echo "gem 'vcr'" >> Gemfile
$ echo "gem 'webmock'" >> Gemfile
$ bundle
```

If we run our script using `bundle exec ruby ./run.rb`, we will see it print out the titles:

```
$ bundle exec ruby ./run.rb
Unable to scrape this file (14)
Unable to scrape this file (43)
Unable to scrape this file (47)
Unable to scrape this file (71)
Unable to scrape this file (94)
Unable to scrape this file (96)
Third day in Salvador
The Hill-Tribes of Northern Thailand
Passion Play of Oberammergau
"Angrezis in Bharat"
Cuba - the good and bad
Nemaste
Mexico/Belize/Guatemala
South Africa
...
```

We print out the errors (when Archive.org does not have a page for a particular URL). Note that as a side effect of caching, things work much faster. If we analyze the time we save using the `time` command, we see these results:

```
$ time bundle exec ruby ./run.rb # before VCR
real    0m29.907s
user    0m2.220s
sys     0m0.170s
$ time bundle exec ruby ./run.rb # after VCR
real    0m3.750s
user    0m3.474s
sys     0m0.194s
```

So, it takes an order of magnitude more time without caching. And, we get these cached responses for free, and inside our IRB sessions as well.

The titles look good, but the fourth one is a little worrisome. Looks like one of the users decided to enclose their title in double quotes. To control the formatting, it would be nice to clean that up. Let's do that, and write tests to verify things work:

```
require './scraper'

describe "#run" do
  before :each do
    @scraper = Scraper.new
  end
```

```
describe "#process_titles" do
  it "should correct titles with double quotes" do
    str = ' something " with a double quote'
    expect( @scraper.process_title( str ) ).to_not match( /"/ )
  end

  it "should strip whitespace from titles" do
    str = '\n\n something between newlines \n\n'
    expect( @scraper.process_title( str ) ).to_not match( /^\n\n/ )
  end
end

end
```

If we run this, we see one test pass and one test fail:

```
$ bundle exec rspec scraper_spec.rb
F.

Failures:

  1) #run #process_titles should correct titles with double quotes
     Failure/Error: expect( @scraper.process_title( ' something " with
     a double quote' ) ).to_not match( /"/ )
       expected "something \" with a double quote" not to match /"/
       Diff:
       @@ -1,2 +1,2 @@
       -/"/
       +"something \" with a double quote"
     # ./scraper_spec.rb:10:in `block (3 levels) in <top (required)>'

Finished in 0.01359 seconds (files took 0.83765 seconds to load)
2 examples, 1 failure

Failed examples:

rspec ./scraper_spec.rb:9 # #run #process_titles should correct titles
with double quotes
```

To fix this test, let's strip out the double quotes by changing one line in the *scraper.rb* file:

```
...

def process_title( row )
  row.strip.gsub( /"/, '' )
end

...
```

Now both tests pass. That line of code might be worrisome if you believe in defensive coding. If this function were called with a nil value, for example, it would crash. Even if we could guarantee that this situation would never occur from our calling context, it is better to make our method safe. Let's make sure it works and write a test to prove it.

Add a test that asserts there is not an error when the argument to `process_title` is nil:

```
...
it "should not crash if the title is nil" do
  expect{ @scraper.process_title( nil ) }.to_not raise_error()
end
...
```

Running `rspec scraper_spec.rb` results in the following error, which we expect since we have not yet fixed the code:

```
..F..

Failures:

  1) #run #process_titles should not crash if the title is nil
     Failure/Error: expect{ @scraper.process_title( nil ) }.to_not raise_error()
       expected no Exception, got #<NoMethodError: undefined method
     `strip' for nil:NilClass> with backtrace:
         # ./scraper.rb:38:in `process_title'
         # ./scraper_spec.rb:20:in `block (4 levels) in <top (required)>'
         # ./scraper_spec.rb:20:in `block (3 levels) in <top (required)>'
     # ./scraper_spec.rb:20:in `block (3 levels) in <top (required)>'

Finished in 0.00701 seconds
5 examples, 1 failure

Failed examples:

rspec ./scraper_spec.rb:19 # #run #process_titles should not crash if the title
# is nil
```

We can fix it with this one simple change:

```
...

def process_title( row )
  row.strip.gsub( /"/, '' ) if row
end
...
```

Now we are in a position to write out the files for our actual posts.

Writing Jekyll Posts

With our titles in hand, we can generate an actual Jekyll post. To keep things simple each post will contain nothing beyond the titles for now, but we will quickly add other content. Getting the skeleton of a post established allows us to use the Jekyll command-line tools to troubleshoot our setup.

First, create a Git repository for our files. When the Jekyll tool runs, it generates all the files into a directory called _site so we should add a .gitignore file, which ignores this directory:

```
$ git init
$ mkdir _posts
$ echo "_site" >> .gitignore
$ git add .gitignore
$ git commit -m "Initial checkin"
```

Jekyll Markdown files are very simple: just a bit of YAML at the beginning, with text content following, formatted as Markdown. To generate Markdown posts, add a method called write to our scraper that writes out the processed information after we have retrieved and parsed the pages from Archive.org.

Jekyll posts are stored inside the _posts directory. As a convention, filenames are generated with the date and title, lowercased, converted to a string without any characters beyond a-z and the hyphen, and terminated by the extension (usually .md for Markdown). In order to properly generate the filename, we will need to scrape the date, so we will do that as well.

As a more concrete example, we want to take something like Cuba - the good and bad that happened on January 12th, 2001, and make a filename like 2001-01-12-cuba-the-good-and-bad.md. Or, Mexico/Belize/Guatemala from the same date, and make it into the filename 2001-01-12-mexico-belize-guatemala.md. These conversions look like good places to write tests, so we can start there:

```
describe "#get_filename" do
  it "should take 'Cuba - the good and bad' on January 12th, 2001" +
     " and get a proper filename" do
    input = 'Cuba - the good and bad'
    date = "January 12th, 2001"
    output = "2001-01-12-cuba-the-good-and-bad.md"
    expect( @scraper.get_filename( input, date ) ).to eq( output )
  end

  it "should `Mexico/Belize/Guatemala` and get a proper filename" do
    input = "Mexico/Belize/Guatemala"
    date = "2001-01-12"
    output = "2001-01-12-mexico-belize-guatemala.md"
    expect( @scraper.get_filename( input, date ) ).to eq( output )
  end
end
```

Let's build the get_filename method. This method uses the handy Ruby Date Time.parse method to convert a string representation of a date into a date object, and then uses the `strfmtime` method to format that date into the format we want in our filename:

```
...
def get_filename( title, date )
  processed_date = DateTime.parse( date )
  processed_title = title.downcase.gsub( /[^a-z]+/, '-' )
  "#{processed_date.strftime('%Y-%m-%d')}-#{processed_title}.md"
end
...
```

If we run our tests now, we will see them both pass.

Now we can add to our scraper so that it can write out the posts:

```
def render( processed ) # ❶
  processed['layout'] = 'post'
  rendered = "#{processed.to_yaml}---\n\n" # ❷
  rendered
end

def write( rendered, processed ) # ❸
  Dir.mkdir( "_posts" ) unless File.exists?( "_posts" )
  filename = get_filename( processed['title'], processed['creation_date'] )
  File.open( "_posts/#{filename}", "w+" ) do |f|
    f.write rendered
  end
end

def process_creation_date( date )
  tuple = date.split( /last updated on:/ ) # ❹
  rv = tuple[1].strip if tuple and tuple.length > 1
  rv
end

def run
  scrape()
  @pages.each do |page| # ❺
    rows = ( page / "table[valign=top] tr" )
    processed = {}
    processed['title'] = process_title( rows[0].text() )
    processed['creation_date'] = process_creation_date( rows[3].text() ) # ❻
    rendered = render( processed )
    write( rendered, processed )
  end
```

❶ We define a `render` method. This takes the processed information (which arrives as a hash) and renders the information into the proper format: the YAML Front Matter (YFM) and then the body (which we don't have yet). We then return the rendered string.

❷ We use the `to_yaml` method on our hash. This method appears when we include the yaml library using `require 'yaml'` (not displayed here, but easy to add to the *scraper.rb* file and present in the samples on GitHub).

❸ The `write` method writes the rendered content to disk. It makes sure the *_posts* directory is available, and if not, creates it. It then writes out the file using our `get_filename` method to get the path, prefixed with the *_posts* directory.

❹ `process_creation_date` takes a piece from the scraped page and breaks it apart by the string "`last updated on:`" and uses the second item in the resultant array.

❺ Inside our `run` method we now build out the processed hash, finding the date and title using rows from the query path we used before.

❻ Once we have our processed array, we can "render" it and then write out the rendered string to our filesystem.

If we generate the posts by calling `bundle exec ruby ./run.rb` we will see our posts generated into the *_posts* directory. Choosing a random one, they look like this:

```
---
title: Beautiful Belize
creation_date: '2003-03-23'
layout: post
---
```

As you can see, for now, posts are nothing more than the YFM, but this is still a perfectly valid Jekyll post.

Now let's use the `jekyll` command-line tool to start looking at our posts and to troubleshoot any issues with our Jekyll repository.

Using the Jekyll Command-Line Tool

Taking a moment to add our files to the Git repository, we can then take a look at our site using the `jekyll` command-line tool. Using the command-line tool locally will spot check our new content as we will see errors immediately (rather than getting notification emails from GitHub after publishing there). Errors can occur if our scraper does not correctly process the HTML retrieved from Archive.org and subsequently generates incorrect Markdown content, for example.

```
$ git add .
$ git commit -m "Make this into a Jekyll site"
...
$ jekyll serve --watch
Configuration file: none
            Source: /home/xrdawson/bytravelers
```

```
      Destination: /home/xrdawson/bytravelers/_site
       Generating...
     Build Warning: Layout 'post' requested in _posts/2000-05-23-third-day-in...
     Build Warning: Layout 'post' requested in _posts/2000-08-28-the-hill-tri...
      ...
                     done.
  Auto-regeneration: enabled for '/home/xrdawson/bytravelers'
 Configuration file: none
     Server address: http://0.0.0.0:4000/
     Server running... press ctrl-c to stop.
```

So, we see a few problems already. First, we don't have a layout for "post." And, there is no configuration file. Let's fix these problems.

Add a file called _config.yml to the root directory:

```
name: ByTravelers.com: Online travel information
markdown: redcarpet
highlighter: pygments
```

Remember, the jekyll tool does not reload the configuration file automatically, so we should restart the tool by hitting Ctrl-C and restarting.

Then, create a directory called _layouts, and place a file called post.html inside it with these contents:

```
---
layout: default
---

<h1>{{ page.title }}</h1>

{{ content }}
```

The post.html layout file is very simple: we use Liquid Markup tags to write out the title of the site (contained in an object called page, which our template has access to) and then the content itself, which is the rendered output from the post page.

We also need to create a "default" layout, so create this inside the _layouts directory with the filename default.html:

```
<html>
<head>
<title>ByTravelers.com</title>
</head>

<body>

{{ content }}

</body>
</html>
```

This file is almost pure HTML, with only the {{ content }} tag. When we specify default as the layout inside YAML for a Markdown file, the Markdown text is converted to HTML, and then this layout file is wrapped around it. You can see that the initial post files specify the post layout, which is wrapped around the content, then the *post.html* layout file specifies the *default.html* layout, which is wrapped around the entire contents.

When we add these files, the Jekyll tool will notice the filesystem has changed and regenerate files. We now have generated posts, but we don't have a master index file, so let's add this now.

Master Index File with Liquid Markup

We now have the posts generated properly, but we don't have an entry page into the blog. We can create an *index.md* file, which just displays an index of all the blog posts:

```
---
layout: default
---

<h1>ByTravelers.com</h1>

Crowd sourced travel information.

<br/>

<div>
{% for post in site.posts %}
<a href="{{ post.url }}"><h2> {{ post.title }} </h2></a>
{{ post.content | strip_html | truncatewords: 40 }}
<br/>
<em>Posted on {{ post.date | date_to_string }}</em>
<br/>
{% endfor %}
</div>
```

Notice that the file combines Markdown (the single # character converts into an H1 tag) with regular HTML. You are free to mix regular HTML inside of Markdown files when there is not a Markdown equivalent.

Output tags use double braces surrounding the content ({{ site.title }}) while logic tags use a brace and percent symbol ({% if site.title %}). As you might expect, output tags place some type of visible output into the page, and logic tags perform some logic operation, like conditionals or loops.

The preceding template has both output and logic tags. We see a logic tag in the form of {% for ... %}, which loops over each post. Jekyll will process the entire posts directory and provide it to pages inside the site.posts variable, and the for logic tag allows us to iterate over them. If we use a {% for ... %} tag we need to "close" the tag with a matching {% endfor %} tag. Inside of our for loop we have several output tags: {{ post.url }} outputs the post URL associated with a post, for example. We also have *filters*, which are methods defined to process data. One such filter is the strip_html filter, which you might guess strips out HTML text, converting it to escaped text. This is necessary when your text could include HTML tags. You'll also notice that filters can be "chained"; we process the body with the strip_html filter and then truncate the text by 40 characters using the truncatewords:40 filter.

If we open *http://localhost:4000* in our browser, we will see a simple index page with the titles of our posts, like Figure 6-6.

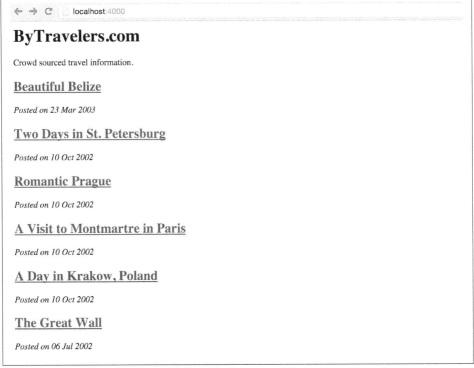

Figure 6-6. The Index Page, for a naked Jekyll blog

This index page lists every post: let's make it display only the last 10 posts. Copy the *index.md* file to a file named *archive.md*. Then, change the {% for post in site.posts %} tag to {% for post in site.posts | limit:10 %}.

Each post has an associated page that is generated by Jekyll. Clicking any of the links displays the post, which is right now just the title. We can now add the rest of the pages from our scraper.

Scraping Body and Author

Use IRB to find the author and body content. Start by searching for the author information:

```
2.0.0-p481 :037 > rows[2].to_s
 => "<tr>\n<td align=\"center\">\n\n\n\n<font size=\"+1\">author:..."
2.0.0-p481 :038 > ( rows[2] / "td font" )[0].text()
 => "author: \n\nMD \n\n\nread more from this author | \nsee maps from this..."
2.0.0-p481 :039 > author = ( rows[2] / "td font" )[0].text()
 => "author: \n\nMD \n\n\nread more from this author | \nsee maps from this..."
2.0.0-p481 :040 > author =~ /author:\s+\n\n([^\s]+)\n\n/
 => 0
2.0.0-p481 :041 > $1
 => "MD"
```

We start by looking at the second row and converting it to raw HTML. We see there is a string `author:`, which is a likely place to reference the author. This string is wrapped by a `font` tag and a `td` tag, so we can use these search queries to eliminate extra information. Then, we convert the HTML to text using the `text()` method and use a regular expression to pull out the text after the `author:` string. If a regular expression matches and has a captured expression, it will be held in the global variable `$1`. There is more than one way to get this information, of course.

Next, we retrieve our body from the scraped page. Add a method called `process_body` and insert this into our processed hash:

```
def render( processed )
  processed['layout'] = 'post'
  filtered = processed.reject{ |k,v| k.eql?('body') } # ❶
  rendered = "#{filtered.to_yaml}---\n\n" + # ❷
    "### Written by: #{processed['author']}\n\n" +
    processed['body']
  rendered
end
 # ❸
def process_body( paragraphs )
  paragraphs.map { |p| p.text() }.join "\n\n"
end

def run
  scrape()
  @pages.each do |page|
    rows = ( page / "table[valign=top] tr" )
    processed = {}
    processed['title'] = process_title( rows[0].text() ) # ❹
    processed['creation_date'] = process_creation_date( rows[3].text() )
    processed['body'] = process_body( rows[4] / "p" ) # ❺
    author_text = ( rows[2] / "td font" )[0].text()
    processed['author'] = $1.strip if author_text =~ /author:\s+\n\n+(.+)\n\n+/
    rendered = render( processed )
```

```
    write( rendered, processed )
  end
```

❶ We need to rewrite `render` slightly. There is no need for the entire body content of a post to be included in the YFM. We can filter this out using the `reject` method.

❷ Then, we append the author and body content to generate the new rendered output.

❸ Our process body is straightforward: we convert each node passed into text (using the `text()` method) and then rejoin them with double newlines. Markdown will properly format paragraphs if they are separated by two newlines.

❹ We then just need to invoke the `process_body` method and insert the results into our processed hash.

❺ Next, we use the query path we found in our IRB session to retrieve the author information, and insert it into our processed hash. The author name will then be inserted into our YFM automatically within the `render` method, and we will insert it into the post.

We can then run `bundle exec ./run.rb` to rewrite our post files.

Adding Images to Jekyll

Jekyll can host any binary files as well, and Markdown files can host the proper markup to include these assets. Let's add the images from the original site:

```
def process_image( title )
  img = ( title / "img" )
  src = img.attr('src').text()
  filename = src.split( "/" ).pop

  output = "assets/images/"
  FileUtils.mkdir_p output unless File.exists? output
  full = File.join( output, filename )

  if not File.exists? full or not File.size? full
    root = "https://web.archive.org"
    remote = root + src
    # puts "Downloading #{full} from #{remote}"
    `curl -L #{remote} -o #{full}`
  end

  filename
end
```

We use the venerable cURL to download our images. Our code makes it so that the file is only downloaded the first time. We use the -L switch to tell cURL to follow redirects, because these images URLs are transparently redirected inside the browser.

We need to customize our run method to invoke the `process_image` call: add `processed['image'] = process_image( rows[0] )` after any of the other process methods.

 I paid an artist for the images used on the original ByTravelers.com. If you are using this technique to scrape images or text content from another site, make sure you are abiding by all local and international copyright laws.

Then, modify our post layout to include the image:

```
---
layout: default
---

<h1>{{ page.title }}</h1>

<img src="/assets/images/{{ page.image }}">

{{ content }}
```

Regenerating this page shows us a white background with an awkwardly juxtaposed colored image. Adding background colors to the entire site will help, so let's now modify the CSS for our site.

Customizing Styling (CSS)

We used Bootstrap in Chapter 9 and will use it again here. We will also layer another CSS file on top of Bootstrap to customize the colors.

First, add a reference to Bootstrap and our custom CSS inside of the master layout file, *default.html*:

```
<html>
<head>
<title>ByTravelers.com</title>

<link href="/assets/css/bootstrap.min.css" rel="stylesheet">
<link href="/assets/css/site.css" rel="stylesheet">

</head>

<body>

{{ content }}
```

```
</body>
</html>
```

Then, download the Bootstrap CSS file into the proper folder:

```
$ mkdir assets/css
$ curl \
https://maxcdn.bootstrapcdn.com/bootstrap/3.3.5/css/bootstrap.min.css \
-o assets/css/bootstrap.min.css
```

Adding a CSS framework like Bootstrap helps things considerably, but we should match the original colors as well. Add a file called *site.css* into the *assets/css* directory:

```
body {
color: #000000;
background-color: #CCCC99;
}

a {
color: #603;
}

.jumbotron {
background-color: #FFFFCC;
}
```

With the Bootstrap library installed, we can slightly modify our *default.html* layout to make the site really stand out. Many Jekyll blogs are quite minimalistic and stark, but you are limited only by your imagination:

```
<html>
  <head>
    <title>ByTravelers.com</title>
    <link href="/assets/css/bootstrap.min.css" rel="stylesheet">
    <link href="/assets/css/site.css" rel="stylesheet">
  </head>

  <body>

    <div class="container">
      <div class="jumbotron">
        <h1>ByTravelers.com</h1>
        Alternative travel information
      </div>
      <div class='row>
        <div class='span12'>
          <div class="container">
            {{ content }}
          </div>
        </div>
      </div>
    </div>
```

```
    </body>
</html>
```

If we reload, we will see a much prettier version of the site (Figure 6-7).

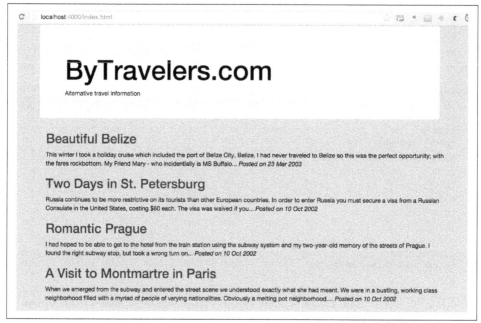

Figure 6-7. Restoring the original colors and images

We've now entirely scraped an old site and built a new Jekyll blog, so there is just one thing left to do: encourage and permit collaboration, which GitHub makes particularly easy.

Inviting Contributions with GitHub "Fork"

When you publish a Jekyll blog, the fact that it is a repository on GitHub makes it simple to manage and track changes. In addition, because forking is a button click away, you can ask people to contribute or make changes with very little friction. You might have seen the banner saying "Fork me on GitHub" on many a software project page hosted on GitHub. We can motivate others to participate in our blog using pull requests. Let's add that as a final touch and invite people to make contributions the GitHub way. The GitHub blog first posted these banners (*https://github.com/blog/273-github-ribbons*), and we'll use its code almost as is inside our *default.html* page, just changing the reference to our repository in the link tag:

```
...
<body>

  <a href="https://github.com/xrd/bytravelers.com">
    <img style="position: absolute; top: 0; right: 0; border: 0;"
          src="https://..."
          alt="Fork me on GitHub"
          data-canonical-src="https://.../forkme_right_gray_6d6d6d.png"></a>

  <div class="container">
    <div class="jumbotron">
      <h1>ByTravelers.com</h1>
      Alternative travel information
...
```

Now anyone can fork our repository, add their own post to the _posts_ directory, and then issue a pull request asking us to incorporate the new post into our Jekyll blog.

Publishing Our Blog to GitHub

Like any other GitHub repository, we can then publish our blog using the same commands we saw with earlier repositories. Obviously you should change the username and blog name to suit your own needs:

```
$ export BLOG_NAME=xrd/bytravelers.com
$ gem install hub
$ hub create $BLOG_NAME # You might need to login here
$ sleep $((10*60)) && open http://bytravelers.com
```

And, don't forget to set up DNS records and give yourself appropriate time to let those records propagate out.

Summary

We've explored the details of Jekyll, looking at the structure of a Jekyll blog. Liquid Markup is a powerful way to use programmatic constructs inside a Markdown file, and we documented the most important concepts around using this templating language. By investigating the internals of a Jekyll post, we explained the intricacies of YAML Front Matter (YFM) and how seamlessly you can mix and match HTML with Markdown syntax. Jekyll blogs can utilize their own custom CSS, and we've shown how easy it is to use a powerful complete library like Bootstrap layered underneath a site-specific small CSS file. And, we built a scraper application that retrieves a remote site in its entirety and converts it into the correct structure of a Jekyll blog. Even though this scraper application was built specifically for a particular site, by adding testing and properly structuring the components it should be evident how to reuse much of the scraper for anything else you want to quickly convert into a Jekyll blog.

In the next chapter we will continue looking at Jekyll by building an Android application that uses the Java GitHub API bindings and allows you to create Jekyll blog posts with the Git Data API.

CHAPTER 7

Android and the Git Data API

You might not use your phone right now as a developer tool, but the odds are that you will soon. At the moment, phones and tablets can be great for reading code, but the editors we developers use on our laptops have not yet been reimagined for mobile devices. We are getting close though: the GitHub API is accessible through the well-written EGit client library for Java, and this library supports both reading data stored on GitHub and writing data back into it. These are a perfect set of building blocks to develop applications for the Android platform, currently the world's most popular mobile OS.

In this chapter, we'll use the Java EGit libraries to develop a small Android application that posts to our blog hosted on GitHub. Our blogging application will allow us to log in to GitHub, and then ask us for a quick note describing how we are feeling. The application will then compose a Jekyll blog post for us and push the post into our blog on GitHub.

Setting Up

To build this application, we need to create a Jekyll blog and then install the necessary Android build tools.

Creating a Jekyll Blog

We are writing an application that adds Jekyll blog entries, and we are writing tests to verify our application works as advertised, so we need a sandbox blog against which we can run commands. There are various ways to create a new Jekyll blog. The simplest is to run a series of Ruby commands documented here; if you want to know more about Jekyll, it is covered in more depth in Chapter 6. There are a few items of note when establishing a Jekyll blog that have some complexity, things like mapping a hostname properly and using the correct branch inside Git. For our purposes here, however, we won't need to make sure all that is established. All we need is to make sure we have a sandbox repository that has the structure of a Jekyll blog:

```
$ echo "source 'https://rubygems.org'" >> Gemfile
$ echo "gem 'github-pages'" >> Gemfile
$ echo "gem 'hub'" >> Gemfile
$ export BLOG_NAME=mytestblog
$ bundle
$ jekyll new $BLOG_NAME
$ cd $BLOG_NAME
$ hub create
$ git push -u origin master
```

These commands install the correct libraries for using Jekyll (and one for our tests as well), generate a new blog using the Jekyll command-line tool, and then create a blog on GitHub with those files. On the second line we specify the name of the blog; you are welcome to change this to any name you'd like, just make sure the tests match the name.

 When you have finished running these commands, you should close the terminal window. There are other commands later in this chapter that should occur in a fresh directory and as such it is best not to run those commands from within the same directory where you created your Jekyll blog. You've pushed all those files into GitHub, so you could safely delete the local repository in this directory.

Android Development Tools

If you don't have a physical Android device, don't fret. You can follow along with this chapter without having an actual Android device by doing development and testing on a virtual device.

Installing the Java SDK

Unfortunately there is no simple shell command to install Java in the same way as there is for Ruby and NodeJS using RVM or NVM. Oracle controls the Java language and distribution of official SDKs, and it restricts access to downloads other than from *java.oracle.com*. Java is freely available, but you need to visit *java.oracle.com* and find the correct download for your needs. Android works with the 1.7 versions of Java or better.

Installing Android Studio

We will use Android Studio, the Google IDE for developing Android applications. To install it, go to *https://developer.android.com/sdk/index.html* and you will see a download button for your platform (OS X, Linux, and Windows supported). Android Studio bundles all the important tools for building Android applications.

Creating a New Project

Let's now create our Android project. When you first open Android Studio, you will see an option in the right pane inviting you to create a new project. Click the "Start a new Android Studio project" option. In the next step, you will see a screen for configuring your new project. Enter GhRU ("GitHub R U?") into the Application Name and use *example.com* as the Company Domain (or use your own domain, but be aware that this will make the directory structure presented in this chapter different than yours). Android Studio should automatically generate the "package name" for you as com.example.ghru.

You will then need to choose a target SDK. The higher the target, the better access to newer Android APIs, but the fewer number of devices that can run the application. The code in this chapter will work with older SDKs, so let's make a balanced choice and use Android 4.4 (KitKat), which runs on phones and tablets. At the moment this means, according to Android Studio, that our application will run on 49.5% of Android devices in the world as shown in Figure 7-1.

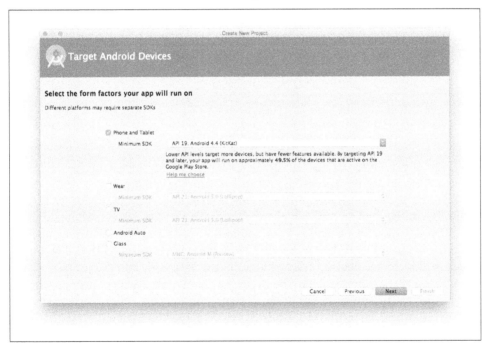

Figure 7-1. Choose an Android SDK

You will then be presented with a choice of activities. Choose "Blank Activity." You will be taken to a screen that allows you to customize the activity. Accept the defaults of "MainActivity" as the Activity Name and the associated files for the layout, title, and menu resource name. Then click the "Finish" button to generate the project.

After completing these steps, Android Studio will create Gradle configuration files and generate the structure of your application. Once this has completed, you can review the file tree of your project by clicking the lefthand vertical tab labeled "Project" as shown in Figure 7-2.

Figure 7-2. Reviewing the Android project structure for the first time

If you have never seen an Android project before, this screen deserves some explanation. The *app* directory contains your application code and resources (layout files, images, and strings). Inside the *app* directory you will see several other directories: The *java* directory contains, quite obviously, any Java code for the project, which includes the application files, and also programs that do not reside in the app when it is published to the app store but perform testing on the app. The *res* directory contains the resources we mentioned. Android Studio lists all build files under the Gradle Scripts section, and groups them regardless of their directory placement. You can see two *build.gradle* files, the first of which you can generally ignore, though the second we will need to adjust.

Now we are ready to start editing our project.

Editing the Gradle Build File

First, we need to add to our Gradle build file and specify the dependent libraries. Gradle is a build system for Java and has become the offical build system for the Android platform. Open the *build.gradle* within the app module (the second of the two *build.gradle* files):

```
apply plugin: 'com.android.application' // ❶

android {
    compileSdkVersion 23 // ❷
    buildToolsVersion "23.0.1"

    defaultConfig {
        applicationId "com.example.ghru"
        minSdkVersion 21
        targetSdkVersion 23
        versionCode 1
        versionName "1.0"
        testInstrumentationRunner
            "android.support.test.runner.AndroidJUnitRunner" // ❸
    }
    buildTypes {
        release {
            minifyEnabled false
            proguardFiles getDefaultProguardFile('proguard-android.txt'),
            'proguard-rules.pro'
        }
    }
}

dependencies {
    compile fileTree(dir: 'libs', include: ['*.jar']) // ❹
    compile 'com.android.support:appcompat-v7:23.0.1'
    compile 'org.eclipse.mylyn.github:org.eclipse.egit.github.core:2.1.5'
    compile( 'commons-codec:commons-codec:1.9' )
    testCompile 'junit:junit:4.12' // ❺
    testCompile 'com.squareup.okhttp:okhttp:2.5.0'
    androidTestCompile 'com.android.support.test:runner:0.4' // ❻
    androidTestCompile 'com.android.support.test:rules:0.4'
    androidTestCompile 'com.android.support.test.espresso:espresso-core:2.2.1'
}
```

❶ First, we load the Android gradle plug-in. This extends our project to allow an android block, which we specify next.

❷ Next, we configure our `android` block, with things like the target version (which we choose when setting up our project) and the actual SDK, which we are using to compile the application.

❸ In order to run UI tests, we need to specify a test runner called the `AndroidJUnitRunner`.

❹ Android Studio automatically adds a configuration to our build file that loads any JARS (Java libraries) from the *lib* directory. We also install the support compatibility library for older Android devices, and most importantly, the EGit library that manages connections to GitHub for us. The commons CODEC library from the Apache Foundation provides tools that help to encode content into Base64, one of the options for storing data inside a GitHub repository using the API.

❺ Next, we install libraries that are only used when we run unit tests. `testCompile` libraries are compiled only when the code is run on the local development machine, and for this situation we need the JUnit library, and the OkHttp library from Square, which helps us validate that our request for a new commit has made it all the way into the GitHub API.

❻ Lastly, we install the Espresso libraries, the Google UI testing framework. The first line (of the three libraries) installs the test runner we configured earlier. We use `androidTestCompile`, which compiles against these libraries when the code runs on Android in test mode.

Creating AVDs for development

Android Studio makes creating AVD (Android Virtual Devices) simple. To start, under the "Tools" menu, click "Android" and then select "AVD Manager." To create a new AVD, click the "Create Virtual Device" button and follow the prompts. You are generally free to choose whatever settings you like. Google produces a real device called the Nexus 5. This is the Android reference device, and is a good option for a generic device with good support across all features. You can choose this one if you are confused about which to use as shown in Figure 7-3.

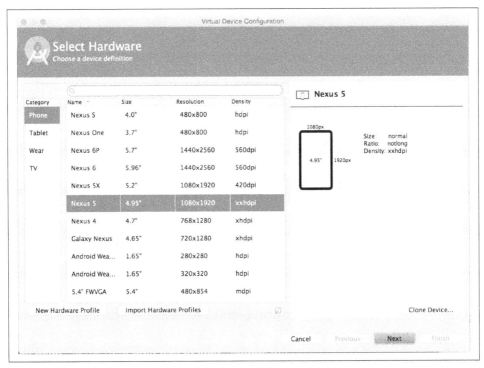

Figure 7-3. Creating a new AVD

Once you have created an AVD, start it up. It will take a few minutes to boot; AVDs emulate the chipset in software and booting up can take a few minutes, unfortunately. There are alternative tools that speed up AVD boot time (Genymotion is one of those), but there are complexities if you stray away from the stock Android tools, so we will stick with AVD.

Default Android Main

When we use the preceding commands to create a new Android application, it creates a sample entry point that is the starting point of our Android application. All Android applications have a file called *AndroidManifest.xml*, which specifies this activity and also supplies a list of permissions to the apps. Open the *AndroidManifest.xml* file from within the *app/src/main* directory. We need to make one change: to add a line that specifies that this app will use the Internet permission (required if our app will be talking to the GitHub API). Note that when viewing this file inside Android Studio the IDE can interpolate strings from resources, so you might see the `android:label` attribute displayed as GhRU with a grey tinge, when in fact the XML file itself has the value displayed here (`@string/app_name`):

```
<manifest xmlns:android="http://schemas.android.com/apk/res/android"
    package="com.example.ghru">

    <uses-permission android:name="android.permission.INTERNET" />

    <application android:allowBackup="true" android:label="@string/app_name"
        android:icon="@mipmap/ic_launcher" android:supportsRtl="true"
        android:theme="@style/AppTheme">

        <activity android:name="MainActivity"
            android:label="@string/app_name">
            <intent-filter>
                <action android:name="android.intent.action.MAIN" />
                <category android:name="android.intent.category.LAUNCHER" />
            </intent-filter>
        </activity>

    </application>

</manifest>
```

When the application is launched, the Android OS will launch this activity and then call the onCreate function for us. Inside this function, our application calls our parent's implementation of onCreate, and then inflates the layout for our application. Layouts are XML files in which the UI of an Android application is declaratively described.

Android Studio created a default layout for us (called *activity_main.xml*), but let's ignore that and create our own layout. To do so, right-click (Ctrl-click on OS X) on the *layouts* directory, and then choose "New" and then "Layout resource file" at the very top of the list (Android Studio nicely chooses the most likely candidate given the context of the click). Enter "main.xml" as the filename, and accept the other defaults.

This application requires that we log in, so we know we at least need a field and a descriptive label for the username, a password field (and associated descriptive label) for the password, a button to click that tells our app to attempt to log in, and a status field that indicates success or failure of the login. So, let's modify the generated *main.xml* to specify this user interface. To edit this file as text, click the tab labeled Text next to the tab labeled Design at the very bottom of the *main.xml* pane to switch to text view. Then, edit the file to look like the following:

```
<?xml version="1.0" encoding="utf-8"?> <-- ❶ -->
<LinearLayout xmlns:android="http://schemas.android.com/apk/res/android"
    android:orientation="vertical"
    android:layout_width="match_parent"
    android:layout_height="match_parent"
    > <-- ❷ -->
<TextView
    android:layout_width="match_parent"
    android:layout_height="wrap_content"
```

```
        android:text="GitHub Username:"
        />
    <EditText
        android:layout_width="match_parent"
        android:layout_height="wrap_content"
        android:id="@+id/username"
        />

    <TextView
        android:layout_width="match_parent"
        android:layout_height="wrap_content"
        android:text="GitHub Password:"
        />

    <EditText
        android:layout_width="match_parent"
        android:layout_height="wrap_content"
        android:id="@+id/password"
        android:inputType="textWebPassword"
        />   <-- ❸ -->

    <Button
        android:layout_width="match_parent"
        android:layout_height="wrap_content"
        android:text="Login"
        android:id="@+id/login"
        />   <-- ❹ -->

    <TextView
        android:layout_width="match_parent"
        android:layout_height="wrap_content"
        android:id="@+id/login_status"
        />

</LinearLayout>
```

You may have complicated feelings about XML files (I know I do), but the Android layout XML files are a straightforward way to design layouts declaratively, and there is a great ecosystem of GUI tools that provide sophisticated ways to manage them. Scanning this XML file, it should be relatively easy to understand what is happening here.

❶ The entire layout is wrapped in a `LinearLayout`, which simply positions each element stacked vertically inside it. We set the height and width layout attributes to `match_parent`, which means this layout occupies the entire space of the screen.

❷ We then add the elements we described previously: pairs of `TextView` and `Edit View` for the label and entry options necessary for the username and password.

❸ The password field customizes the type to be a password field, which means the entry is hidden when we enter it.

❹ Some elements in the XML have an ID attribute, which allows us to access the items within our Java code, such as when we need to assign a handler to a button or retrieve text entered by the user from an entry field. We will demonstrate this in a moment.

You can review the visual structure of this XML file by clicking the "Design" tab to switch back to design mode.

We also need a layout once we have logged in. Create a file called *logged_in.xml* using the same set of steps. Once logged in, the user is presented with a layout asking him to choose which repository to save into, to enter his blog post into a large text field, and then to click a button to submit that blog post. We also leave an empty status box beneath the button to provide context while saving the post:

```xml
<?xml version="1.0" encoding="utf-8"?>
<LinearLayout xmlns:android="http://schemas.android.com/apk/res/android"
    android:orientation="vertical"
    android:layout_width="match_parent"
    android:layout_height="match_parent"
    >
  <TextView
      android:layout_width="match_parent"
      android:layout_height="wrap_content"
      android:text="Logged into GitHub"
      android:layout_weight="0"
      android:id="@+id/status" />

  <EditText
      android:layout_width="match_parent"
      android:layout_height="wrap_content"
      android:hint="Enter the blog repository"
      android:id="@+id/repository"
      android:layout_weight="0"
      />

  <EditText
      android:layout_width="match_parent"
      android:layout_height="wrap_content"
      android:hint="Enter the blog title"
      android:id="@+id/title"
      android:layout_weight="0" />

  <EditText
    android:gravity="top"
    android:layout_width="match_parent"
    android:layout_height="match_parent"
    android:hint="Enter your blog post"
```

```
        android:id="@+id/post"
        android:layout_weight="1"
        />

    <Button
        android:layout_width="match_parent"
        android:layout_height="wrap_content"
        android:layout_weight="0"
        android:id="@+id/submit"
        android:text="Send blog post"/>

</LinearLayout>
```

Most of this should be familiar once you have reviewed the *main.xml* file (and be sure to copy this from the associated sample repository on GitHub if you don't want to copy it in yourself).

Now that we have our XML established, we can ready our application for testing.

Android Automated Testing

Android supports three types of tests: unit tests, integration tests, and user interface (UI) tests. Unit tests validate very tightly defined and isolated pieces of code, while integration tests and UI tests test larger pieces of the whole. On Android, integration tests generally mean instantiation of data managers or code that interacts with multiple components inside the app, while UI testing permits testing of user-facing elements like buttons or text fields. In this chapter we will create a unit test and a UI test.

One important note: Unit tests run on your development machine, not the Android device itself. UI tests run on the Android device (or emulator). There can be subtle differences between the Java interpreter running on your development machine and the Dalvik interpreter running on your Android device, so it is worthwhile to use a mixture of the three types of tests. Stated another way, write at least one test that runs on the device or emulator itself!

Unit Tests for Our GitHub Client

Let's start by defining a unit test. Since the unit test runs on our development machine, our test and implementation code should be written such that they do not need to load any Android classes. This forces us to constrain functionality to only the GitHub API. We will define a helper class that will handle all the interaction with the GitHub API but does not know about Android whatsoever. Then, we can write a test harness that takes that class, instantiates it, and validates our calls to GitHub produce the right results.

You might legitimately ask: is a unit test the right place to verify an API call? Will this type of test be fast, given that slow-running unit tests are quickly ignored by software developers? Would it be better to mock out the response data inside our unit tests? These are all good questions!

To set up unit tests, we need to switch the build variant to unit tests. Look for a vertical tab on the lefthand side of Android Studio. Click this, and then where it says "Test Artifact" switch to "Unit Tests." From the project view (click the "Project" vertical tab if project view is not already selected) you can expand the "java" directory, and you should then see a directory with "(test)" in parentheses indicating this is where tests go. If this directory is not there, create a directory using the command line (this command would work: `mkdir -p app/src/test/java/com/example/ghru`).

Then, create a test file called *GitHubHelperTest.java* that looks like the following:

```java
package com.example.ghru;

import com.squareup.okhttp.OkHttpClient; // ❶
import com.squareup.okhttp.Request;
import com.squareup.okhttp.Response;

import org.junit.Test; // ❷

import java.util.Date;

import static org.junit.Assert.assertTrue;

/**
 * To work on unit tests, switch the Test Artifact in the Build Variants view.
 */
public class GitHubHelperTest { // ❸
    @Test
    public void testClient() throws Exception {

        String login = System.getenv("GITHUB_HELPER_USERNAME"); // ❹
        String password = System.getenv("GITHUB_HELPER_PASSWORD");
        String repoName = login + ".github.io";

        int randomNumber = (int)(Math.random() * 10000000);
        String randomString = String.valueOf( randomNumber );
        String randomAndDate = randomString + " " +
          (new Date()).toString() ; // ❺

        GitHubHelper ghh = new GitHubHelper( login, password ); // ❻
        ghh.SaveFile(repoName,
            "Some random title",
            "Some random body text",
            randomAndDate );
```

```
        Thread.sleep(3000); // ❼

        String url = "https://api.github.com/repos/" +  // ❽
        login + "/" + repoName + "/events";
        OkHttpClient ok = new OkHttpClient();
        Request request = new Request.Builder()
                .url( url )
                .build();
        Response response = ok.newCall( request ).execute();
        String body = response.body().string();

        assertTrue( "Body does not have: " + randomAndDate,   // ❾
            body.contains( randomAndDate ) );
    }

}
```

❶ First, we import the OkHttp library, a library for making HTTP calls. We will verify that our GitHub API calls made it all the way into GitHub by looking at the event log for our repository, a log accessible via HTTP.

❷ Next, we import JUnit, which provides us with an annotation @Test we can use to indicate to a test runner that certain methods are test functions (and should be executed as tests when in test mode).

❸ We create a class called GitHubHelperTest. In it, we define a sole test case test Client. We use the @Test annotation to indicate to JUnit that this is a test case.

❹ Now we specify our login information and the repository we want to test against. In order to keep the password out of our source code, we use an environment variable we can specify when we run the tests.

❺ Next, we build a random string. This unique string will be our commit message, a beacon that allows us to verify that our commit made it all the way through and was stored on GitHub, and to differentiate it from other commits made recently by other tests.

❻ Now, to the meat of the test: we instantiate our GitHub helper class with login credentials, then use the SaveFile function to save the file. The last parameter is our commit message, which we will verify later.

❼ There can be times when the GitHub API has registered the commit but the event is not yet displayed in results coming back from the API; sleeping for a few seconds fixes this.

❽ Next, we go through the steps to make an HTTP call with the OkHttp library. We load a URL that provides us with the events for a specified repository, events that will have the commit message when it is a push type event. This repository happens to be public so we don't require authentication against the GitHub API to see this data.

❾ Once we have the body of the HTTP call, we can scan it to verify the commit message is there.

The final steps deserve a bit more investigation. If we load the event URL from cURL, we see data like this:

```
$ curl https://api.github.com/repos/burningonup/burningonup.github.io/events
[
  {
    "id": "3244787408",
    "type": "PushEvent",
    ...
    "repo": {
      "id": 44361330,
      "name": "BurningOnUp/BurningOnUp.github.io",
      "url":
      "https://api.github.com/repos/BurningOnUp/BurningOnUp.github.io"
    },
    "payload": {
      ...
      "commits": [
        {
          "sha": "28f247973e73e3128737cab33e1000a7c281ff4b",
          "author": {
            "email": "unknown@example.com",
            "name": "Unknown"
          },
          "message": "207925 Thu Oct 15 23:06:09 PDT 2015",
          "distinct": true,
          "url":
      "https://api.github.com/repos/BurningOnUp/BurningOnUp.github.io/..."
        }
      ]
    }
  },
  ...
]
```

This is obviously JSON. We see the type is PushEvent for this event, and it has a commit message that matches our random string format. We could reconstitute this into a complex object structure, but scanning the JSON as a string works for our test.

Android UI Tests

Let's now write a UI test. Our test will start our app, find the username and password fields, enter in the proper username and password text, then click the login button, and finally verify that we have logged in by checking for the text "Logged into Git-Hub" in our UI.

Android uses the Espresso framework to support UI testing. We already installed Espresso with our Gradle configuration, so we can now write a test. Tests are written by deriving from a generic test base class (`ActivityInstrumentationTestCase2`). Any public function defined inside the test class is run as a test.

In Android Studio, from the "Build Variant" window, select "Android Instrumentation Test," which will then display a test directory called "androidTest." These are tests that will run on the emulator or actual device. Inside the directory, make a new file called *MainActivityTest.java*:

```
package com.example.ghru;

import android.support.test.InstrumentationRegistry; // ❶
import android.test.ActivityInstrumentationTestCase2;
import static android.support.test.espresso.Espresso.onView;
import static android.support.test.espresso.action.ViewActions.*;
import static android.support.test.espresso.assertion.ViewAssertions.matches;
import static android.support.test.espresso.matcher.ViewMatchers.*;

public class MainActivityTest  // ❷
    extends ActivityInstrumentationTestCase2<MainActivity> {

    public MainActivityTest() {
        super( MainActivity.class ); // ❸
    }

    public void testLogin() { // ❹
        injectInstrumentation( InstrumentationRegistry.
        getInstrumentation() ); // ❺
        MainActivity mainActivity = getActivity();
        String username = mainActivity // ❻
                .getString( R.string.github_helper_username );
        onView( withId( R.id.username ) ) // ❼
            .perform( typeText( username ) ); // ❽
        String password = mainActivity
                .getString( R.string.github_helper_password );
        onView( withId( R.id.password ) )
            .perform( typeText( password ) );
        onView( withId( R.id.login ) )
            .perform( click() );
        onView( withId( R.id.status ) ) // ❾
            .check( matches( withText( "Logged into GitHub" ) ) );
```

```
    }
}
```

❶ We import the instrumentation registry (for instrumenting the tests of our app), the base class, and matchers that will be used to make assertions in our tests.

❷ We create a test class that derives from the `ActivityInstrumentationTestCase2` generic.

❸ The constructor of an Espresso test implementation needs to call the parent constructor with the class of the activity for test, in this case `MainActivity`.

❹ Our test verifies that we can log in to GitHub, so we name it accordingly.

❺ We then load the instrumentation registry, and also call `getActivity`, which actually instantiates and starts the activity. In many Espresso tests these two steps will occur in a function annotated as a `@Before` function if they are used across multiple tests (in which case they will be run before each test). Here to simplify our function count we can call them inside the single test function.

❻ It is never a good idea to store credentials inside of a code repository, so we retrieve the username and password from a resource XML file using the `get` `String` function available using the activity. We will show what the contents of this secret file could look like presently.

❼ Once we have the username, we can enter it in the text field in our UI. With the `onView` function we can interact with a view (for example: a button or text field). `withId` finds the view using the resource identifier inside the XML layout files. Once we have the view, we can then perform an action (using the `perform` function) like typing in text. This chain of calls enters the GitHub username into the first text field.

❽ We then complete our interaction with the UI, entering in the password and then clicking the login button.

❾ If all is successful, we should see the text "Logged into GitHub." Under the hood, this test will verify that we are logged in to GitHub and display the successful result.

To provide a username and password to our test and to keep these credentials out of our source code, create a file called *secrets.xml* inside our *strings* directory inside the resource folder. This file should look like this:

```
<?xml version="1.0" encoding="utf-8"?>
<resources>
    <string name="github_helper_login">MyUsername</string>
    <string name="github_helper_password">MyPwd123</string>
</resources>
```

Make sure this is not checked into your source code by adding an exception to *.gitignore* (the command echo "secrets.xml" >> .gitgnore is a quick way to add this to your *.gitignore* file).

Our tests will not even compile yet because we have not yet written the other parts of the application. As such, we will skip the setup required to run our tests within Android Studio for now.

Let's now build the application itself to pass these tests.

Application Implementation

Now we can start writing some Java code for our application. Let's make it so our MainActivity class will inflate the layouts we defined earlier:

```java
package com.example.ghru;

import android.app.Activity;
import android.os.Bundle;
import android.widget.Button;
import android.widget.LinearLayout;
import android.widget.EditText;
import android.widget.TextView;
import android.view.View;

public class MainActivity extends Activity
{
    /** Called when the activity is first created. */
    @Override
    public void onCreate(Bundle savedInstanceState)
    {
        super.onCreate(savedInstanceState);
        setContentView( R.layout.main);

        Button login = (Button)findViewById( R.id.login );
        login.setOnClickListener(new View.OnClickListener() { // ❶
            public void onClick(View v) {
                login(); // ❷
            }
        });
    }

    private void login() {

        setContentView(R.layout.logged_in); // ❸
```

```
    Button submit = (Button)findViewById( R.id.submit );
    submit.setOnClickListener(new View.OnClickListener() {
        public void onClick(View v) { // ❹
            doPost(); (4)
        }
    });
}

private void doPost() {
    TextView tv = (TextView)findViewById( R.id.post_status ); // ❺
    tv.setText( "Successful jekyll post" );
}

}
```

This code mocks out the functionality we will be building and shows us exactly what the UI will look like once that code is completed.

❶ We register a click handler for our login button.

❷ When the login button is clicked, we call the login() function that triggers a login flow.

❸ Once we have logged in, we inflate the logged-in layout, suitable for making a blog post.

❹ We then set up another click handler for the submit button; when clicked, we call the doPost() function.

❺ Our doPost() function updates the status message at the bottom of our application.

Even though our code is not functionally complete, this application will compile. This is a good time to play with this application and verify that the UI looks appropriate. Our login form looks like Figure 7-4.

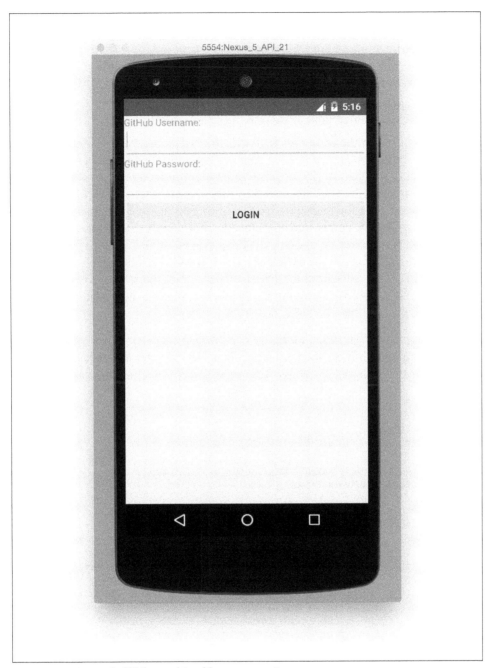

Figure 7-4. A simple UI for making blog post entries

Code to Log In to GitHub

Now we can wire in the GitHub API. Let's first work on the login() function. Poking into the EGit libary reference (*http://bit.ly/1SQ93Qf*), we can write GitHub login code, which is as simple as the following:

```
GitHubClient client = new GitHubClient();
client.setCredentials("us3r", "passw0rd");
```

The context in which the code runs makes as much of a difference as the code. The Android OS disallows any code from making network connections unless it runs inside a background thread. If you are not a Java developer already, and the thought of using threads with Java sounds daunting, dispell your worries. The Android SDK provides a great class for managing background tasks called AsyncTask. This class provides several entry points into the lifecycle of a thread that is managed by the Android OS. We implement a class and then override two functions provided by AsyncTask: the first function is doInBackground(), which handles operations off the main thread (our background thread code), and the second function is onPostExecute(), which runs on the UI thread and allows us to update the UI with the results of the code that ran inside doInBackground().

Before we implement the login, we need to update our onCreate function of the Main Activity. Our login button handles logging in, so let's register a click handler on the login button that will call the login task we will define inside our class based off AsyncTask:

```
...
    @Override
    public void onCreate(Bundle savedInstanceState)
    {
        super.onCreate(savedInstanceState);
        setContentView(R.layout.main);

        Button login = (Button)findViewById( R.id.login );
        login.setOnClickListener(new View.OnClickListener() {
                public void onClick(View v) {
                    EditText utv = (EditText)findViewById( R.id.username );
                    EditText ptv = (EditText)findViewById( R.id.password );
                    username = (String)utv.getText().toString();
                    password = (String)ptv.getText().toString(); // ❶
                    TextView status =
                      (TextView)findViewById( R.id.login_status );
                    status.setText( "Logging in, please wait..." ); // ❷
                    new LoginTask().execute( username, password );  // ❸
                }
            });
    }
...
```

❶ We retrieve the username and password from our UI elements.

❷ Our UI should notify the user that a login is occurring in a background task, so we grab the status text element and update the text in it.

❸ We then start the background thread process to do our login. This syntax creates a new thread for us with the username and password as parameters. Android will manage the lifecycle of this thread for us, including starting the new thread separate from the main UI thread.

Now we can implement `LoginTask`:

```
...
    class LoginTask extends AsyncTask<String, Void, Boolean> {   // ❶
        @Override
            protected Boolean doInBackground(String... credentials) { // ❷
            boolean rv = false;
            UserService us = new UserService();
            us.getClient().setCredentials( credentials[0], credentials[1] );
            try {
                User user = us.getUser( credentials[0] );   // ❸
                rv = null != user;
            }
            catch( IOException ioe ) {}
            return rv;
        }

        @Override
            protected void onPostExecute(Boolean result) {
            if( result ) {
                loggedIn();  // ❹
            }
            else { // ❺
                TextView status = (TextView)findViewById( R.id.login_status );
                status.setText( "Invalid login, please check credentials" );
            }
        }
    }
...
```

❶ Here we define our class derived from `AsyncTask`. You see three types in the generics signature: `String`, `Void`, and `Boolean`. These are the parameters to our entry point, an intermediate callback and the final callback, which returns control to the calling thread. The first type allows us to parameterize our instantiated task; we need to provide a username and password to the background task, and the first type in the signature allows us to pass an array of Strings. You can see in the actual function definition that the ellipsis notation provides a way to parameterize a function with a variable number of arguments (called varargs). Inside our defined function we expect we will send two Strings in, and we make sure to do that in our call.

❷ Once inside the doInBackground() function, we instantiate a UserService class, a wrapper around the GitHub API, which interacts with the user service API call. In order to access this information, we have to retrieve the client for this service call and provide the client with the username and password credentials. This is the syntax to do that.

❸ We wrap the call to getUser() in a try block as the function signature can throw an error (if the network were down, for example). We don't really need to retrieve information about the user using the User object, but this call verifies that our username and password are correct, and we store this result in our return value. GitHub will not use the credentials you set until you make an API call, so we need to use our credentials to access something in order to verify that those credentials work.

❹ Let's call our function loggedIn() instead of login() to more accurately reflect the fact that when we call this, we are already logged in to GitHub.

❺ If our login was a failure, either because of network failure, or because our credentials were incorrect, we indicate this in the status message. A user can retry if they wish.

loggedIn updates the UI once logging in has completed and then initiates the post on GitHub:

```
...
    private void loggedIn() {

        setContentView(R.layout.logged_in);  // ❶

        Button submit = (Button)findViewById( R.id.submit );
        submit.setOnClickListener(new View.OnClickListener() { // ❷
            public void onClick(View v) {

                TextView status = (TextView) findViewById(R.id.login_status);
                status.setText("Logging in, please wait...");

                EditText post = (EditText) findViewById(R.id.post); // ❸
                String postContents = post.getText().toString();

                EditText repo = (EditText) findViewById(R.id.repository);
                String repoName = repo.getText().toString();

                EditText title = (EditText) findViewById(R.id.title);
                String titleText = title.getText().toString();
```

```
                    doPost(repoName, titleText, postContents); // ❹
                }
            });
        }
    ...
```

❶ Inflate the logged-in layout to reflect the fact we are now logged in.

❷ Then, install a click handler on the submit button so that when we submit our post information, we can start the process to create the post on GitHub.

❸ We need to gather up three details the user provides: the post body, the post title, and the repository name.

❹ Using these three pieces of data, we can then call into doPost and initiate the asynchronous task.

Building out doPost() should be more familiar now that we have experience with AsyncTask. doPost() makes the commit inside of GitHub, and it performs the network activity it needs to run on a background thread:

```
    ...
    private void doPost( String repoName, String title, String post ) {
        new PostTask().execute( username, password, repoName, title, post );
    }

    class PostTask extends AsyncTask<String, Void, Boolean> {

        @Override
        protected Boolean doInBackground(String... information) { // ❶
            String login = information[0];
            String password = information[1];
            String repoName = information[2];
            String titleText = information[3];
            String postContents = information[4];

            Boolean rv = false; // ❷
            GitHubHelper ghh = new GitHubHelper(login, password); // ❸
            try {
                rv = ghh.SaveFile(repoName, titleText,
                postContents, "GhRu Update"); // ❹
            } catch (IOException ioe) { // ❺
                Log.d(ioe.getStackTrace().toString(), "GhRu");
            }
            return rv;
        }

        @Override
        protected void onPostExecute(Boolean result) {
            TextView status = (TextView) findViewById(R.id.status);
```

```
            if (result) { // ❻
                status.setText("Successful jekyll post");

                EditText post = (EditText) findViewById(R.id.post);
                post.setText("");

                EditText repo = (EditText) findViewById(R.id.repository);
                repo.setText("");

                EditText title = (EditText) findViewById(R.id.title);
                title.setText("");
            } else {
                status.setText("Post failed.");
            }
        }
    }
    ...
```

❶ First, we retrieve the parameters we need to send off to the GitHub API. Notice that we don't attempt to retrieve these from the UI. Background threads don't have access to the Android UI functions.

❷ This function returns a true or false value indicating success or failure (using the variable rv for "return value"). We assume that it fails unless everything we need to do inside our function works exactly as expected, so set the expectation to false to start. The value of our return statement is passed to the next stage in the lifecycle of the thread, a function called onPostExecute (an optional stage in the thread lifecycle we will use to report status of the operation back to the user).

❸ Now, we instantiate the GitHubHelper class. This instantiation and usage should look very familiar as it is the same thing we did inside our unit test.

❹ Our helper class returns success or failure. If we have reached this point, this is our final return value.

❺ We will wrap the call to SaveFile inside a try/catch block to make sure we handle errors; these will most likely be network errors.

❻ onPostExecute() is the function we (optionally) return to once our background task has completed. It receives the return value from our previous function. If we have a true value returned from doInBackground(), then our save file succeeded and we can update the UI of our application.

We need to import the support classes. The JARs and classes for EGit have already been added to our project automatically using Gradle. Make sure you add these import statements to the top of the file, under the other imports:

```
...
import android.view.View;
import android.os.AsyncTask;
import org.eclipse.egit.github.core.service.UserService;
import org.eclipse.egit.github.core.User;
import java.io.IOException;
...
```

Now we are ready to write the code to write data into GitHub.

Code to Talk to GitHub

Our last step is to write the code that handles putting content into GitHub. This is not a simple function, because the GitHub API requires you build out the structure used internally by Git. A great reference for learning more about this structure is the free and open-source book called *Pro Git* (*https://progit.org/*) and specifically the last chapter called Git Internals (*http://git-scm.com/book/en/Git-Internals*).

In a nutshell, the GitHub API expects you to create a Git "tree" and then place a "blob" object into that tree. You then wrap the tree in a "commit" object and then create that commit on GitHub using a data service wrapper. In addition, writing a tree into GitHub requires knowing the base SHA identifier, so you'll see code that retrieves the last SHA in the tree associated with our current branch. This code will work regardless of whether we are pushing code into the master branch, or into the gh-pages branch, so this utility class works with real Jekyll blogs.

We'll write a helper class called GitHubHelper and add a single function that writes a file to our repository.

The GitHub API requires that files stored in repositories be either Base64 encoded or UTF-8. The Apache Foundation provides a suite of tools published to Maven (the same software repository where we grabbed the EGit libraries), which can do this encoding for us, and which were already installed in our Gradle file previously (the "commons-codec" declaration).

We will start by defining a series of high-level functions inside SaveFile to get through building a commit inside of GitHub. Each function itself contains some complexity so let's look first at the overview of what it takes to put data into GitHub using the Git Data API:

```
package com.example;

import android.util.Log;

import org.eclipse.egit.github.core.*;
import org.eclipse.egit.github.core.client.GitHubClient;
import org.eclipse.egit.github.core.service.CommitService;
import org.eclipse.egit.github.core.service.DataService;
import org.eclipse.egit.github.core.service.RepositoryService;
```

```
import org.eclipse.egit.github.core.service.UserService;
import org.apache.commons.codec.binary.Base64;

import java.text.SimpleDateFormat;
import java.util.Date;
import java.io.IOException;
import java.util.*;

class GitHubHelper {

    String login;
    String password;

    GitHubHelper( String _login, String _password ) {
        login = _login;
        password = _password;
    }

    public boolean SaveFile( String _repoName,
                             String _title,
                             String _post,
                             String _commitMessage ) throws IOException {
        post = _post;
        repoName = _repoName;
        title = _title;
        commitMessage = _commitMessage;

        boolean rv = false;

        generateContent();
        createServices();
        retrieveBaseSha();

        if( null != baseCommitSha && "" != baseCommitSha ) {
            createBlob();
            generateTree();
            createCommitUser();
            createCommit();
            createResource();
            updateMasterResource();
            rv = true;
        }

        return rv;
    }

    ...
```

The SaveFile function goes through each step of writing data into a repository using the GitHub API. We will walk through each of these functions. As you can see, the SaveFile function has the same signature as the function we call inside our unit test.

Let's implement each of the functions specified in the `GitHubHelper` class.

Writing the Blog Content

First, we implement `generateContent()`. The following code snippet shows the functions defined to generate the content we will place into our remote Git repository stored on GitHub:

```
...
    String commitMessage; // ❶
    String postContentsWithYfm;
    String contentsBase64;
    String filename;
    String post;
    String title;
    String repoName;

    private void generateContent() { // ❷
        postContentsWithYfm =  // ❸
        "---\n" +
        "layout: post\n" +
        "published: true\n" +
        "title: '" + title + "'\n---\n\n" +
        post;
        contentsBase64 =  // ❹
        new String( Base64.encodeBase64( postContentsWithYfm.getBytes() ) );
        filename = getFilename();
    }

    private String getFilename() {
        String titleSub = title.substring( 0,  // ❺
                        post.length() > 30 ?
                        30 :
                        title.length() );
        String jekyllfied = titleSub.toLowerCase() // ❻
        .replaceAll( "\\W+", "-")
        .replaceAll( "\\W+$", "" );
        SimpleDateFormat sdf = new SimpleDateFormat( "yyyy-MM-dd-" ); // ❼
        String prefix = sdf.format( new Date() );
        return "_posts/" + prefix + jekyllfied + ".md"; // ❽
    }

    String blobSha;
    Blob blob;
...
```

You will notice many similarities between this Java code and the Ruby code we used in Chapter 6 when generating filenames and escaping whitespace.

❶ First, we set up several instance variables we will use when storing the data into GitHub: the commit message, the full post including the YAML Front Matter

(YFM), the post contents encoded as Base64, the filename, and then the three parameters we saved from the call to SaveFile(): the post itself, the title, and the repository name.

❷ The generateContent function creates the necessary components for our new post: the full content Base64 encoded, and the filename we will use to store the content.

❸ Here we create the YAML Front Matter (see Chapter 6 for more details on YFM). This YAML specifies the "post" layout and sets publishing to "true." We need to terminate the YAML with two newlines.

❹ Base64 encodes the contents of the blog post itself using a utility class found inside the Apache Commons library. Contents inside a Git repository are stored either as UTF-8 content or Base64; we could have used UTF-8 since this is text content but Base64 works losslessly, and you can always safely use Base64 without concerning yourself about the content.

❺ Next, inside getFilename(), create the title by using the first 30 characters of the post.

❻ Convert the title to lowercase, and replace the whitespace with hyphens to get the Jekyll post title format.

❼ Jekyll expects the date to be formatted as yyyy-MM-dd, so use the java SimpleDate Format class to help create a string of that format.

❽ Finally, create the filename from all these pieces, prepending _posts to the filename, where Jekyll expects posts to reside.

Now we will set up the services necessary to store a commit inside GitHub.

GitHub Services

Next, we implement createServices(). There are several services (wrappers around Git protocols) we need to instantiate. We don't use them all immediately, but we will need them at various steps during the file save process. The createServices call manages these for us:

```
    ...
    RepositoryService repositoryService;
    CommitService commitService;
    DataService dataService;

    private void createServices() throws IOException {
        GitHubClient ghc = new GitHubClient();
```

```
        ghc.setCredentials( login, password );
        repositoryService = new RepositoryService( ghc );
        commitService = new CommitService( ghc );
        dataService = new DataService( ghc );
    }
```

...

As a side note, writing things this way would allow us to specify an enterprise end-point instead of GitHub.com. Refer to the Appendix A for specific syntax on how to do this.

The Base SHA from the Repository and Branch

Now we implement retrieveBaseSha(). A Git repository is a directed acyclic graph (DAG) and as such, (almost) every node in the graph points to another commit (or potentially two if it is a merge commit). When we append content to our graph, we need to determine the prior node in that graph and attach the new node. retrieveBaseSha does this: it finds the SHA hash for our last commit, a SHA hash that is functionally an address inside our tree. To determine this address, our application needs to have a reference to the repository, and we use the repository service we instantiated earlier to get this reference. Once we have the repository, we need to look inside the correct branch: getBranch does this for us:

...

```
    private void createServices() throws IOException {
        GitHubClient ghc = new GitHubClient();
        ghc.setCredentials( login, password );
        repositoryService = new RepositoryService( ghc );
        commitService = new CommitService( ghc );
        dataService = new DataService( ghc );
    }

    Repository repository;
    RepositoryBranch theBranch;
    String baseCommitSha;
    private void retrieveBaseSha() throws IOException {
        // get some sha's from current state in git
        repository = repositoryService.getRepository(login, repoName);
        theBranch = getBranch();
        baseCommitSha = theBranch.getCommit().getSha();
    }

    public RepositoryBranch getBranch() throws IOException {
        List<RepositoryBranch> branches =
          repositoryService.getBranches(repository);
        RepositoryBranch master = null;
        // Iterate over the branches and find gh-pages or master
        for( RepositoryBranch i : branches ) {
```

```
            String theName = i.getName().toString();
            if( theName.equalsIgnoreCase("gh-pages") ) {
                theBranch = i;
            }
            else if( theName.equalsIgnoreCase("master") ) {
                master = i;
            }
        }
        if( null == theBranch ) {
            theBranch = master;
        }
        return theBranch;
    }

    . . .
```

This SHA commit is very important. Without it, we cannot create a new commit that links into our existing commit graph. In our starting point function `SaveFile()` we discontinue our commit steps if the SHA hash is not retrieved properly.

Creating the Blob

Contents inside a Git repository are stored as blobs. `createBlob` manages storing our content as a blob object, and then uses the `dataService` to store this blob into a repository. Until we have called `dataService.createBlob`, we have not actually placed the object inside GitHub. Also, remember that blobs are not linked into our DAG by themselves; they need to be associated with our DAG vis-a-vis a tree and commit object, which we do next:

```
    . . .
    String blobSha;
    Blob blob;
    private void createBlob() throws IOException {
        blob = new Blob();
        blob.setContent(contentsBase64);
        blob.setEncoding(Blob.ENCODING_BASE64);
        blobSha = dataService.createBlob(repository, blob);
    }

    . . .
```

Generating a Tree

Next, we generate a tree by implementing `generateTree()`. A tree wraps a blob object and provides basically a path to our object: if you were designing an operating system, the tree would be the filename path and the blob is an inode. Our data service manager uses a repository name and a base SHA address, one that we retrieved earlier, to validate that this is a valid starting point inside our repository. Once we have a tree, we fill out the necessary tree attributes, like tree type (blob) and tree mode (blob), and set the SHA from the previously created blob object along with the size. Then we store the tree into our GitHub account using the data service object:

```
...
    Tree baseTree;
    private void generateTree() throws IOException {
        baseTree = dataService.getTree(repository, baseCommitSha);
        TreeEntry treeEntry = new TreeEntry();
        treeEntry.setPath( filename );
        treeEntry.setMode( TreeEntry.MODE_BLOB );
        treeEntry.setType( TreeEntry.TYPE_BLOB );
        treeEntry.setSha(blobSha);
        treeEntry.setSize(blob.getContent().length());
        Collection<TreeEntry> entries = new ArrayList<TreeEntry>();
        entries.add(treeEntry);
        newTree = dataService.createTree( repository, entries,
          baseTree.getSha() );
    }

...
```

Creating the Commit

We are getting close to actually finalizing the creation of content: next, implement createCommit(). We have created a blob that stores the actual content, and created a tree that stores the path to the content (more or less), but since Git is a version control system, we also need to store information about who wrote this object and why. A commit object stores this information. The process should look familiar coming from the previous steps: we create the commit and then add relevant metadata, in this case the commit message. We also need to provide the commit user with the commit. We then use the data service to create the commit inside our repository in GitHub at the correct SHA address:

```
...
    CommitUser commitUser;
    private void createCommitUser() throws IOException {
        UserService us = new UserService(); // ❶
        us.getClient().setCredentials( login, password );
        commitUser = new CommitUser(); // ❷
        User user = us.getUser(); // ❸
        commitUser.setDate(new Date());
        String name = user.getName();
        if( null == name || name.isEmpty() ) { // ❹
            name = "Unknown";
        }

        commitUser.setName( name ); // ❺
        String email = user.getEmail();
        if( null == email || email.isEmpty() ) {
            email = "unknown@example.com";
```

```
        }
        commitUser.setEmail( email );
    }

    Commit newCommit;
    private void createCommit() throws IOException {
        // create commit
        Commit commit = new Commit(); // ❻
        commit.setMessage( commitMessage );
        commit.setAuthor( commitUser); // ❼
        commit.setCommitter( commitUser );
        commit.setTree( newTree );
        List<Commit> listOfCommits = new ArrayList<Commit>(); // ❽
        Commit parentCommit = new Commit();
        parentCommit.setSha(baseCommitSha);
        listOfCommits.add(parentCommit);
        commit.setParents(listOfCommits);
        newCommit = dataService.createCommit(repository, commit); // ❾
    }
    ...
```

❶ Create a user service object. We will use this to get back user data for the logged-in user from GitHub.

❷ We then create a commit user. This will be used to annotate the commit object (twice in fact, as we will use it for both the author and committer).

❸ Retrieve the user from the service, loading it from GitHub.

❹ Now, attempt to get the name for the logged-in user. If the name does not exist (the user has not set a name in their GitHub profile) set the name to unknown. Then, store the name in the commit user object.

❺ Do the same process to establish the email for the commit user.

❻ Now, return to the `createCommit` function and create a commit object.

❼ We need to use an author and committer, so pass in the commit user we created in the `createCommitUser` function.

❽ Next, generate a list of commits. We will only use one, but you might recall commits can have multiple parents (a merge, for example) and we need to specify the parent or parents. We create the list, create a parent, and set the base SHA we determined earlier, and then indicate in our new commit that it is the parent.

❾ Finally, we create the commit using our data service object.

Updating the Master Resource

Our final step is to take the new commit SHA and update our branch reference to point to it:

```
...
    TypedResource commitResource;
    private void createResource() {
        commitResource = new TypedResource(); // ❶
        commitResource.setSha(newCommit.getSha());
        commitResource.setType(TypedResource.TYPE_COMMIT);
        commitResource.setUrl(newCommit.getUrl());
    }

    private void updateMasterResource() throws IOException {
        Reference reference =
                dataService.getReference(repository,
                        "heads/" + theBranch.getName() ); // ❷
        reference.setObject(commitResource);
        dataService.editReference(repository, reference, true) ; // ❸
    }
...
```

❶ First, we create the new commit resource. We then associate the new commit SHA, indicate it is a resource of commit type, and then link it to our commit using its URL.

❷ We use the data service object to get the current branch reference from GitHub. Branch references are retrieved by appending "heads" to the branch (we determined the branch in a previous step).

❸ Finally, we update the branch reference to our new commit resource.

This is the complete code to add data to GitHub using the Git Data API. Good work!

Passing All Our Tests

Our code is complete. Let's make sure our tests run successfully.

We need to set up our test configuration to run within Android Studio. Select the "Build Variants" vertical tab on the left, and in Test Artifact select Unit Tests. Then, open the Run menu, and select "Edit configurations". Click the plus symbol, and choose JUnit. You will be presented with space to create a unit test run configuration. First, click "Use classpath of module" and select "app". Make sure the Test Kind is set to class, and then click the selector to the right of the class field. It should display your test class "GitHubHelperTest.java". We will need to store the username and password as environment variables, so click to add these. Your final configuration should look like Figure 7-5.

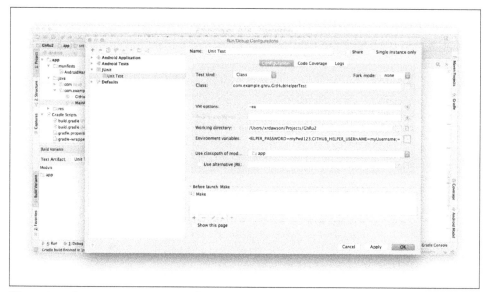

Figure 7-5. Creating a unit test configuration

Now, create the UI tests configuration: switch to "Android Instrumentation Tests" in the "Test Artifact" of the "Build Variants" tab. Then, click the "Run" menu, and again go to "Edit configurations". Click the plus symbol, and this time choose "Android Tests." Choose "app" as the module, and then select "android.support.test.runner.AndroidJUnitRunner" as the specific instrumentation runner. You can choose whichever target device you prefer, an emulator, or a physical device if you have one. Give the configuration a name like "Android Test."

To run your tests, switch to the appropriate test artifact and then from the "Run" menu, select "Debug" and choose the proper test configuration. You can set breakpoints and step through code in your test or implementation from within Android Studio.

I personally find it annoying to switch between build variants when I want to run my tests, so if you prefer, you can use the command line instead (and ignore the need to change build variants):

```
$ GITHUB_HELPER_USERNAME=MyUsername \
GITHUB_HELPER_PASSWORD=MyPwd123 \
./gradlew testDebugUnitTest
...
:app:mockableAndroidJar UP-TO-DATE
:app:assembleDebugUnitTest UP-TO-DATE
:app:testDebugUnitTest UP-TO-DATE

BUILD SUCCESSFUL
$ ./gradlew connectedAndroidTest
```

```
...
:app:compileDebugAndroidTestNdk UP-TO-DATE
:app:compileDebugAndroidTestSources
:app:preDexDebugAndroidTest
:app:dexDebugAndroidTest
:app:packageDebugAndroidTest
:app:assembleDebugAndroidTest
:app:connectedDebugAndroidTest

BUILD SUCCESSFUL
```

You will see similar results with the Android Studio test runner windows. Our tests pass and our application is complete.

 If you want to see a more complicated version of the GitHub API on Android, take a look at Teddy Hyde (*https://github.com/xrd/ TeddyHyde.git*) (also available on the Google Play Store). Teddy Hyde uses OAuth to log in to GitHub, and has a much richer set of features for editing Jekyll blogs.

Summary

This application will allow you to write into a real Jekyll blog, adding posts, upon which GitHub will regenerate your site. This little application manages quite a few things: formatting the filename correctly, encoding the data for submission to Git-Hub, and we have a unit test and UI test that help to verify the functionality.

In the next chapter we will use CoffeeScript to create our own chat robot that requests pull request reviews from chat room members using the Activity API.

CHAPTER 8

CoffeeScript, Hubot, and the Activity API

Though the phrase has now been removed from its marketing materials, GitHub used to call itself a tool for "social coding." This idea is still central to the services GitHub provides—intimate access to the social layer inside of GitHub through the Activity API.

In this chapter we'll investigate the Activity API by extending a chat robot. You might find it odd that a robot, generally considered an antisocial invention despite all best attempts, would play nicely with a social API, but this is a social robot. GitHubbers use an extensible chat robot called Hubot to record and automate their tasks, and to have fun on the Internet. If there were any robot suited for interacting with the Git-Hub Activity API, it's Hubot, described on the site *https://hubot.github.com/* as "a customizable, kegerator-powered life embetterment robot."

The Activity API

The Activity API includes:

- Notifications (comments issued to users through various events)
- Stargazing tools (Facebook has "likes" while GitHub has "stars" to indicate approval or interest)
- Watching (a way to track GitHub data)
- Events (a higher-level activity stream useful for following actions of users)

The Activity API section also includes *feeds*. While feeds are grouped within the Activity API, they are not programmatic in the same way an API is, and we won't cover them in depth here. Feeds are actually Atom feeds and not interactive beyond that. Atom feeds are similar to RSS feeds: a static feed you can subscribe to with an Atom client.

Planning for PR Satisfaction Guaranteed

We are going to build an extension to Hubot. When we are done, Hubot will be transformed into a robot that…

- listens for pull request events from GitHub by subscribing to notifications using the GitHub Activity API;

- invites people in the chat room to comment on those pull requests;

- guarantees that communication between it and GitHub is securely delivered (with an unfortunate bug as caveat);

- retrieves vital information from an external service (the Slack API);

- has functionality fully described by automated tests;

- allows easy simulation of inputs and outputs that map to the inputs and outputs it gets from APIs and services; and

- runs with ease on a major PaaS (Heroku).

Hubot provides the skeleton for our chat robot. We'll add the preceding functionality to Hubot and see how easy it is to combine these features into a coherent whole that solves a real problem.

Considerations and Limitations

If you want stability with your Hubot, you need to host it on a server. Hubot is written in NodeJS and requires a hosting service that supports NodeJS. Our Hubot needs to sit on a public IP address (not inside the firewall) because we receive notifications from GitHub. It is not strictly required that you host Hubot on a public server; if your Hubot does not need to receive requests from the outside world, you can host on a private internal server as well.

The simplest and cheapest hosting service for Hubot is Heroku. Once we generate our Hubot, we can simply do a git-push into Heroku to publish our chat robot for free. We'll show these steps later in the chapter.

Hubot works with many chat endpoints. Your Hubot can connect to almost any popular chat service or protocol: IRC, XMPP, and many commercial services like Gchat, Basecamp, and even Twitter. Slack is a relatively new entrant into the world of chat services, but despite its youth, the Slack API is solid and connecting third-party clients to the Slack service is simple and straightforward. We'll use Slack as our chat endpoint.

Now let's create our Hubot and configure it to use Slack.

Creating a Vanilla Hubot

To build a Hubot you will need a working NodeJS installation, as specified in Appendix B. The following commands create a directory with a barebones Hubot:

```
$ npm install -g generator-hubot ❶
$ mkdir slacker-hubot ❷
$ cd slacker-hubot/
$ yo hubot ❸
$ npm install hubot-slack --save ❹
```

You may not be familiar with these commands, so let's go over the important ones.

❶ npm is the tool that installs packages for NodeJS (documented in Appendix B). The npm install -g generator-hubot command installs a command-line tool called yeoman and a plug-in for yeoman that scaffolds Hubot.

❷ You should create a new directory and enter it so that when you create your Hubot you can store it entirely in its own space.

❸ You run the generator using the yo hubot command. This builds out the set of files for a minimal Hubot.

❹ We then install the slack adapter and save the package to the *package.json* file.

Now that we have a simple Hubot created we need to create the Slack site where our Hubot will live.

Creating a Slack Account

Going to *https://slack.com/* starts the process of creating your own Slack site. You'll need to step through creating an account. Slack sites are segmented by organization, and you'll want to establish a URL prefix for your Slack site. Typically this is the name of your organization.

Naming the channel

Once you have your slack site created, you need to create a channel as in Figure 8-1.

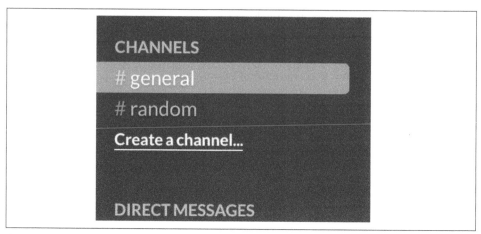

Figure 8-1. Creating a channel from the Slack sidebar

You can name the channel anything you want, but it is often a good mnemonic to use a name that suggests this is a channel where more serious work gets done. You could use a name like "PR Discussion" to indicate this is the channel where PRs are discussed. To keep things simple, we will use the name "#general." Once you click the link to create a channel, you'll see a popup asking for the name and an optional description. After you have created the channel, you will see a link to "Add a service integration" as shown in Figure 8-2.

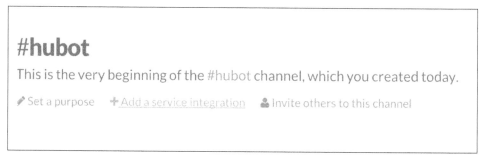

Figure 8-2. Adding service integrations to Slack

Slack supports many different service integrations, and one of them is Hubot as shown in Figure 8-3.

Figure 8-3. Service integration options for Slack

Choosing Hubot takes you to a settings screen for your Hubot integration.

Slack automatically generates an authentication token for you. This token is used to verify the connection from your Hubot. This token can be revoked, and in fact the token from Figure 8-4 has been revoked and can no longer be used to authenticate into Slack. If you ever accidentally publicize this token, you can easily revoke and reassign a token to your Hubot on this screen.

You will also need to specify a name. Use "probot" and if you'd like, change the avatar associated with the Hubot (these options are shown in Figure 8-4).

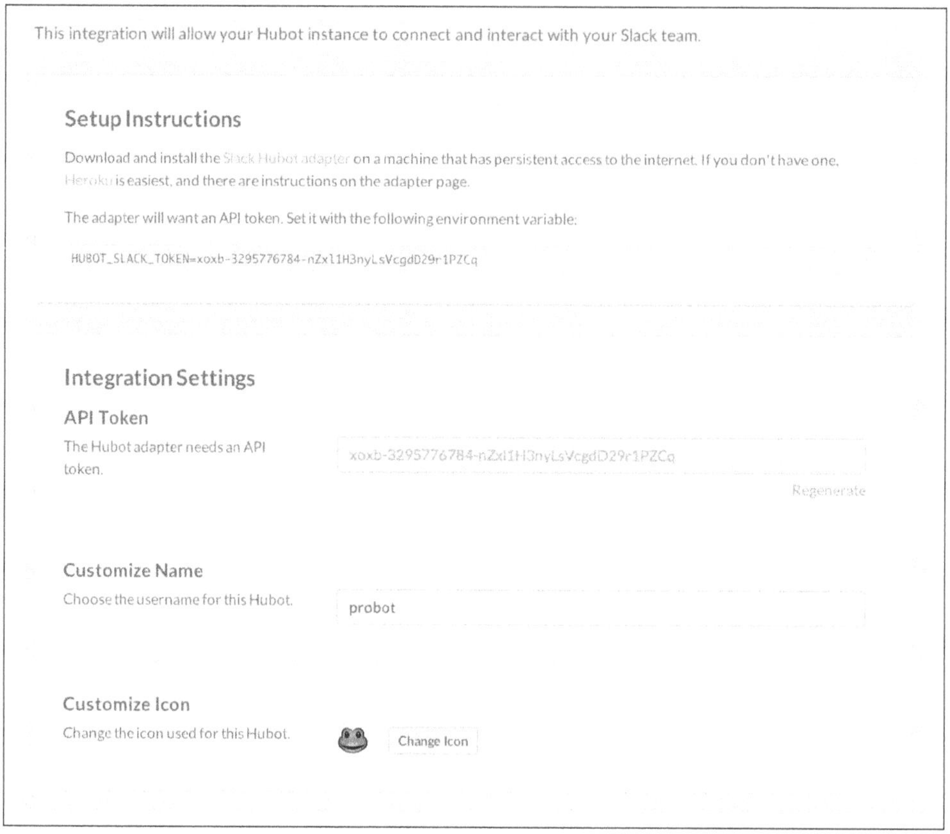

This integration will allow your Hubot instance to connect and interact with your Slack team.

Setup Instructions

Download and install the Slack Hubot adapter on a machine that has persistent access to the internet. If you don't have one, Heroku is easiest, and there are instructions on the adapter page.

The adapter will want an API token. Set it with the following environment variable:

```
HUBOT_SLACK_TOKEN=xoxb-3295776784-nZxl1H3nyLsVcgdD29r1PZCq
```

Integration Settings

API Token

The Hubot adapter needs an API token.

```
xoxb-3295776784-nZxl1H3nyLsVcgdD29r1PZCq
```

Regenerate

Customize Name

Choose the username for this Hubot.

```
probot
```

Customize Icon

Change the icon used for this Hubot. Change Icon

Figure 8-4. Hubot configuration page for Slack

Make sure you save your integration before continuing.

Running Hubot Locally

Eventually you will want to run your Hubot on a server, but Hubot can run from a laptop behind a firewall as well. At the beginning of development, while testing and developing your bot and the changes are fast and furious, you probably want to run Hubot locally. In fact, Hubot behind a firewall is almost identical in its feature set with one major exception: anything behind the firewall is inaccessible, obviously, to external services. We are eventually going to be configuring GitHub to send events to us when a pull request is created, and Hubot behind the firewall cannot receive those events. But, for almost all other functionality, running Hubot locally speeds up development cadence.

To run your bot locally, make sure you specify the variables on the command line:

```
$ HUBOT_SLACK_TOKEN=xoxb-3295776784-nZxl1H3nyLsVcgdD29r1PZCq \
./bin/hubot -a slack
```

This command runs the Hubot script with the Slack adapter. The Slack adapter knows how to interact with the Slack.com service. It requires an authentication token, and this is provided via the environment variable at the beginning of the line.

A first conversation

Your bot should be set up and waiting in the #general room inside your Slack site. Go to the #general room. Then, you can test that Hubot is properly connectd by typing in the name of your Hubot and then a command like the rules. For example, if our Hubot is named probot, then we would type probot the rules, which then displays the following conversation as shown in Figure 8-5.

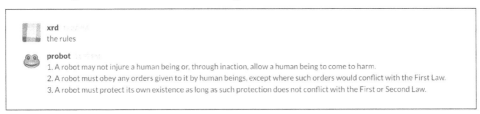

Figure 8-5. Hubot's built-in repartee

We see that our Hubot printed out the rules it abides by (published originally by Isaac Asimov in his "Runaround" short story in 1942).

Exploring the Hubot vocabulary

Hubot out-of-the-box supports many commands. To get a list, type help to see a list like that shown in Figure 8-6.

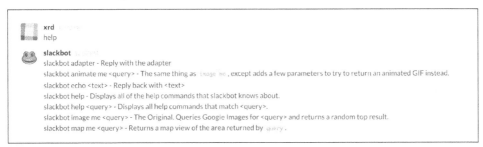

Figure 8-6. Listing the Hubot vocabulary

The pug me command is a favorite. Many people new to Hubot quickly get sucked into spending hours looking at cute pictures of pugs. Beware!

Installation on Heroku

Now that we've successfully started our Hubot locally, we can move it to Heroku and keep it running even when our laptop is turned off.

Setting Up Heroku

Heroku requires registration before using it. Heroku offers free plans and everything we'll do here can be done using one of them. Once you have created an account, install the Heroku toolbelt found here: *https://toolbelt.heroku.com/*. The toolbelt provides a set of tools useful for managing Heroku applications. You will need to have Ruby set up as explained in Chapter 1.

If your chatbot is working per the instructions given in the previous section, then it is almost ready to deploy to Heroku. You'll need to add the same environment variable using the Heroku tools. In addition to the authentication token for Slack, you will need to configure a URL for your site. Heroku will generate a URL for you from the name of your project (in this case `inqry-chatbot`); so as long as the name has not been claimed already by someone else, you can name it as you will:

```
$ heroku create inqry-chatbot
$ heroku config:add HEROKU_URL=https://inqry-chatbot.herokuapp.com/
$ heroku config:add HUBOT_SLACK_TOKEN=xxbo-3957767284-ZnxlH1n3ysLVgcD2dr1PZ9Cq
$ git push heroku master
Fetching repository, done.
Counting objects: 5, done.
Delta compression using up to 8 threads.
Compressing objects: 100% (3/3), done.
Writing objects: 100% (3/3), 317 bytes | 0 bytes/s, done.
Total 3 (delta 2), reused 0 (delta 0)

-----> Node.js app detected
-----> Requested node range:  0.10.x
...
-----> Compressing... done, 6.8MB
-----> Launching... done, v9
       https://inqry-chatbot.herokuapp.com/ deployed to Heroku

To git@heroku.com:inqry-chatbot.git
   d32e2db..3627218  master -> master
```

If you need to troubleshoot issues with your Hubot, you can always run the heroku log command to view logs for your application, `heroku logs -t`:

```
$ heroku logs -t
2014-11-18T07:07:18.716943+00:00 app[web.1]: Successfully 'connected'
as hubot
2014-11-18T07:07:18.576287+00:00 app[web.1]: Tue, 18 Nov 2014 07:07:18
GMT connect deprecated limit: Restrict request size at location of
read at
```

```
node_modules/hubot/.../express/.../connect/.../middleware/multipart.js:86:15
...
```

When you send commands into your chat room you will notice events inside of Heroku. This is a good way to verify that your bot is wired into Slack properly.

You might also want to publish this repository into GitHub. Heroku, as a part of hosting your live application, also hosts the full Git repository of your Hubot (Hubot, as friendly as it tries to be, is just another NodeJS application in the end). Heroku can host the entirety of the source code for your Hubot for you, but does not have the additional tools, like user management, that GitHub does. For this reason, use your GitHub account as your code repository, the place where team members develop new features of your chatbot. Build and test locally, and then push into Heroku using the ease of the Git workflow as a deployment layer.

Now that we have created and installed Hubot, let's look at the Activity API and determine how we want to code our extension.

Activity API Overview

The Activity API centers around notifications: notifications are similar to the notifications you see on social networking sites, events that occur that document important points of interest inside a timeline of activity. GitHub activity events are often tied to important milestones inside of a developer's day, activities like pushing commits into the main remote repository, asking questions on discussion threads associated with a repository, or assigning issues to a developer for review.

These notifications are accessible to team members without programmatically accessing the GitHub API. Team members are notified of events inside of their workflow using email based on several rules. GitHub will automatically send out notification emails when a user has watched a repository and issues or comments are added, a pull request is made, or there are comments made on a commit. In addition, even if a user has not watched a repository, they will be notified if that user is *@mentioned* (prefixing the @ character to a team member's name inside a comment), when an issue is assigned to them, or when that user participates in a discussion associated with any repository.

The GitHub policy for notification is definitely to err on the side of being overly verbose. Many people live in their email, and making sure that all important activities are distributed to the right people involved makes sense. GitHub has a good set of rules for making sure the correct notifications get to the right parties.

Email does falter as a to-do list, however, and at times the ease in which email can be delivered breeds a secondary problem: overwhelm. It can be very easy to lose focus (vital to building software) when you are constantly context switching by checking email, and notifications can often fly by. In addition, email is privately directed and prevents easy collaboration; generally people don't share email inboxes. Let's extend our Hubot to help us resolve these problems by taking our GitHub notifications into a shared and "opt-in when you are logged-in" communication channel.

Writing a Hubot Extension

Hubot extensions are written in either JavaScript or CoffeeScript. CoffeeScript is a intermediate language that compiles directly to JavaScript. Many people prefer writing in CoffeeScript because it has a cleaner syntax and writes "safer" JavaScript (the syntax helps you avoid common tricky pitfalls in the JavaScript language, like what "this" refers to). CoffeeScript is an indentation-based language (much like Python), and after the initial learning curve, can feel easier to read than JavaScript, especially when you have many nested function callbacks (common in JavaScript programming); it is easier to see where a function begins and ends given the indentation levels. Hubot is itself written in CoffeeScript, and we'll write our extension in CoffeeScript as well.

CoffeeScript is a language where indentation is important. For readability purposes, when we display a snippet of code from a longer file, there are times where we have changed the indentation of that snippet and removed the initial indentation. If you were to copy the code without realignment, the snippet would not work until you reindented it to fit the context into which it sits.

The Hubot extension module format is exceedingly simple. You write JavaScript modules (using the export syntax) and Hubot passes you in a robot object you program using several API methods.

There are a few concepts useful to programming Hubot. You can find an example of each of these methods inside the *example.coffee* file inside the *scripts* directory:

- Hubot has a "brain." This is an internal state object, which means these values persist across chat messages. This state is not persisted into a database by default, so this state is not restored if you restart Hubot. However, a persistence mechanism is exposed via Redis, though this is optional and requires configuration. The brain is the way you set and get values that are saved across discrete messages.

- Hubot has different response mechanisms. They can choose to respond only when they hear exact phrases or when keywords are found in any message, and you don't need to do the grunt work inside your code to determine the differences between these communication types.

- Hubot includes an HTTP server. You might need your Hubot to accept requests from additional services beyond the chat service, and Hubot makes it easy to accept these kinds of requests.

- Hubot has a built-in HTTP client. You can easily access HTTP resources within Hubot; many popular extensions to Hubot access a web service when Hubot receives a request.

- Hubot commands can include parameters. You can tell a Hubot to do something multiple times and write a generic function that accepts options.

- Hubot can handle events. Each chat service has a generalized set of events that are normalized to a common API. Hubot can be programmed to interact with these events. For example, Hubot can perform actions when a room topic changes or when users leave rooms.

- Hubot can handle generic errors at the top level. Hubot can be programmed with a catch-all error handler so that no matter where your code failed, you can catch it without crashing your bot.

Hubot will use the first five of these features:

- We will use the Hubot brain to store a PR review request. If Hubot asks a user to review a PR, it needs to keep track of this so that when the user responds it has some context of the request.

- We will use the `respond` method to program our Hubot to handle a request when a user accepts or declines the review request.

- We will use the HTTP server to accept PR notifications from GitHub webhooks.

- We will use the HTTP client to get a list of users from Slack.

- We will use the parameterization of requests to Hubot to retrieve the specific pull request ID from a chat user message.

There are examples of the other two features (events and generic errors) inside the examples script that ship with the Hubot source code but we won't use those APIs in our Hubot.

Code Reviews via Pull Requests

As we've seen in other chapters, pull requests are the mechanism used on GitHub to easily integrate code changes into a project. Contributors either fork the master repository and then issue a pull request against that repository, or, if they have write permission to the main repository, make a "feature" branch and then issue a pull request against the "master" branch.

Pull requests often come with a chat message indicating several people who should review the request. This tribal knowledge about who should be involved is only in the head of the developer who created the code. It could be that they invited the correct people. Or, it could be that they invited the people they prefer to review their code for various (and completely rational reasons). This can be an effective way to engage the right people around a new piece of code.

And inviting reviewers this way can have downsides as well: if the person is otherwise engaged, pull requests can linger when a notification email goes unread. And, there is good research to indicate that the best performing teams are those who share all tasks and responsibilities equally. It often does not scale to ask everyone to participate in all code reviews associated with a pull request. But it might be the case that randomly selecting developers involved in a project is a better (and more efficient) way to review code than asking the developer who created the code to determine these people.

Hubot will assign active chat room users to do code reviews when a new pull request is created. We will use the GitHub Activity API to subscribe to pull request events. When Hubot becomes aware that a pull request needs review, it will randomly assign a user in the chat room to do the review and then ask that user if they want to accept the challenge. If they accept, we will note that in the pull request comments.

Extension boilerplate

We will start writing our extension by defining the high-level communication format we expect from our users. Our script has a simple vocabulary: look for responses indicating acceptance or refusal of our review requests. Our extension script should be in the *scripts* directory and named *pr-delegator.coffee*. This is just the back and forth we will be having with users; we are not yet writing any code to handle the pull request notifications:

```
module.exports = (robot) -> ❶
    robot.respond /accept/i, (res) -> ❷
        accept( res )
    robot.respond /decline/i, (res) -> ❸
        decline( res )
    accept = ( res ) -> ❹
        res.reply "Thanks, you got it!"
        console.log "Accepted!" ❺
    decline = ( res ) -> ❻
        res.reply "OK, I'll find someone else"
        console.log "Declined!"
```

This is a dense piece of code and can be confusing if you are new to CoffeeScript. At the same time, hopefully you will agree that this is amazingly powerful code for such a small snippet after reading these notes.

❶ All NodeJS modules start by defining entrypoints using the `exports` syntax. This code defines a function that expects a single parameter; when the function is executed, the parameter will be called a robot. The Hubot framework will pass in a `robot` object for us that we will program further down.

❷ The Hubot API defines a method on the `robot` object called `respond`, which we use here. It takes two parameters: a regular expression to match against and a function that receives an instance of the chat response object (called `res` here). The second line uses the API for this response object to call a method `accept` with the response object. We define `accept` in a moment.

❸ We setup a response matcher for a `decline` response.

❹ Now we define the `accept` method. The `accept` method receives the response object generated by the Hubot framework and calls the `reply` method, which, you guessed it, sends a message back into the chat channel with the text "Thanks, you got it!"

❺ The `accept` method then also calls `console.log` with information that is displayed on the console from which we started Hubot. This is a simple way for us to assure everything worked correctly; if we don't see this message, our code before this was broken. The `console.log` is not visible to any users in the channel. It is good practice to remove this code when you finalize your production code, but if you forget, it won't affect anything happening in the channel.

❻ We then define the `decline` method using the same APIs as for the `accept` method.

If Hubot is running, you will need to restart it to reload any scripts. Kill Hubot (using Ctrl-C), and then restart it, and then play with commands inside your Slack site. Enter the commands `probot accept` and `probot decline` and you'll see Hubot responding inside the channel. You'll also see the message `Accepted!` or `Declined!` printed to the console on which Hubot is running.

Writing tests for Hubot extensions

Now that we have the basics of our Hubot working, let's make sure we certify our code with some tests. We'll use the Jasmine testing framework for NodeJS. It offers an elegant behavior-driven testing syntax where you specify a behavior as the first parameter to an `it` function, and as a second parameter, a function that is run as the test itself. Jasmine manages running each `it` call and displays a nice output of passing and failed tests at the end of your run. Jasmine tests are typically written in JavaScript, but the latest versions of Jasmine support tests are also written in CoffeeScript. Hubot is written in CoffeeScript, so let's write our tests in CoffeeScript as well. We need to put our tests inside a directory called *spec* and make sure our filename ends with *.spec.coffee*. Let's use *spec/pr-delegator.spec.coffee* as the complete filename. Jasmine expects spec files to have *.spec.* at the end of their filename (before the extension, either *.js* or *.coffee*); if your filename does not match this pattern Jasmine won't recognize it as a test.

```
Probot = require "../scripts/pr-delegator"
Handler = require "../lib/handler"

pr = undefined
robot = undefined

describe "#probot", ->
        beforeEach () ->
                robot = {
                        respond: jasmine.createSpy( 'respond' )
                        router: {
                                post: jasmine.createSpy( 'post' )
                                }
                        }

        it "should verify our calls to respond", (done) ->
                pr = Probot robot
                expect( robot.respond.calls.count() ).toEqual( 2 )
                done()
```

The first line in our test requires, or loads, the Hubot extension module into our test script, giving us a function we save as a `Probot` variable. We then create a `describe` function, which is an organizing function to group tests. `describe` functions take an indentifier (in this case #probot) and a function that contains multiple `it` calls. In addition, a `describe` function can also contain a `beforeEach` function that configures common elements inside our `it` calls; in this case we create a faked `robot` object we will pass into our `Probot` function call. When we are running Hubot itself, Hubot creates the `robot` and passes it into the `Probot` function, but when we run our tests, we generate a fake one and query it to make sure it is receiving the proper configuration. If we make a change inside our actual Hubot code and forget to update our tests to verify those changes, our tests will fail and we'll know we need to either augment our tests, or something broke inside our `robot`, a good automated sanity check for us when we are feverishly coding away, animating our helpful Hubot.

You should see some similarities between the calls made to our `robot` (`robot.respond` and `robot.router.post`) and the tests. We set up "spies" using Jasmine that generate fake function calls capable of recording any interaction from outside sources (either our production code or the test code harness). Inside our `it` call, we then verify that those calls were made. We use the `expect` function to verify that we made two calls to the `respond` function defined on the `robot`, and that `robot.router.post` has been called as well.

We need to install Jasmine, and we do this by adding to our *package.json* file. Append `"jasmine-node": "^1.14.5"` to the file, and make sure to add a comma to the tuple above it. Adding this code specifies that the minimum version of Jasmine node we will use is "1.14.5".

```
    ...
    "hubot-shipit": "^0.1.1",
    "hubot-slack": "^3.2.1",
    "hubot-youtube": "^0.1.2",
    "jasmine-node": "^2.0.0"
  },
  "engines": {
    ...
```

Runing the following commands will then install Jasmine (the library and a test runner command-line tool) and run our tests. We abbreviate some of the installation output to save space:

```
$ npm install
...
hubot-slack@3.2.1 node_modules/hubot-slack
└── slack-client@1.2.2 (log@1.4.0, coffee-script@1.6.3, ws@0.4.31)
...
$ ./node_modules/.bin/jasmine-node --coffee spec/

.

Finished in 0.009 seconds
1 test, 1 assertions, 0 failures, 0 skipped
```

Our tests pass and we now have a way to document and verify that our code does what we think it does.

Setting up our webhook

We are now in a position to start adding the actual functionality to our Hubot. Our first requirement is to register for pull request events. We could do this from within the GitHub website, but another way is to use the cURL tool to create the webhook from the command line. In order to do this, we need to first create an authorization token, and then we can use that token to create a webhook.

To create the token, run this command, setting the proper variables for your username instead of mine ("xrd"):

```
$ export USERNAME=xrd
$ curl https://api.github.com/authorizations --user $USERNAME --data
'{"scopes":["repo"], "note": "Probot access to PRs" }' -X POST
```

This call can return in one of three ways. If your username or password is incorrect, you will get an error response message like this:

```
{
  "message": "Bad credentials",
  "documentation_url": "https://developer.github.com/v3"
}
```

If your username and password are correct and you don't have two-factor authentication turned on, the request will succeed and you will get back a token inside the JSON response:

```
{
  "id": 238749874,
  "url": "https://api.github.com/authorizations/9876533",
  "app": {
    "name": "Probot access to PRs",
    "url": "https://developer.github.com/v3/oauth_authorizations/",
    "client_id": "00000000000000000000"
  },
  "token": "fakedtoken1234",
  "hashed_token": "fakedhashedtoken7654",
  ...
```

If you are using two-factor authentication then you will see a response message like this:

```
{
  "message": "Must specify two-factor authentication OTP code.",
  "documentation_url":
  "https://developer.github.com/v3/auth#working-with-two-factor-authentication"
}
```

If you get this message in response to the prior cURL command, then you will be receiving a one-time password via your choice of a two-factor authentication alternative endpoint (either SMS or a two-factor authentication app like Google Authenticator or recovery codes that you printed out). If you use text messaging, check your text messages and then resend the request appending a header using cURL:

```
$ curl https://api.github.com/authorizations --user $USERNAME --data
'{"scopes":["repo"], "note": "Probot access to PRs" }' -X POST
--header "X-GitHub-OTP: 423584"
Enter host password for user 'xrd':
```

If all these steps complete successfully (regardless of whether you are using two-factor authentication or not) you will then receive an OAuth token:

```
{
  "id": 1234567,
  "url": "https://api.github.com/authorizations/1234567",
  "app": {
    "name": "Probot access to PRs (API)",
    "url": "https://developer.github.com/v3/oauth_authorizations/",
```

```
      "client_id": "00000000000000000000"
    },
    "token": "ad5a36c3b7322c4ae8bb9069d4f20fdf2e454266",
    "note": "Probot access to PRs",
    "note_url": null,
    "created_at": "2015-01-13T06:23:53Z",
    "updated_at": "2015-01-13T06:23:53Z",
    "scopes": [
      "notifications"
    ]
}
```

Using the OAuth Token to Register for Events

Once this is completed we now have our token we can use to create a webhook. Make sure to use the correct repository name and access token before running the cURL command. We will also need the endpoint we created when we published into Heroku (in our case `https://inqry-chatbot.herokuapp.com`):

```
$ REPOSITORY=testing_repostory
$ TOKEN=ad5a36c3b7322c4ae8bb9069d4f20fdf2e454266
$ WEBHOOK_URL=https://inqry-chatbot.herokuapp.com/pr
$ CONFIG=$(echo '{
  "name": "web",
  "active": true,
  "events": [
    "push",
    "pull_request"
  ],
  "config": {
    "url": "'$WEBHOOK_URL'",
    "content_type": "form",
    "secret" : "XYZABC"
  }
}')
$ curl -H "Authorization: token $TOKEN" \
-H "Content-Type: application/json" -X POST \
-d "$CONFIG" https://api.github.com/repos/$USERNAME/$REPOSITORY/hooks
{
  "url": "https://api.github.com/repos/xrd/testing_repostory/hooks/3846063",
  "test_url":
  "https://api.github.com/repos/xrd/testing_repostory/hooks/3846063/test",
  "ping_url":
  "https://api.github.com/repos/xrd/testing_repostory/hooks/3846063/pings",
  "id": 3846063,
  "name": "web",
  "active": true,
  "events": [
    "push",
    "pull_request"
  ],
  "config": {
```

```
        "url": "https://inqry-chatbot.herokuapp.com/pr",
        "content_type": "json"
      },
      "last_response": {
        "code": null,
        "status": "unused",
        "message": null
      },
      "updated_at": "2015-01-14T06:23:59Z",
      "created_at": "2015-01-14T06:23:59Z"
    }
```

There is a bit of bash cleverness here, but nothing to be overly disturbed by. We create a few variables we use in the final command. Since the $CONFIG variable is particularly long, we use echo to print out a bunch of information with the webhook URL in the middle. If you want to see the result of that variable, type echo $CONFIG and you'll notice the snippet ... "url": "https://inqry-chatbot.herokuapp.com/pr" ... properly interpolated.

Here we use the Heroku API URL as our webhook endpoint. This means we need to have things hosted on Heroku for the webhook to talk to our HTTP server properly. We can do some things (like connecting the Hubot to the Slack service) from behind a firewall and have it talk with other chat room participants, but any webhook request will fail unless the chat client is running on a publicly available server.

Be careful to make sure you use the content_type set to "form" (which is the default, so you could leave it blank). Setting this to json will make it difficult to retrieve the raw body inside your Hubot when the post request is received and validate the request using a secure digest. We want to make sure all requests are real requests from GitHub and not a cracker attempting to maliciously inject themselves into our conversations. To protect from this possible situation, we verify each request back into GitHub by using the secret generated when we created the webhook. We'll discuss this in detail later in this chapter, but for now, establish a secret when you create the hook. A cracker might be able to guess about where our endpoint exists, but unless Heroku or GitHub is compromised, they won't know our webhook secret.

We should update our tests to make sure we anticipate this new functionality. We will be using the Hubot HTTP server, which piggybacks on the built-in express server running inside of Hubot. Our new test should reflect that we use the router.post method exposed to our Hubot, and that it is called once. We add this next test to the end of our spec file:

```
it "should verify our calls to router.post", (done) ->
    pr = Probot robot
    expect( robot.router.post ).toHaveBeenCalled()
    done()
```

This additional test will fail should we run it. Now we can add to our Hubot and have it handle webhook callbacks from GitHub. Add this to the end of the file:

```
robot.router.post '/pr', ( req, res ) ->
    console.log "We received a pull request"
```

Now if we run our tests, they all pass. If they do, publish our new version of the app into Heroku. We'll omit this step in the future, but if you want to receive pull requests on the router you have set up, remember that you need to publish your files into Heroku so the endpoint is public.

```
$ ./node_modules/.bin/jasmine-node --coffee spec/
..
$ git commit -m "Working tests and associated code" -a
...
$ heroku push

Finished in 0.009 seconds
2 tests, 2 assertions, 0 failures, 0 skipped
$ git push heroku master
Fetching repository, done.
Counting objects: 5, done.
Delta compression using up to 8 threads.
...
```

We now have an end-to-end Hubot setup, ready to receive webhook notifications.

Triggering Real Pull Requests

We can now start testing our Hubot with real GitHub notifications. First, let's set up a repository we can use for testing. Creating the new repository on GitHub is a quick task if we use the hub tool described in Chapter 6:

```
$ mkdir testing_repository
$ cd testing_repository
$ git init
$ touch test.txt
$ git add .
$ git commit -m "Initial checkin"
$ hub create
...
```

Now we can create a real pull requests for our repository from the command line and test our Hubot. A typical pull request flow looks like the following:

1. Create a new branch

2. Add new content

3. Commit the content

4. Push the new branch into GitHub

5. Issue a pull request

All of this can be automated using a combination of Git commands and cURL. We've seen some of these commands before and can reuse the previous command-line invocations and variables we used when generating our webhook using the API via cURL. Our config variable is similar, but the required fields in this case are: the title and body for the pull request, the "head" key that matches the name of the branch, and where to merge it to using the "base" key.

Creating a new branch, adding some content, and then issuing a pull request against the branch might be something we need to do several (or more) times as we experiment and learn about the Hubot extension API. The examples here work right out of the box, but don't be fooled into thinking that it all went exactly as we expected the first time. Given that, these are commands you might want to perform multiple times as you are experimenting, so let's put the commands described in the previous paragraph into a bash script that is generic and can be run multiple times. We can call it issue-pull-request.sh and place the script inside the test directory:

```
# Modify these three variables
AUTH_TOKEN=b2ac1f43aeb8d73b69754d2fe337de7035ec9df7
USERNAME=xrd
REPOSITORY=test_repository

DATE=$(date "+%s")
NEW_BRANCH=$DATE
git checkout -b $NEW_BRANCH
echo "Adding some content" >> test-$DATE.txt
git commit -m "Adding test file to test branch at $DATE" -a
git push origin $NEW_BRANCH
CONFIG=$(echo '
{ "title": "PR on '$DATE'",
  "body" : "Pull this PR'$DATE'",
  "head": "'$NEW_BRANCH'",
  "base": "master"
}' )
URL=https://api.github.com/repos/$USERNAME/$REPOSITORY/pulls
curl -H "Authorization: token $AUTH_TOKEN" \
-H "Content-Type: application/json" -X POST -d "$CONFIG" "$URL"
```

This script generates a unique string based on the current time. It then creates and checks out a new branch based on that name, adds some content to a unique file, commits it, pushes it into GitHub, and generates a pull request using the API. All you will need to do is make a one-time update to the three variables at the top of the script to match your information. This script is resilient in that even if your auth token were incorrect (or had expired) this command would do nothing other than add testing data to your test repository, so you can experiment safely. Just be sure to pay attention to whether you see a successful JSON request as shown in the following code or an error message. And, as we are going to run this script as a command, make it executable using the chmod command.

Now, let's run it and see what happens:

```
$ chmod +x ./issue-pull-request.sh
$ ./issue-pull-request.sh
{
  "url": "https://api.github.com/repos/xrd/testing_repostory/pulls/1",
  "id": 27330198,
  "html_url": "https://github.com/xrd/testing_repostory/pull/1",
  "diff_url": "https://github.com/xrd/testing_repostory/pull/1.diff",
  "patch_url": "https://github.com/xrd/testing_repostory/pull/1.patch",
  "issue_url": "https://api.github.com/repos/xrd/testing_repostory/issues/1",
  "number": 1,
  "state": "open",
  "locked": false,
  "title": "A PR test",
      "open_issues_count": 1,
...
```

This returns a huge JSON response (abbreviated here), but you can see the first item is a link to the pull request. For a human-readable link, we should use the link called html_url. Were we to visit this link, we could merge the pull request from within the GitHub web UI.

To see more context on what is happening with this pull request, once we are looking at this pull request inside of GitHub, we can then navigate to the settings for our repository, follow the link to "Webhooks and Services" on the left navigation bar, and we will then find at the very bottom of the page a list of recent deliveries to our webhook, as in Figure 8-7.

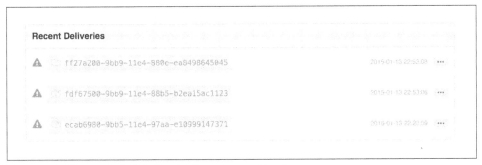

Figure 8-7. Recent failed deliveries from our webhook

These requests all failed; our Hubot is not correctly configured to handle real HTTP requests from GitHub. This does show that GitHub is trying to do something when a pull request is received. We'll work on getting our handler code written and pushed into Heroku, and then issue another PR.

Handling PR Notifications as Post Requests over HTTP

Let's build our HTTP handler when PR notifications arrive from GitHub. At first glance, we might take the easy route, adding it directly into the top-level script. But given the fact that JavaScript handles events inside of callbacks and the fact that Hubot extensions only export a single constructor (using the `module.exports` syntax), it is easier to create, and more importantly test, a separate module, which we require in our main extension script.

We start by writing our tests. We've already created a test that verifies the call to `robot.router.post`. Our new functionality will actually handle the PR notification, so let's add a new grouping using the describe syntax and call it `"#pr"`. The new functionality is simple: if the Hubot receives the proper parameters (most importantly that the internal secret matches the secret sent on the request) then we accept the PR as valid and message our room with further instructions, namely inviting some user to review this pull request. Our handler then needs to expose two methods: `prHandler`, which is where we delegate any information coming from an HTTP request to the `/pr` route, and a method where we can configure the secret, which we call `setSecret`. Once we have established this internal signature for our handler library, we can add two simple tests and then our library.

We have two tests: one that handles the correct flow and one that handles the incorrect flow. In a before block (this happens before each test) we set up a fake `robot`, and set the secret on our handler module. Our faked `robot` implements the same methods a real Hubot `robot` does (the `messageRoom` and `send` methods), but we create Jasmine spies to verify these functions are called inside our implementation code:

```coffeescript
describe "#pr", ->
        secret = "ABCDEF"
        robot = undefined
        res = undefined

        beforeEach ->
                robot = {
                        messageRoom: jasmine.createSpy()
                        }
                res = { send: jasmine.createSpy() }
                Handler.setSecret secret

        it "should disallow calls without the secret", (done) ->
                req = {}
                Handler.prHandler( robot, req, res )
                expect( robot.messageRoom ).not.toHaveBeenCalled()
                expect( res.send ).toHaveBeenCalled()
                done()

        it "should allow calls with the secret", (done) ->
                req = { body: { secret: secret } }
```

```
Handler.prHandler( robot, req, res )
expect( robot.messageRoom ).toHaveBeenCalled()
expect( res.send ).toHaveBeenCalled()
done()
```

Now, add a file called *./lib/handler.coffee*:

```
_SECRET = undefined

exports.prHandler = ( robot, req, res ) ->
        secret = req.body?.secret
        if secret == _SECRET
                console.log "Secret verified, let's notify our channel"
                room = "general"
                robot.messageRoom room, "OMG, GitHub is on my caller-id!?!"
        res.send "OK\n"

exports.setSecret = (secret) ->
        _SECRET = secret
```

As you can see, the Hubot API does a lot of work for us: it processes the JSON POST request to the /pr endpoint and provides us with the parsed parameters inside the body object. We use that to retrieve the secret from the request. Even if you have used CoffeeScript before, you may not be familiar with the ?. syntax: this just tests to see if body is defined and if so, has a key named secret. This prevents us from crashing if the secret is not sent in with the request. If the secret from the request matches the configured secret, then we message the room; otherwise we ignore the request. In either case, we need to respond to the calling server by using the send method (send is provided by the built-in *express* server Hubot uses to provide an HTTP server). For debugging purposes we output that the secret was validated, if it was in fact validated, but otherwise the behavior of our response to the calling client is the same regardless of whether they provided a correct secret or not. We don't want to provide an attacker with anything extra if they pass in an incorrect secret.

If we run our tests we will see them all pass:

```
$ node_modules/jasmine-node/bin/jasmine-node \
--coffee spec/pr-delegator.spec.coffee
....

Finished in 0.01 seconds
4 tests, 6 assertions, 0 failures, 0 skipped
```

Hubot will spawn the HTTP server wherever it runs so we can talk to it on our local machine (though this will likely be inside a firewall and inaccessible to GitHub), so we can test it using cURL locally. Remember that our robot router accepts commands as HTTP POST requests, so we need to specify a post request (using the --data switch with cURL):

```
$ ( HUBOT_SLACK_TOKEN=xoxb-3295776784-nZxl1H3nyLsVcgdD29r1PZCq \
./bin/hubot -a slack 2> /dev/null | grep -i secret & )
$ curl --data '' http://localhost:8080/pr
Invalid secret
OK
$ curl --data 'secret=XYZABC' http://localhost:8080/pr
Secret verified
OK
$ kill `ps a | grep node | grep -v grep | awk -F ' ' '{ print $1 }'`
```

These commands verify that things are working properly. First, we start the server, piping the output to grep to constrain output related to our secret processing (we also background the entire chain using an ampersand and parentheses, a bash trick). Then, we hit the server running locally without the secret: the server (as it is running in the same shell) prints out the message "Invalid secret" using console.log, and then cURL prints out "OK," which is what was returned from our server. If we run the command again, this time including the secret as post parameters, we see that Hubot verified the secret internally against its own secret, and then cURL again prints "OK," which was what the express server inside of Hubot returned to the calling client. The final line quits Hubot: this command finds the PID for the Hubot client (which runs as a node process) and then sends it a SIGHUP signal, signaling to Hubot that it should quit.

Provided you connected correctly to your Slack site, you'll also see a message inside your #general channel, which says "OMG, GitHub is on my caller-id!?!" We now have a simple way to trigger a pull request notification without going through the formality of actually generating a pull request. Between our script, which issues real pull requests through the GitHub API, and this one that fakes a webhook notification, we have the ability to test our code externally as we develop it. Of course, our tests are valuable, but sometimes it is impossible to understand what is happening inside of our Hubot without running against the real Hubot and not a test harness.

Assigning an active chat room user

Now that we have an incoming pull request (albeit one we are faking), we need to write the code to find a random user and assign them to the pull request.

This next section is redundant; our Hubot will function exactly as we need it to if you were to disregard any code from this section. As I was writing this book, I mistakenly missed the fact that the Hubot brain contains a list of users and found another avenue to get that data, the Slack API. I wrote the chapter using the Slack API, and then discovered my mistake.

Initially I planned to remove this entire section. However, it does demonstrate the ease of using an external service through the built-in HTTP client, which is a powerful feature of Hubot. And it also demonstrates how powerful tests aid you when developing a Hubot extension; I was able to refactor to use a radically different internal code path for getting the list of users and maintain faith that the end-to-end process of my code works by refactoring and then fixing broken tests. And, though not important for this section per se, the Slack API provides much richer data on the users logged in to a room, which could be valuable in other situations. If you want to skip to the next section, you will have all the code to build our Hubot as we described earlier. But I think it is a worthwhile read for general Hubot understanding.

To find a user in the room, one option is to go outside the Hubot API and use the Slack API to query for a list of users. The Slack API provides an endpoint, giving you all users currently in a room. To access the Slack API, we will use the built-in Hubot HTTP client. Once we have the list of members in the room we can look over this list and randomly choose a member and deliver the PR request to them:

```
_SECRET = undefined

anyoneButProbot = (members) ->   ❶
        user = undefined
        while not user
                user = members[ parseInt( Math.random() * \
                        members.length ) ].name
                user = undefined if "probot" == user
        user

sendPrRequest = ( robot, body, room, url ) ->   ❷
        parsed = JSON.parse( body )
        user = anyoneButProbot( parsed.members )
        robot.messageRoom room, "#{user}: Hey, want a PR? #{url}"

exports.prHandler = ( robot, req, res ) ->
        slack_users_url =   ❸
                "https://slack.com/api/users.list?token=" +
                process.env.HUBOT_SLACK_TOKEN
        secret = req.body?.secret   ❹
        url = req.body?.url
```

```
            if secret == _SECRET and url
                    room = "general"
                    robot.http( slack_users_url ) ❺
                            .get() (err, response, body) ->
                                    sendPrRequest( robot, body, \
                                                    room, url ) unless err
            else
                    console.log "Invalid secret or no URL specified"
            res.send "OK\n"

    exports.setSecret = (secret) ->
            _SECRET = secret
```

❶ We define a method called `anyoneButProbot` that takes a list of users and finds a random one, as long as it is not the Hubot.

❷ The `sendPrRequest` method parses the JSON returned from the Slack API and then sends the members inside of the object into the `anyoneButProbot` call. It then uses the Hubot API to send a message to the room asking if that user will accept the pull request review invitation.

❸ We build the URL to the Slack service by tacking on the Slack API token to the base Slack API URL.

❹ As we did before, we pull out the secret and the PR URL, and then make sure they both exist.

❺ We use the built-in HTTP client to make a GET request to the Slack API. Unless we receive an error in the response callback, we use the data provided by the Slack API to initiate the PR review request.

To test this using our cURL command, we need to modify the invocation slightly:

```
$ curl --data 'secret=XYZABC&url=http://pr/1' \
http://localhost:8080/pr
```

Our randomly selected user will see the text `username: Hey, want a PR? http://pr/1` (and the Slack client will format that link as a clickable URL).

Unfortunately, our tests are now broken: we now have the failure `TypeError: Object #<Object> has no method 'http'`. Our mocked `robot` object that we pass into our tests does not have the HTTP interface that comes with Hubot, so we should add it to our custom Robot. The method signature for the HTTP client (which comes from the `node-scoped-http-client` NodeJS package) is hairy: you chain calls together to build up an HTTP client request and end up with a function returned into which you pass a callback where you handle the response body. This module makes you write code that is not particularly testable (said another way, it was challenging for me to understand what the faked test implementation should look like), but the setup code does work and the test itself documents an interface to our robot, which is easily understandable. We simulate the same chain, defining an `http` attribute on the mocked `robot` object, an attribute that resolves to a function call itself. Calling that function returns an object that has a `get` method, and calling that function returns a function callback that when called executes that function with three parameters. In real life that function callback would contain the error code, the response object, and the JSON. In our case, as long as the error code is empty, our implementation will parse the JSON for members, and then issue the PR request:

```
json = '{ "members" : [ { "name" : "bar" } , { "name" : "foo" } ] }'

httpSpy = jasmine.createSpy( 'http' ).and.returnValue(
        { get: () -> ( func ) ->
                func( undefined, undefined, json ) } )

beforeEach ->
        robot = {
                messageRoom: jasmine.createSpy( 'messageRoom' )
                http: httpSpy
                }

        res = { send: jasmine.createSpy( 'send' ) }
        Handler.setSecret secret

it "should disallow calls without the secret", (done) ->
        req = {}
        Handler.prHandler( robot, req, res )
        expect( robot.messageRoom ).not.toHaveBeenCalled()
        expect( httpSpy ).not.toHaveBeenCalled()
        expect( res.send ).toHaveBeenCalled()
        done()

it "should disallow calls without the url", (done) ->
        req = { body: { secret: secret } }
        Handler.prHandler( robot, req, res )
        expect( robot.messageRoom ).not.toHaveBeenCalled()
        expect( httpSpy ).not.toHaveBeenCalled()
        expect( res.send ).toHaveBeenCalled()
        done()

it "should allow calls with the secret", (done) ->
        req = { body: { secret: secret, url: "http://pr/1" } }
        Handler.prHandler( robot, req, res )
        expect( robot.messageRoom ).toHaveBeenCalled()
        expect( httpSpy ).toHaveBeenCalled()
        expect( res.send ).toHaveBeenCalled()
        done()
```

The code we write here was definitely not a piece of code where testing came easy; I refactored this multiple times to find a balance between an easy-to-read test and easy-to-read code. Writing test code takes effort, but when both your tests and code are readable and minimal, you generally can be sure you have a good implementation.

We now have a functional and complete implementation of the code to retrieve a list of users and assign an incoming pull request out to a randomly selected user from that list.

The user list from the Hubot brain

Instead of using the Slack API, we can replace the code with a much simpler call to `robot.brain.users`. Calling into the Slack users API takes a callback, but the `brain.users` call does not, which simplifies our code. We do verify inside our tests that we make a call to the HTTP Jasmine spy on the `get` function, so we will want to remove that inside our tests. We will need to provide a new function called `users` to the Hubot inside the faked `brain` we created.

Unfortunately, things don't just work when we change our code to this:

```
...
users = robot.brain.users()
sendPrRequest( robot, users, room, url, number )
...
```

It is likely that what we got back from the Slack API and what Hubot stores inside its brain for users are functionally the same information, but structurally stored very differently. How can we investigate whether this assumption is correct? NodeJS has a standard library module called `util`, which includes useful utility functions, as you might expect from the name. One of them is `inspect`, which will dig into an object and create a pretty printed view. If we use this module and `console.log` we can see the full contents of a live response object passed into our `accept` function. A line like `console.log( require( 'util' ).inspect( users ) )` displays the following:

```
{ U04FVFE97:
   { id: 'U04FVFE97',
     name: 'ben',
     real_name: 'Ben Straub',
     email_address: 'xxx' },
  U038PNUP2:
   { id: 'U038PNUP2',
     name: 'probot',
     real_name: '',
     email_address: undefined },
  U04624M1A:
   { id: 'U04624M1A',
     name: 'teddyhyde',
     real_name: 'Teddy Hyde',
     email_address: 'xxx' },
```

```
U030YMBJY:
 { id: 'U030YMBJY',
   name: 'xrd',
   real_name: 'Chris Dawson',
   email_address: 'xxx' },
USLACKBOT:
 { id: 'USLACKBOT',
   name: 'slackbot',
   real_name: 'Slack Bot',
   email_address: null } }
```

Ah, we were right: the Slack API returns an array while this is an associative array (called a hash in other languages). So, we need to refactor our inputs to the test to take an associative array instead of an array, and then we need a function to flatten it out (after that our code will work the same as before). We will return that when the user calls robot.brain.users so add a new spy as the users key inside our fake robot:

```
...
users = { CDAWSON: { name: "Chris Dawson" }, BSTRAUB: { name: "Ben Straub" } }
brainSpy = {
        users: jasmine.createSpy( 'getUsers' ).and.returnValue( users ),
        set: jasmine.createSpy( 'setBrain' ),
...
```

Inside our implementation code, flatten out the user associative array and find the user inside the new flattened array:

```
...
flattenUsers = (users) ->
        rv = []
        for x in Object.keys( users )
                rv.push users[x]
        rv

anyoneButProbot = ( users ) ->
        user = undefined
        flattened = flattenUsers( users )
        while not user
                user = flattened[ parseInt( Math.random() * \
                        flattened.length ) ].name
                user = undefined if "probot" == user
        user

...
```

Sending PR data via webhook

Our wiring is almost complete, so let's actually send real pull request information. If we run our script issue-pull-request.sh we will see it sending data out to our Hubot. Once we have deployed to Heroku, our Hubot is listening on a public hostname. GitHub will accept the pull request and then send a JSON inside the body of a POST request made to our Hubot. This JSON looks very different from the URL-encoded parameters we provide in our cURL script, so we need to modify our code to fit.

If we retrieve the JSON from a POST, it will look something like this (reformatted for clarity and brevity):

```
{
    "action":"opened",
    "number":13,
    "pull_request": {
      "locked" : false,
      "comments_url" :
      "https://api.github.com/repos/xrd/test_repository/issues/13/comments",
      "url" : "https://api.github.com/repos/xrd/test_repository/pulls/13",
      "html_url" : "https://github.com/xrd/test_repository/pulls/13",
      }
      ...
}
```

Most importantly, you see a URL (the html_url more specifically) we will use inside our Hubot message to the user. Retrieving the JSON and parsing it is trivial inside our Hubot:

```
...
exports.prHandler = ( robot, req, res ) ->
        body = req.body
        pr = JSON.parse body if body
        url = pr.pull_request.html_url if pr
        secret = pr.secret if pr

        if secret == _SECRET and url
              room = "general"
...
```

Here you see we pull out the body contents, process them as JSON, extract the secret and the URL from the parsed JSON, and then go through our normal routine.

Our tests are simple, and require that we send in JSON:

```
...
it "should disallow calls without the secret and url", (done) ->
        req = {}
        Handler.prHandler( robot, req, res )
        expect( robot.messageRoom ).not.toHaveBeenCalled()
        expect( httpSpy ).not.toHaveBeenCalled()
        expect( res.send ).toHaveBeenCalled()
        done()

it "should allow calls with the secret and url", (done) ->
        req = { body: '{ "pull_request" : { "html_url" : "http://pr/1" },
```

```
    "secret": "ABCDEF" }' }
    Handler.prHandler( robot, req, res )
    expect( robot.messageRoom ).toHaveBeenCalled()
    expect( httpSpy ).toHaveBeenCalled()
    expect( res.send ).toHaveBeenCalled()
    done()
...
```

We are putting the secret inside the JSON as a convenience. The secret will not come
in with the JSON when GitHub sends us JSON via the webhook, but this is an easy
way to provide it to our handler for the moment. If we run our tests, they should pass
now.

Securing the webhook

Our Hubot is now in a position where it will operate correctly if the secret passes validation and the webhook data is passed properly. Now we need to secure the webhook.
GitHub signs your data inside the webhook payload, which provides you with a way
to verify the data really came from an authorized host. We need to decode it inside
our handler. To do this, we will need to retrieve the secure hash GitHub provides
inside the request headers. Then, we will need to calculate the hash ourselves using
the secret we maintain internally. If these hashes match, then we know the incoming
request and JSON is truly from GitHub and not an attacker:

```
...
getSecureHash = (body, secret) ->
        hash = crypto.
                createHmac( 'sha1', secret ).
                update( "sha1=" + body ).
                digest('hex')
        console.log "Hash: #{hash}"
        hash

exports.prHandler = ( robot, req, res ) ->
        slack_users_url =
                "https://slack.com/api/users.list?token=" +
                process.env.HUBOT_SLACK_TOKEN
        body = req.body
        pr = JSON.parse body if body
        url = pr.pull_request.html_url if pr
        secureHash = getSecureHash( body, _SECRET ) if body
        webhookProvidedHash = req.headers['HTTP_X_HUB_SIGNATURE' ] \
                        if req?.headers
        secureCompare = require 'secure-compare'

        if secureCompare( secureHash, webhookProvidedHash ) and url
                room = "general"
                robot.http( slack_users_url ) ->
                        .get() (err, response, body) ->
                                sendPrRequest( robot, body, \
```

```
                                    room, url ) unless err
        else
    ...
```

The signature is a *hash message authentication code* (HMAC). HMAC cryptography is vulnerable to timing attacks. When you use this encryption technique, the time it takes to complete a comparison of the computed hash and the sent hash can be the starting point for an attacker to gain forced access to a server. More specifically to JavaScript, naive comparison operators like == will leak this timing information. To eliminate the risk that this information could be used to compromise the host system, we use a module called secure-compare that obscures this timing information when making a comparison. To load this module, we need to add it to our *package.json* manifest file with the command npm install secure-compare --save.

Now we can adjust our tests to fit the new reality of our handler:

```
    ...
    it "should disallow calls without the secret and url", (done) ->
        req = {}
        Handler.prHandler( robot, req, res )
        expect( robot.messageRoom ).not.toHaveBeenCalled()
        expect( httpSpy ).not.toHaveBeenCalled()
        expect( res.send ).toHaveBeenCalled()
        done()

    it "should allow calls with the secret and url", (done) ->
        req = { body: '{ "pull_request" : { "html_url" : "http://pr/1" }}',
        headers: { "HTTP_X_HUB_SIGNATURE" :
            "cd970490d83c01b678fa9af55f3c7854b5d22918" } }
        Handler.prHandler( robot, req, res )
        expect( robot.messageRoom ).toHaveBeenCalled()
        expect( httpSpy ).toHaveBeenCalled()
        expect( res.send ).toHaveBeenCalled()
        done()
    ...
```

You'll notice we moved the secret out of the JSON and into the headers. This is the same structure our Hubot will see when the GitHub webhook encodes the content of the JSON and provides us with a secure hash in the HTTP_X_HUB_SIGNATURE key. Inside our test we will need to provide the same signature inside our mocked request object. We could duplicate our secure hash generation code from the handler implementation, or we could be lazy and just run our tests once (knowing they will fail this time), watch for the console.log output that says "Hash: cd970490d83c..." and copy this hash into our mocked request object. Once we do this, our tests will pass.

Now, after reloading our Hubot, if we issue a pull request using our issue-pull-request.sh script, we should see the matching hashes. But we won't (at least if you used the same *package.json* file as we specified earlier) because of a critical bug inside of Hubot at the time of this writing.

As we mentioned earlier, Hubot bundles Express.js, a high-performance web framework for NodeJS. Express.js has a modular architecture, where middleware is inserted into a request and response chain. This approach to building functionality and the wide array of middleware allows web developers to string together various standardized middleware components to use only those features needed for the problem at hand. Common middleware includes static file handlers (for serving static files), cookie handlers, session handlers, and body parsers. You can imagine circumstances where you would not need all of these (or you might need others) and this flexibility makes Express.js a popular choice for building NodeJS web applications.

The body parser middleware is of particular interest to us here: the body parser middleware is used to convert the "body" of a request into a JavaScript object attached to the request object. Previously you saw us access it inside a variable we called `req` inside our callback; obviously this stands for request. The body parser takes on converting whatever data content comes from inside the body of the HTTP request into a structured JavaScript associative array inside the `body` object within our `request` object. If the body is URL encoded (as the PR information is encoded if we create the webhook with the `content_type` set to `form`), then the body parser URL decodes the content, parses it as JSON, and then sets the inflated object to the `body` attribute on our `request` object. Normally, this is a very handy process that removes a lot of grunt work for web application authors.

Unfortunately, because the `express` object is bundled and configured for us long before our extension is loaded, we cannot interrupt the load order of the body parser middleware inside our extension, which means we cannot get access to the raw body content. The body parser middleware processes the stream of data by registering for events inside the HTTP request flow. NodeJS made a mark on web application development by providing a network application toolkit centered around one of the most controversial features of JavaScript: the asynchronous callback. In NodeJS, processes register for events and then return control to the host program. In other languages, like Ruby, for example, when building services that receive data from clients, by default, you listen for incoming data, and the moment you tell your program to listen, you have blocked other processing. Asynchronous programming is by no means a new concept (threading in many languages, for example), but NodeJS offers a simple way to interact with asynchronous functions through event registration. In the case of express middleware, however, this event registration process bites us, because middleware loaded first gets first access to incoming data, and once the body parser has processed our body content, we can no longer access the original content. We need access to the raw body content, and there is no way to install our own middleware that would provide it inside our Hubot extension when a PR request is received on the router.

What options do we have then? Well, fortunately, every bit of our stack here is open source, and we can modify the code inside Hubot that sets up our express server to fit our needs. This code is installed by the npm tool in the *node_modules* directory, and we can easily find where express is configured inside of Hubot. There are issues with doing it this way: if we rerun npm install we will blow away our *node_modules* directory, and this is something Heroku will do if it is not told otherwise. A better way might be to fork Hubot and store our own copy of Hubot inside of GitHub and then specify our forked copy inside of the *package.json*? file. This has issues too; if Hubot gets updated with a critical security flaw, we need to merge those changes into our fork, a maintenance issue we would avoid if we use tagged releases from the main repository. There is, unfortunately, no perfect way to resolve this problem that does not itself create other problems.

If you do choose to modify the built-in Hubot code, modify the file *robot.coffee* inside the *node_modules/hubot/src/* directory. The *node_modules* directory, in case memory fails, is where the NodeJS package manager (npm) builds out the local dependency tree for libraries, and this is the file Hubot uses internally to build the robot object and set up the express HTTP server. If we add the following code at line 288 (this line number might vary if you are not using the same version of Hubot we specify in our *package.json*), we can install a custom middleware callback that will provide us with the raw body we can use when verifying the HMAC signature:

```
...
app.use (req, res, next) =>
  res.setHeader "X-Powered-By", "hubot/#{@name}"
  next()

app.use (req, res, next) =>
  req.rawBody = ''
  req.on 'data', (chunk) ->
    req.rawBody += chunk
  next()

app.use express.basicAuth user, pass if user and pass
app.use express.query()


...
```

Express middleware have a very simple interface: they are nothing more than a Java-Script function callback that receives a request, response, and continuation function passed as parameters. We register a listener when data content (the body) is propagated, and then add the body content to a variable on the request object. When the request object is passed in to our handler for pull requests within our Hubot, we have the raw data prefilled. The next() function is used to indicate to the middleware host that the next middleware can proceed.

We now need to adjust our tests to fit this new requirement. We prime the pump with a request object that has this rawBody inside it, and we should properly encode the content using encodeURIComponent to match the format in which it will be appearing from GitHub:

```
...
it "should allow calls with the secret and url", (done) ->
        payload =  '{ "pull_request" : { "html_url" : "http://pr/1" } }'
        bodyPayload = "payload=#{encodeURIComponent(payload)}"
        req = { rawBody: bodyPayload,
        headers: { "x-hub-signature" : \
                "sha1=dc827de09c5b57da3ee54dcfc8c5d09a3d3e6109" } }

        Handler.prHandler( robot, req, res )
        expect( robot.messageRoom ).toHaveBeenCalled()
        expect( httpSpy ).toHaveBeenCalled()
        expect( res.send ).toHaveBeenCalled()
        done()
...
```

Our implementation breaks our tests, so we will need to modify the cost to use the rawBody attribute on the request object, break it apart from the payload key/value pair, URI decode it, and then if all that works, parse the JSON and start the verification process. Our tests describe all this for us. The new prHandler method looks like this:

```
...
exports.prHandler = ( robot, req, res ) ->

        rawBody = req.rawBody
        body = rawBody.split( '=' ) if rawBody
        payloadData = body[1] if body and body.length == 2
        if payloadData
                decodedJson = decodeURIComponent payloadData
                pr = JSON.parse decodedJson

                if pr and pr.pull_request
                        url = pr.pull_request.html_url
                        secureHash = getSecureHash( rawBody )
                        signatureKey = "x-hub-signature"
                        if req?.headers
                                webhookProvidedHash =
                                        req.headers[ signatureKey ]
                        secureCompare = require 'secure-compare'
                        if url and secureCompare( "sha1=#{secureHash}",
                                webhookProvidedHash )
                                room = "general"
                                users = robot.brain.users()
                                sendPrRequest( robot, users, room, url )
                        else
                                console.log "Invalid secret or no URL specified"
                else
                        console.log "No pull request in here"
```

```
        res.send "OK\n"

    _GITHUB = undefined

    ...
```

When all is said and done, is verifying the signature even worth it? If we are not hosting our Hubot on a service that handles our router requests over HTTPS, this HMAC verification could be compromised. And, given the issues with maintaining our own copy of the Hubot code in order to permit the validation inside our Hubot extension, it might be best to ignore the validation header. The worst case, as our extension is written now, would be that an attacker could fake a pull request notification, and falsely engage chat room users around it. If the PR the attacker used was fake, it might confuse our Hubot, but no real harm would be done. If they used an existing real PR, an attacker could trick our Hubot into adding data to the PR, adding confusion in the comments about who accepted the review request. We won't solve that potential problem with this code, but you can imagine adding code to our Hubot that handles a case like this (for example, by checking first to see if someone was already tagged on the PR, and ignoring successive incoming webhooks associated with that PR).

Responding to the PR request

Our Hubot is now programmed to generate a pull request review message and send it to a random user. What happens when they respond? They can respond in two ways obviously: accepting the request or declining the request. We put placeholders in our Hubot extension to notify us with a debugging message when the user responds and send a message back to whoever sent us a message, but now we can actually wire up handling the response and adding to the pull request on GitHub based on the user we are interacting with (provided they accepted).

There are multiple ways in which a Hubot can interact with chat room messages. We chose the respond method, but there is another method called hear we could have used. respond is used when the message is preceded by the Hubot name, so only messages that look like probot: accept or @probot decline or / accept (if the Hubot name alias is enabled) will be processed by our Hubot. We could have used hear but in our case we are processing a simple response, and without a clear direction for the message, it would be difficult to always make sure we were interpreting the message in the correct context. respond makes more sense here.

If they decline the request, let's just graciously note that the offer was declined:

```
    ...
    exports.decline = ( res ) ->
            res.reply "No problem, we'll go through this PR in a bug scrub"

    ...
```

We are asking someone to accept a pull request, and there is a possible situation where two could come in within a very short period of time. For this reason, it probably makes sense for us to indicate the pull request identifier in the communication with the target user. And, users should be told to reply with a string like accept 112. The Hubot can then interpret this to mean they are accepting PR #112 and not the other pull request the Hubot invited John to respond to 10 seconds later.

If we do this, our Hubot does need to save the state of pull request invitations. Fortunately, there is an extremely easy way to do this using the "brain" of our Hubot. The brain is a persistent store, typically backed by Redis, into which you can keep any type of information. You simply reference the robot.brain and use methods like get or set to retrieve and store information. The set method takes any key and any value but note that the Hubot brain does not do much with your value if that value happens to be a complex object; if you want to properly serialize something beyond a flat value, you should probably call JSON.stringify on the object to maintain full control over the roundtrip storing and retrieval.

Let's modify our Hubot handler to deal with accepting or declining responses (and change our extension file to deal with this new interface). Of course, we will need to add to our tests. Finally, we will need to set up a way to provide the GitHub API key to our Hubot handler, so we'll add a method to do that that looks almost exactly like the one for setting our secret key.

We'll use a GitHub API NodeJs module called node-github, found on GitHub at *https://github.com/mikedeboer/node-github*. If we look at the API documentation, we see that it supports authentication using an OAuth token (using the git hub.authenticate({ 'type' : 'oauth': 'token' : '...' } syntax), and has methods we can use to add a comment to an issue or pull request associated with a repository (using the github.issues.createComment method).

Knowing that this module handles most of the work for us between these two methods, we can start by writing our tests. We'll create a new describe block called #response that groups our tests together. As we noted earlier, our Hubot can take affirmative and negative responses, so our tests should reflect these two code paths. Our setup block (the beforeEach section) in both cases should do the same thing for each response—make the pull request invitation to a random user: this all happens inside our prHandler code. We don't need to verify the expectations of this method since that got that covered by prior tests. After we get our handler to the right state, we need to test that the handler works correctly with an accept and decline method (they don't yet exist in our handler code so we'll add them next).

Our accept request handler triggers our Hubot to contact GitHub and add a comment to the pull request noting our targeted chat user accepted the request. The network connection to the GitHub API uses the GitHub API bindings from within the node-github module. We want to make this testable, so we should pass in the GitHub binding object inside our interface, and during the test, pass in a mocked object. If we review the documentation for the createComment in the GitHub API binding, we see it requires information about the repository such as the user or organization that owns the repository, the repository name, the issue number (pull requests are also referenced by issue numbers), and the comment itself. To get this information we simply need to decode it from the Hubot handler that receives the pull request information, and we will add code that does this (and is exposed in our handler for testing). We saw that a pull request comes in through a large JSON response, and we can use the URL we used earlier as the way we decode this information. So, we'll need to have two more tests inside our #response block, one for the decoding of the URL into a message object, and another to retrieve the username we insert into the comment stored in the pull request on the repository. We know what our test URL looks like since we saw it in our PR webhook message, but we don't yet have the structure of the chat message from which we can pull out our username, so our test will need to be adjusted when we know what it really looks like.

Declining the request means nothing happens. If we mock out our GitHub API binding, acceptance should log in (using the authenticate method) and then call create Comment. These are directly pulled from the GitHub API NodeJS documentation. Finally, we should record the result of this operation inside the chat room, which happens using the reply method on our response object:

```
...
describe "#response", ->
        createComment = jasmine.createSpy( 'createComment' ).and.
                callFake( ( msg, cb ) -> cb( false, "some data" ) )
        issues = { createComment: createComment }
        authenticate = jasmine.createSpy( 'ghAuthenticate' )
        responder = { reply: jasmine.createSpy( 'reply' ),
        send: jasmine.createSpy( 'send' ) }
        beforeEach ->
                githubBinding = { authenticate: authenticate, \
                                                 issues: issues }
                github = Handler.setApiToken( githubBinding, \
                                                  "ABCDEF" )
                req = { body: '{ "pull_request" : \
                        { url : "http://pr/1" } }', \
                        headers: { "HTTP_X_HUB_SIGNATURE" : \
                        "cd970490d83c01b678fa9af55f3c7854b5d22918" } }
                Handler.prHandler( robot, req, responder )

        it "should tag the PR on GitHub if the user accepts", (done) ->
                Handler.accept( responder )
                expect( authenticate ).toHaveBeenCalled()
                expect( createComment ).toHaveBeenCalled()
                expect( responder.reply ).toHaveBeenCalled()
                done()
```

```
it "should not tag the PR on GitHub if the user declines", \
    (done) ->
      Handler.decline( responder )
      expect( authenticate ).toHaveBeenCalled()
      expect( createComment ).not.toHaveBeenCalledWith()
      expect( responder.reply ).toHaveBeenCalled()
      done()

it "should decode the URL into a proper message object " + \
    "for the createMessage call", (done) ->
      url = "https://github.com/xrd/testing_repository/pull/1"
      msg = Handler.decodePullRequest( url )
      expect( msg.user ).toEqual( "xrd" )
      expect( msg.repository ).toEqual( "testing_repository" )
      expect( msg.number ).toEqual( "1" )
      done()

it "should get the username from the response object", (done) ->
      res = { username: { name: "Chris Dawson" } }
      expect( Handler.getUsernameFromResponse( res ) ).toEqual \
                                                "Chris Dawson"

      done()
```

Note that this code was indented to save space, but yours will be nested in several deeper levels of indentation. Refer to the sample repository for the exact code if there is confusion.

Our tests will fail if we run them now. So, let's write the code at the end of our delegator extension. We need code that parses the URL into the appropriate structured message object, code to put the reminder into the pull request comment on GitHub, and code that pulls the user out of the response object passed to us. The first two of these are within reach; basic JavaScript and reading the GitHub API binding documentation will get us to these two. The third one requires a little more investigation, so we will leave this as a placeholder for now.

To convert the URL into the object necessary for the createMessage call, we just need to split the message into pieces by the slash character, and then retrieve the correct items by index. We probably could add some additional tests that cover passing in empty strings, or other edge cases, but we'll leave it as an exercise to the reader. Our code does not crash in these cases, but it would be nice to have coverage of our expectations represented in our tests:

```
...
_GITHUB = undefined
_PR_URL = undefined

exports.decodePullRequest = (url) ->
    rv = {}
    if url
```

```
                    chunks = url.split "/"
                    if chunks.length == 7
                            rv.user = chunks[3]
                            rv.repository = chunks[4]
                            rv.number = chunks[6]
            rv

exports.getUsernameFromResponse = ( res ) ->
        "username"

exports.accept = ( res ) ->

        msg = exports.decodePullRequest( _PR_URL )
        username = exports.getUsernameFromResponse( res )
        msg.body = "@#{username} will review this (via Probot)."

        _GITHUB.issues.createComment msg, ( err, data ) ->
                unless err
                        res.reply "Thanks, I've noted that in a PR comment!"
                else
                        res.reply "Something went wrong, " + \
                                "I could not tag you on the PR comment."

exports.decline = ( res ) ->
        res.reply "OK, I'll find someone else."
        console.log "Declined!"

exports.setApiToken = (github, token) ->
        _API_TOKEN = token
        _GITHUB = github
        _GITHUB.authenticate type: "oauth", token: token

exports.setSecret = (secret) ->
        _SECRET = secret
```

To summarize, we added an internal variable called _GITHUB where we will store a reference to our instantiation of the GitHub API binding. Our interface to the setApiToken call passes in the instantiation; this method takes our OAuth token and the binding because using an interface like this means we can pass in a mocked binding inside our tests. When we are not running inside a test, this method call authenticates against the GitHub API, readying the API binding to make connections to the GitHub API itself.

Our top-level extension script looks like this now:

```
handler = require '../lib/handler'

handler.setSecret "XYZABC"
github = require 'node-github'
handler.setApiToken github, "12345ABCDEF"

module.exports = (robot) ->
```

```
robot.respond /accept/i, ( res ) ->
        handler.accept( res )

robot.respond /decline/i, ( res ) ->
        handler.decline( res )

robot.router.post '/pr', ( req, res ) ->
        handler.prHandler( robot, req, res )
```

If you were to look only at this code, the interface is clean, and the bulk of the work is handled by our very testable handler.

Peering into the response object

We need to get the username, and it stands to reason that the object passed to us when we get a respond callback might have it in there. The respond method provided by the Hubot API is documented mostly by way of the example scripts that come with Hubot. There is very little information on what the parameter passed to your callback looks like. Let's use the util library to inspect the data and print it to the console. We abbreviate the full output here, and show you that it contains information on the user who sent the message to our Hubot. We can access this information by using response.message.user.name if, for example, we wanted to retrieve the name of the user:

```
{ robot:
  { name: 'probot',
    brain:
      { data: [Object],
  ...
  message:
  { user:
      { id: '...',
        name: 'xrd',
        real_name: 'Chris Dawson',
        email: 'chrisdawson@example.com'
    ...
    text: 'probot accept',
    rawText: 'accept',
    rawMessage:
      { _client: [Object],
  ...
  match: [ 'probot accept', index: 0, input: 'probot accept' ],
  ...
}
```

Inside it all we can find information we need, specifically the username and email. So, let's update our test and our handler code. The last test in our spec file can be modified to look like this:

```
    ...
    it "should get the username from the response object", (done) ->
        res = { message: { user: { name: "Chris Dawson" } } }
        expect( Handler.getUsernameFromResponse( res ) ).toEqual "Chris Dawson"
        done()

    ...
```

And, our handler code defining getUsernameFromResponse simply turns into this:

```
    ...
    exports.getUsernameFromResponse = ( res ) ->
        res.message.user.name

    ...
```

With this information in hand, we can properly comment on the pull request. Well, almost.

Unifying usernames via the Collaborators API

If the Slack username for the person who accepted the pull request is an exact match with their GitHub username, then we can assume they are the same person in real life and create a comment inside the pull request reminding them (and anyone else) that they will be reviewing the PR. We can use the collaborator subsection of the Repository API to look up their name on GitHub.

If we don't find them inside the list of users and there is not an exact match with their Slack name then we have at least one problem, maybe two. First, we could just have a mismatch in their identities (their usernames are different on each site). If this is the case, we could ask them to clarify this inside the Slack room. We do have another case: the user is not a collaborator on the repository hosted on GitHub. If this is the case, clarifying their username is not going to help. The Repository API does support adding a user to the list of collaborators so we could do that here, but this arguably is a moment where a larger discussion should happen (write access to a repository is a big resposibility in a way that being inside a chat room is not). Adding a user as a repository collaborator should not be automated inside a chat room. Because of the complexity here, we will write code to unify a username inside the chat room, but we won't handle the case where there is no clarification to be made because they are not in the repository collaborator list.

Using the GitHub API binding we passed into our setApiToken call we will verify the user exists as a collaborator on the repository. The API binding provides a method called getCollaborator inside the repos namespace we can use to verify that a username is on the list of collaborators. It takes as the first parameter a message that is used to specify the repository and owner, and then an attribute called collabuser, which is the name you want to ensure is a collaborator. The second parameter to the function is a callback that is executed once the request has completed. If the callback returns without an error code, then our Hubot should tag the pull request with a comment confirming and message the room.

Our new test reflects usage of the `repos.getCollaborator` call. In our test setup block we mock out the call to `getCollaborator` and use Jasmine to "spy on" it so we can assure it was called later in our actual test. Our setup is more beefy than before, but we are following the same patterns of generating spies to watch methods, and implementing our fake callbacks when necessary. We can also move our message inside the response object into the one created in our setup block so that we can use it inside all of our subtests, rather than creating a new object for each test inside the test body:

```
...
send: jasmine.createSpy( 'send' ),
message: { user: { name: "Chris Dawson" } } }
getCollaborator = jasmine.createSpy( 'getCollaborator' ).and.
        callFake( ( msg, cb ) -> cb( false, true ) )
repos = { getCollaborator: getCollaborator }

...

it "should tag the PR on GitHub if the user accepts", (done) ->
        Handler.accept( robot, responder )
        expect( authenticate ).toHaveBeenCalled()
        expect( createComment ).toHaveBeenCalled()
        expect( responder.reply ).toHaveBeenCalled()
        expect( repos.getCollaborator ).toHaveBeenCalled()
        done()
```

Our handler can then implement the **accept** and **decline** methods in full:

```
...
exports.accept = ( robot, res ) ->

        prNumber = res.match[1]
        url = robot.brain.get( prNumber )

        msg = exports.decodePullRequest( url )
        username = exports.getUsernameFromResponse( res )
        msg.collabuser = username

        _GITHUB.repos.getCollaborator msg, ( err, collaborator ) ->
                msg.body = "@#{username} will review this (via Probot)."

                _GITHUB.issues.createComment msg, ( err, data ) ->
                        unless err
                                res.reply "Thanks, I've noted that " + \
                                        "in a PR comment. " + \
                                        "Review the PR here: #{url}"
                        else
                                res.reply "Something went wrong."  + \
```

```
                                            "I could not tag you " + \
                                            "on the PR comment: " +
                    "#{require('util').inspect( err )}"

    exports.decline = ( res ) ->
            res.reply "No problem, we'll go through this PR in a bug scrub"
    ...
```

We now have a full implementation of both the accept and decline methods inside our Hubot.

Sanitizing our source code

It is typically bad form to save passwords (or other access credentials, like OAuth tokens or secrets) inside of source code. Right now we have hardcoded them into our application inside of the *pr-delegator.coffee* file. We could instead retrieve them from the environment of the running process:

```
    ...
    handler.setSecret process.env.PROBOT_SECRET
    github = require 'github'
    ginst = new github version: '3.0.0'
    handler.setApiToken ginst, process.env.PROBOT_API_TOKEN
    ...
```

When we launch our Hubot from the command line, we will need to use a command like this as we are testing locally from our laptop:

```
$ PROBOT_SECRET=XYZABC \
PROBOT_API_TOKEN=926a701550d4dfae93250dbdc068cce887531 \
HUBOT_SLACK_TOKEN=xoxb-3295776784-nZxl1H3nyLsVcgdD29r1PZCq \
./bin/hubot -a slack
```

When we publish into Heroku, we will want to set these as environment variables using the appropriate Heroku commands:

```
$ heroku config:set PROBOT_API_TOKEN=926a701550d4dfae93250dbdc068cce887531
Adding config vars and restarting myapp... done, v12
PROBOT_API_TOKEN=926a701550d4dfae93250dbdc068cce887531

$ heroku config:set PROBOT_SECRET=XYZABC
Adding config vars and restarting myapp... done, v12
PROBOT_SECRET=XYZABC
```

Don't forget that when we run our tests, we will need to specify the environment variables on the command line as well:

```
$ PROBOT_SECRET=XYZABC \
PROBOT_API_TOKEN=926a701550d4dfae93250dbdc068cce887531 \
node_modules/jasmine-node/bin/jasmine-node --coffee \
spec/pr-delegator.spec.coffee
```

Summary

Our Hubot is alive! We went through building a robot that can interact with us inside a chat room, then refactored the robot so that its functionality is contained into a highly testable module. Along the way, we got intimate with the Hubot API, and even discussed how to modify (and the drawbacks surrounding) modifying the source code to Hubot itself. Finally, we demonstrated how to use the Activity API receiving (and faking data) coming from a GitHub webhook.

In the next chapter we will look at building a single-page application that edits information inside a GitHub repository using JavaScript and the GitHub.js library talking to the Pull Request API.

CHAPTER 9

JavaScript and the Git Data API

Applications utilizing the GitHub API will typically reside inside a server. You are not limited, however, to accessing the API from within server-side programming languages exclusively. The GitHub API works perfectly well from within a web browser context as well, and the UI to your application comes for free if you know a little HTML. In this chapter we discuss how to use the unofficial JavaScript client library to access the GitHub API and build a single-page application (SPA), which we host entirely on GitHub.

The main weakness of JavaScript has always been testability. Mainly due to the asynchronous nature of JavaScript, writing tests has never been easy; polling for changes when a callback returns was until recently the best way to test nonlinear code. But recent toolkits like AngularJS and promise-based libraries have made testing not only easy, but elegant as well. Building applications on top of third-party services makes testing even more important than it already was, and we'll make sure to add testing to our application to verify the functionality works as we expect.

JavaScript should be generally accessible to most people who know other imperative programming languages. There is one feature, however, that can be challenging: the callback function. In JavaScript, functions are first-class objects, meaning they can be passed as arguments to other functions and stored as the value of a variable. You will find callbacks everywhere in JavaScript programming. Callbacks make debugging and understanding JavaScript code more challenging at times. As we stated earlier, writing code that includes tests makes understanding the entire picture easier, and we will do that in this chapter to further explain sections where necessary function callbacks may initially look confusing.

Building a Coffee Shop Database on GitHub

Like many software developers, I suffer from an almost disturbing obsession with coffee. Perhaps it is really my family that suffers: when we travel to a new city, I drag my wife and children through questionable neighborhoods just to find the perfect brew and complementary gluten-free desserts.

Google Maps is a great help on these quests, in that it will find me a coffee shop and reviews, but the granularity of information about that coffee shop is often poor and limited in scope. Do they offer rice milk as a dairy-free alternative? What special details should I know when considering a place? Many guidance and mapping applications exist, but if they don't fit my own personalized informational niche, I might miss a unique experience. With such a pressing and dire problem in front of us, let's use the GitHub API to solve it.

We'll build a coffee shop single-page web app that allows anyone to add information on coffee shops, information that is flexible and dynamic, and search and filter through that information about a coffee shop. All files, such as the HTML, images, and JavaScript will be hosted on GitHub. And we'll be using the GitHub API to allow contributors to add data to our database, a database we will also host on GitHub. And as GitHub developers write code with tests, we will write tests to validate our Java-Script code as well as the expectations we have of the GitHub API.

More specifically, we'll use these technologies:

- An (unofficial) GitHub API JavaScript library (*https://github.com/michael/github*)
- AngularJS (*http://angularjs.org*), a "superpowered framework" for writing JS applications that are testable
- Bootstrap (*http://getbootstrap.com*), a CSS library that simplifies building beautiful webapps

You don't need to know these technologies in advance of working on this chapter.

Set Up

To create our app, let's first create our main web page and push it into our repository:

```
$ mkdir coffeete.ch
$ cd coffeete.ch
$ git init
$ git checkout -b gh-pages
$ printf "<html>\n<body>Hello from CoffeeTe.ch</body>\n</html>\n" > index.html
$ git commit -m "Add starting point index.html" -a
$ git config push.default gh-pages
```

Notice that we created a new repository, and then created and entered the gh-pages branch. We'll do all our work there. And by using the git config command, we specified that we want the default push branch to be gh-pages. This allows us to use git push to push our branch up instead of the longer git push origin gh-pages.

Mapping Hostnames

Once we publish these files into GitHub inside a repository we can connect the repository to a real hostname. There are two steps to take to do this:

- Add a CNAME file that tells GitHub under which server name this service should resolve.
- Set up DNS records so that the hostname maps to the correct IP address at Git-Hub.

Imagine you have the hostname *myspecialhostname.com*. If you map this repository to a subdomain called *coffeetech*, then you would do something like this:

```
$ echo 'coffeetech.myspecialhostname.com' > CNAME
$ git commit -m "Added CNAME mapping" -a
$ git push
```

Remember that you need to wait about 10 minutes before GitHub regenerates its database to establish the connection between your gh-pages site and the mapping on their frontend servers. This is only the first time you connect a repository to a hostname; you will see subsequent changes almost instantaneously.

 Generally it takes several hours to even a few days to propagate DNS settings out into the wild, so make sure you choose and set up a hostname far in advance if your site has to be live by a certain point.

Now we can install the libraries needed for this application.

Adding the Support Libraries

As we mentioned, we will use the GitHub.js library, AngularJS, and Bootstrap. Let's add those to our project now. Using whatever editor you prefer, edit the *index.html* file to look like this:

```
<html>
<head>
<title>CoffeeTe.ch</title>
<meta name="viewport" content="width=device-width, initial-scale=1.0"> ❶
<link rel="stylesheet" type="text/css" href="bootstrap.min.css"></link>
</head>
```

```
<body ng-app> ❷
<div class="container">
{{'Welcome to Coffeete.ch'}} ❸
</div>
<script src="angular.js"></script>
<script src="github.js"></script>
</body>
</html>
```

I am assuming you have a firm grasp on most HTML concepts, but a few of the advanced topics are included here:

❶ The meta tag makes our page work well with mobile browsers and enables the responsive features of Bootstrap.

❷ The ng-app attribute in the body tag tells AngularJS to initialize and compile our page from the body tag downward.

❸ The {{ }} (double brackets) are an AngularJS two-way data binding directive. You'll see two-way data binding in action very soon if it is not already familiar. Adding this code here sanity checks whether AngularJS is working for us; if we see "Welcome to Coffeete.ch" without the braces then we know AngularJS is loading and working properly. If we see the braces, then there is some error in our setup to resolve. Two-way data binding solves a significant pain point when building JS apps: marshalling data back and forth between network events, into HTML and out of HTML forms. AngularJS does all this heavy lifting for you. In a moment we'll show how to use two-way data binding as it was intended by defining a variable on the AngularJS scope. We then access the variable using the same {{ }} data binding directives.

Then, download the necessary files locally using these commands. We include AngularJS, GitHub.js, and Bootstrap CSS:

```
$ wget https://ajax.googleapis.com/ajax/libs/angularjs/1.2.10/angular.js
$ wget https://maxcdn.bootstrapcdn.com/bootstrap/3.3.5/css/bootstrap.min.css
$ wget https://github.com/michael/github/raw/master/github.js
```

Now we are ready to use the GitHub library inside our SPA.

An AngularJS Application Using GitHub.js

Now let's implement a *coffeetech.js* file, which is where we will build our single-page application functionality. Create a new file called *coffeetech.js* in the root of your repository:

```
var mod = angular.module( 'coffeetech', [] ) ❶
mod.controller( 'GithubCtrl', function( $scope ) { ❷
    var github = new Github({} ); ❸
```

```
    var repo = github.getRepo( "gollum", "gollum" ); ➍
    repo.show( function(err, repo) { ➎
      $scope.repo = repo;
      $scope.$apply(); ➏
    });
  })
```

➊ Define a module named "coffeetech." Save a reference to the module we will use next in defining a controller, a smaller bundle of functions. Modules are an AngularJS feature for grouping related functionality, and we will keep all our code for this application inside this module.

➋ We define a controller called GithubCtrl that bundles up functions and data. When we use the controller syntax, we name the controller, and then define a function with at least a single parameter: the scope object. I think of scope as the "world" available to the controller. The controller knows only of data and functions defined on its scope, and AngularJS does its magic as long as your functions or variables are defined on the scope.

➌ We create a new Github() object using the constructor. This constructor can take user credentials, but for now, we can just create it without those since we are accessing a public repository.

➍ Once we have our github object, we call the method getRepo() with an owner and a name. This returns our repository object.

➎ To actually load the data for this repository object, we call the show method and pass it a callback that uses the two parameters err and repo to handle errors or otherwise provide us with details of the repository specified. In this case we are using the Gollum wiki public repository to display some sample data.

➏ Once we have loaded the repository data, we need to call $apply to tell AngularJS a change has occurred to data stored within the scope variable. As we mentioned before, AngularJS knows only about functions and data defined on its scope. The show function is defined on the GitHub object, and any changes are not tracked by AngularJS, so we need to use $apply().

GitHub.js handles making the proper request to GitHub for us, and AngularJS handles putting the results into our web page. To modify our HTML to use this data, we change *index.html* to look like the following:

```
<html>
<head>
<title>CoffeeTe.ch</title>
<meta name="viewport" content="width=device-width, initial-scale=1.0">
<link rel="stylesheet" type="text/css" href="bootstrap.min.css"></link>
```

```
    </head>
    <body ng-app="coffeetech"> ❶
    <div class="container" ng-controller="GithubCtrl">
    {{ repo }} ❷
    </div>
    <script src="angular.js"></script>
    <script src="github.js"></script>
    <script src="coffeetech.js"></script> ❸
    </body>
    </html>
```

❶ Change the `ng-app` reference to use the module we defined in our *coffeetech.js* file.

❷ Remove our data binding to the `Welcome to CoffeeTech` string and replace it with a binding to the variable `repo` (by default AngularJS will filter complex objects and convert them to JSON).

❸ Add a reference to our *coffeetech.js* file beneath our other JS references.

If you load this up in your browser, you will see something like Figure 9-1.

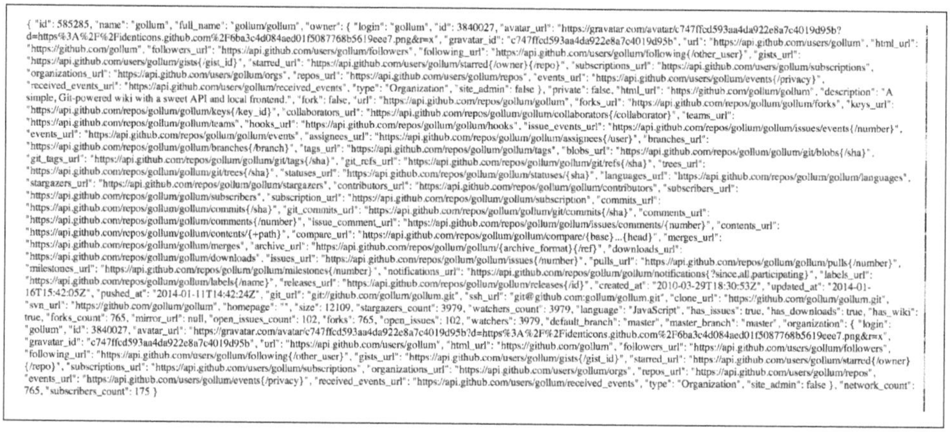

{ "id": 585285, "name": "gollum", "full_name": "gollum/gollum", "owner": { "login": "gollum", "id": 3840027, "avatar_url": "https://gravatar.com/avatar/c747ffcd593aa4da922e8a7c4019d95b?d=https%3A%2F%2Fidenticons.github.com%2F6ba3c4d084aed01f5087768b5619eee7.png&r=x", "gravatar_id": "c747ffcd593aa4da922e8a7c4019d95b", "url": "https://api.github.com/users/gollum", "html_url": "https://github.com/gollum", "followers_url": "https://api.github.com/users/gollum/followers", "following_url": "https://api.github.com/users/gollum/following{/other_user}", "gists_url": "https://api.github.com/users/gollum/gists{/gist_id}", "starred_url": "https://api.github.com/users/gollum/starred{/owner}{/repo}", "subscriptions_url": "https://api.github.com/users/gollum/subscriptions", "organizations_url": "https://api.github.com/users/gollum/orgs", "repos_url": "https://api.github.com/users/gollum/repos", "events_url": "https://api.github.com/users/gollum/events{/privacy}", "received_events_url": "https://api.github.com/users/gollum/received_events", "type": "Organization", "site_admin": false }, "private": false, "html_url": "https://github.com/gollum/gollum", "description": "A simple, Git-powered wiki with a sweet API and local frontend.", "fork": false, "url": "https://api.github.com/repos/gollum/gollum", "forks_url": "https://api.github.com/repos/gollum/gollum/forks", "keys_url": "https://api.github.com/repos/gollum/gollum/keys{/key_id}", "collaborators_url": "https://api.github.com/repos/gollum/gollum/collaborators{/collaborator}", "teams_url": "https://api.github.com/repos/gollum/gollum/teams", "hooks_url": "https://api.github.com/repos/gollum/gollum/hooks", "issue_events_url": "https://api.github.com/repos/gollum/gollum/issues/events{/number}", "events_url": "https://api.github.com/repos/gollum/gollum/events", "assignees_url": "https://api.github.com/repos/gollum/gollum/assignees{/user}", "branches_url": "https://api.github.com/repos/gollum/gollum/branches{/branch}", "tags_url": "https://api.github.com/repos/gollum/gollum/tags", "blobs_url": "https://api.github.com/repos/gollum/gollum/git/blobs{/sha}", "git_tags_url": "https://api.github.com/repos/gollum/gollum/git/tags{/sha}", "git_refs_url": "https://api.github.com/repos/gollum/gollum/git/refs{/sha}", "trees_url": "https://api.github.com/repos/gollum/gollum/git/trees{/sha}", "statuses_url": "https://api.github.com/repos/gollum/gollum/statuses{/sha}", "languages_url": "https://api.github.com/repos/gollum/gollum/languages", "stargazers_url": "https://api.github.com/repos/gollum/gollum/stargazers", "contributors_url": "https://api.github.com/repos/gollum/gollum/contributors", "subscribers_url": "https://api.github.com/repos/gollum/gollum/subscribers", "subscription_url": "https://api.github.com/repos/gollum/gollum/subscription", "commits_url": "https://api.github.com/repos/gollum/gollum/commits{/sha}", "git_commits_url": "https://api.github.com/repos/gollum/gollum/git/commits{/sha}", "comments_url": "https://api.github.com/repos/gollum/gollum/comments{/number}", "issue_comment_url": "https://api.github.com/repos/gollum/gollum/issues/comments{/number}", "contents_url": "https://api.github.com/repos/gollum/gollum/contents/{+path}", "compare_url": "https://api.github.com/repos/gollum/gollum/compare/{base}...{head}", "merges_url": "https://api.github.com/repos/gollum/gollum/merges", "archive_url": "https://api.github.com/repos/gollum/gollum/{archive_format}{/ref}", "downloads_url": "https://api.github.com/repos/gollum/gollum/downloads", "issues_url": "https://api.github.com/repos/gollum/gollum/issues{/number}", "pulls_url": "https://api.github.com/repos/gollum/gollum/pulls{/number}", "milestones_url": "https://api.github.com/repos/gollum/gollum/milestones{/number}", "notifications_url": "https://api.github.com/repos/gollum/gollum/notifications{?since,all,participating}", "labels_url": "https://api.github.com/repos/gollum/gollum/labels{/name}", "releases_url": "https://api.github.com/repos/gollum/gollum/releases{/id}", "created_at": "2010-03-29T18:30:53Z", "updated_at": "2014-01-16T15:42:05Z", "pushed_at": "2014-01-11T14:42:24Z", "git_url": "git://github.com/gollum/gollum.git", "ssh_url": "git@github.com:gollum/gollum.git", "clone_url": "https://github.com/gollum/gollum.git", "svn_url": "https://github.com/gollum/gollum", "homepage": "", "size": 12109, "stargazers_count": 3979, "watchers_count": 3979, "language": "JavaScript", "has_issues": true, "has_downloads": true, "has_wiki": true, "forks_count": 765, "mirror_url": null, "open_issues_count": 102, "forks": 765, "open_issues": 102, "watchers": 3979, "default_branch": "master", "master_branch": "master", "organization": { "login": "gollum", "id": 3840027, "avatar_url": "https://gravatar.com/avatar/c747ffcd593aa4da922e8a7c4019d95b?d=https%3A%2F%2Fidenticons.github.com%2F6ba3c4d084aed01f5087768b5619eee7.png&r=x", "gravatar_id": "c747ffcd593aa4da922e8a7c4019d95b", "url": "https://api.github.com/users/gollum", "html_url": "https://github.com/gollum", "followers_url": "https://api.github.com/users/gollum/followers", "following_url": "https://api.github.com/users/gollum/following{/other_user}", "gists_url": "https://api.github.com/users/gollum/gists{/gist_id}", "starred_url": "https://api.github.com/users/gollum/starred{/owner}{/repo}", "subscriptions_url": "https://api.github.com/users/gollum/subscriptions", "organizations_url": "https://api.github.com/users/gollum/orgs", "repos_url": "https://api.github.com/users/gollum/repos", "events_url": "https://api.github.com/users/gollum/events{/privacy}", "received_events_url": "https://api.github.com/users/gollum/received_events", "type": "Organization", "site_admin": false }, "network_count": 765, "subscribers_count": 175 }

Figure 9-1. The whole messy JSON

That is a lot of data. AngularJS's JSON filter pretty-printed it for us, but this is a bit too much. Let's change the HTML to reduce some noise:

```
    <html>
    <head>
    <title>CoffeeTe.ch</title>
    <meta name="viewport" content="width=device-width, initial-scale=1.0">
    <link rel="stylesheet" type="text/css" href="bootstrap.min.css"></link>
    </head>
    <body ng-app="coffeetech">
    <div class="container" ng-controller="GithubCtrl">
```

```
<div>Subscriber count: {{ repo.subscribers_count }}</div>
<div>Network count: {{ repo.network_count }}</div>
</div>
<script
src="angular.js"></script>
<script src="github.js"></script>
<script src="coffeetech.js"></script>
</body>
</html>
```

We can filter this information by modifying the HTML to show just a few vital pieces of information from the repository JSON. Let's display the `subscriber_count` and the `network_count`. Now we see something more palatable (Figure 9-2).

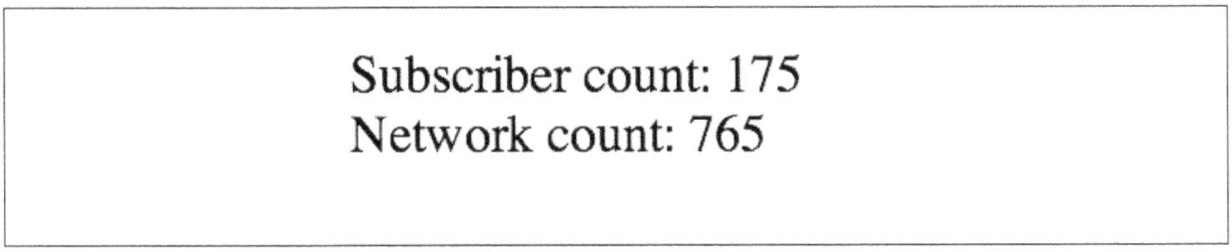

Subscriber count: 175
Network count: 765

Figure 9-2. Pulling out what we want

We've just extracted the subscriber and network count from the Gollum repository hosted on GitHub using the GitHub API and placed it into our single-page app.

Visualize Application Data Structure

We are going to be building a coffee shop database. We want to use Git as our data-store, but Git and its associated tools (either command-line tools or GitHub) don't offer the same features as a standard relational database. So, we need to think and plan how we will structure our data inside our repository to make it easily searchable.

This application allows us to search coffee shops. These coffee shops will be, for the most part, in larger cities. If we keep all the data stored as JSON files named after the city, we can keep data located in a file named after the city, and then either use geolocation on the client side to retrieve a set of the data, or ask the user to choose their city manually.

If we look at the GitHub.js JavaScript documentation on GitHub (*https://github.com/ michael/github*) we can see that there are some options for us to pull content from a repository. We'll store a data file in JSON named after the city inside our repository and retrieve this from that repository. It looks like the calls we need to use are `git hub.getRepo( username, reponame )`, and once we have retrieved the repository, `repo.contents( branch, path, callback )`.

Now that we have a barebones application let's pause and make sure we are building something we can refactor and maintain long term. This means adding tests to our project.

Making Our App Testable

Testing not only builds better code by making us think clearly about how our code will be used from the outside, but makes it easier for an outsider (meaning other team members) to use our code. Testing facilitates "social coding."

We'll use a JavaScript testing tool called "Karma." Karma simplifies writing JavaScript unit tests. We need to first install the tool, then write a test or two. Karma can easily be installed using npm (installation of which is documented in Appendix B):

```
$ npm install karma -g
$ wget https://ajax.googleapis.com/ajax/libs/angularjs/1.2.7/angular-mocks.js
```

The *angular-mocks.js* file makes it easy to mock out Angular dependencies in our tests.

Then, create a file called *karma.config.js* and enter the following contents:

```
module.exports = function(config) {
  config.set({
    basePath: '',
    frameworks: ['jasmine'],
    files: [ ❶
        'angular.js',
        'fixtures-*.js',
        'angular-mocks.js',
        'firebase-mock.js',
        'github.js',
        '*.js'
    ],
    reporters: ['progress'],
    port: 9876,
    colors: true,
    logLevel: config.LOG_INFO,
    autoWatch: true,
    browsers: ['Chrome'], ❷
    captureTimeout: 60000,
    singleRun: false
  });
};
```

This is more or less a default Karma configuration file.

❶ The files section specifying the load order of our JavaScript implementations and the test scripts. You can see a few of the files we've added specified directly and wildcards to cover the remaining files.

❷ Note also that we've specified Chrome as our test browser (so you should have it installed), which is a safe bet because it works on just about any desktop platform you might be running. Know that you can always choose Safari or Firefox if you want Karma to test inside those as well. Karma will start a new instance of each browser specified and run your tests inside a test harness in those browsers.

To write the test, let's clarify what we want our code to do:

- When a user first visits the application, we should use the geolocation features of their browser to determine their location.
- Pull a file from our repository that contains general latitude and longitude locations of different cities.
- Iterate over the list of cities and see if we are within 25 miles of any of the cities. If so, set the current city to the first match.
- If we found a city, load the JSON data file from GitHub.

Concretely, let's assert that we load the list of cities and have two of them, then we load a matching city named "Portland," a city that has three shops available.

We'll use an ng-init directive, which is the mechanism to tell AngularJS we want to call the function specified when the controller has finished loading. We'll call this function init so let's test it.

First, we will write the setup code for an AngularJS test written using the Jasmine test framework. Jasmine is a "behavior-driven JavaScript" library that provides functions to group and create expectation-based tests. Within the Jasmine framework are "matchers" that allow for the most common assertions (comparing a variety of expected types to the resultant types from function calls) and the ability to define your own custom matchers. Jasmine also gives you the ability to "spy" on functions, which is another way of saying Jasmine can intercept function calls to validate that those calls were made in the way you anticipate. It is easiest to explain the power of Jasmine by showing the elegance of the tests themselves, so let's do that now:

```
describe( "GithubCtrl", function() {
    var scope = undefined; ❶
    var ctrl = undefined;
    var gh  = undefined;
    var repo = undefined;
    var geo = undefined;

    beforeEach( module( "coffeetech" ) ); ❷

    beforeEach( inject( function ($controller, $rootScope ) { ❸
            generateMockGeolocationSupport(); ❹
            generateMockRepositorySupport();
            scope = $rootScope.$new(); ❺
```

```
        ctrl = $controller( "GithubCtrl",
      { $scope: scope, Github: gh, Geo: geo } ); ❻
      } )
    );
    ...
```

❶ We declare our variables at the top of the function. If we did not do this, Java-
    Script would silently define them inside the functions the first time the variable is
    used. Then our variables would be different inside our setup code and the actual
    tests.

❷ We load our `coffeetech` module into our tests using the `module` method inside a
    `beforeEach` call, code that is executed before our tests run.

❸ `inject` is the AngularJS way to provide our before functions with the
    `$controller` and `$rootScope` objects, which we use to set up our tests.

❹ We will be creating two functions that generate the mock objects required for our
    tests. We'll discuss these two functions in a bit.

❺ `scope` is the AngularJS convention for the object into which all functionality and
    state is stored. We create a new `scope` using the AngularJS utility function `$root`
    `Scope.$new()` and store a reference to this `scope` so we can test functionality
    we've implemented in our actual code.

❻ We pass in the mocked objects (created by the mocked function calls) as well as
    the `scope` object and instantiate a controller object. This controller uses the
    `scope` to define functions and data, and since we have a reference to it, we can
    call those functions and inspect that data and assert our implementation is cor-
    rect.

Now, let's write an actual test:

```
describe( "#init", function() { ❶
    it( "should initialize, grabbing current city", function() { ❷
        scope.init(); ❸
        expect( geo.getCurrentPosition ).toHaveBeenCalled(); ❹
        expect( gh.getRepo ).toHaveBeenCalled();
        expect( repo.read ).toHaveBeenCalled();
        expect( scope.cities.length ).toEqual( 2 ); ❺
        expect( scope.city.name ).toEqual( "portland" );
        expect( scope.shops.length ).toEqual( 3 );
    });
  });
});
```

❶ Describe functions are used to group tests defined inside it functions. Since we are testing the init function, it seems logical to use an identifier called #init.

❷ describe blocks group tests while it blocks actually specify code that is run as a test.

❸ Our controller code begins with an init call, so we mimic that inside our test to set up the controller state.

❹ We assert that our code uses the various interfaces we defined on our injected objects: getCurrentPosition on the geo object, and read on the repository object.

❺ Then we assert that the data is properly loaded. Our test verifies that there are two cities, that a default city has been loaded and the name of the default city is equal to the string "portland". In addition, the test verifies there are three shops loaded for the default city. Behind the scenes in our implementation we will load these via JSON, but all we care about is that the interface and data matches our expectations.

This syntax initially can look confusing if you have never written Jasmine tests for JavaScript, but it actually solves a lot of problems in an elegant way. Most importantly, Jasmine provides a spyOn function that will intercept a call to it, and then allow you to assert that it was called. Any place in our tests you see toHaveBeenCalled() is an assertion that spyOn provides to us proving that a call was made.

Now we can implement the two mocking functions vital for the test. Put them in between the beforeEach(module("coffeetech")) line and the beforeEach(inject(...)) functions to provide proper visibility to Karma:

```
...
beforeEach( module( "coffeetech" ) );

function generateMockGeolocationSupport( lat, lng ) { ❶
    response = ( lat && lng ) ?
        { coords: { lat: lat, lng: lng } } :
   { coords: CITIES[0] };
    geo = { getCurrentPosition: function( success, failure ) { ❷
        success( response );
    } };
    spyOn( geo, "getCurrentPosition" ).andCallThrough(); ❸
}

function generateMockRepositorySupport() { ❹
    repo = { read: function( branch, filename, cb ) { ❺
        cb( undefined,
       JSON.stringify( filename == "cities.json" ?
```

```
                    CITIES : PORTLAND ) );
        } };
        spyOn( repo, "read" ).andCallThrough();

        gh = new Github({});
        spyOn( gh, "getRepo" ).andCallFake( function() { ❻
            return repo;
        } );
    }

    beforeEach( inject( function ($controller, $rootScope ) {
    ...
```

❶ We first implement the generateMockLocation function.

❷ Mock location involves creating a geo object that has a single function getCurrentPosition, which is a function that calls back into a success callback function provided. This exactly matches the native browser support for Geolocation, which has the same function defined.

❸ We then spyOn the function so we can assert that it was called in our actual tests.

❹ Next, we implement generateMockRepositorySupport.

❺ Again, we implement a mock object: this one to provide a method called read. This function matches the function of the same name contained in the API provided by the JavaScript GitHub.js library. Just like in the previous mock, we spyOn the function so we can validate it was called. However, this is not the "top-level" repository object—this is the object returned from the call to getRepo. We will take this mock object and return it from the getRepo call.

❻ We spy on the getRepo call, and then return our next mock object, the repository object. This object is used to retrieve the actual information using the read call.

Now that we have a set of tests, run the test suite from the command line and watch them fail:

```
$ karma start karma.conf.js
Chrome 32.0.1700 (Mac OS X 10.9.1) GithubCtrl #init should initialize,
        grabbing current city FAILED
  Error: [$injector:modulerr] Failed to instantiate module...:
  Error: [$injector:nomod] Module 'coffeetech' is not available!
    You either misspelled the module name or forgot to load it.
    If registering a module ensure that you specify the
    dependencies as the second argument.
  ...
```

We now need to provide some test fixtures.

Test Data

We need to build our support fixtures, data files that have test data. Add the *fixtures-cities.js* file into the same directory as your other code:

```
var CITIES = [{
    name: "portland",
    latitude: 45,
    longitude: 45
}, {
    name: "seattle",
    latitude: 47.662613,
    longitude: -122.323837
}]
```

And the *fixtures-portland.js* file:

```
var PORTLAND = [{
    "name": "Very Good Coffee Shop",
    "latitude": 45.52292,
    "longitude": -122.643074
}, {
    "name": "Very Bad Coffee Shop",
    "latitude": 45.522181,
    "longitude": -122.63709
}, {
    "name": "Mediocre Coffee Shop",
    "latitude": 45.520437,
    "longitude": -122.67846
}]
```

CoffeeTech.js

Then, add the *coffeetech.js* file. We'll focus just on the setup code and the changes to the init function for now:

```
var mod = angular.module( 'coffeetech', [] );

mod.factory( 'Github', function() {  // ❶
    return new Github({});
});

mod.factory( 'Geo', [ '$window', function( $window ) {  // ❷
    return $window.navigator.geolocation;
} ] );

mod.factory( 'Prompt', [ '$window', function( $window ) {
    return $window.prompt;
} ] );

mod.controller( 'GithubCtrl', [ '$scope', 'Github', 'Geo', 'Prompt',  // ❸
        function( $scope, ghs, Geo, Prompt ) {
```

```
$scope.messages = []

$scope.init = function() { // ❹
    $scope.getCurrentLocation( function( position ) {
        $scope.latitude = position.coords.latitude;
        $scope.longitude = position.coords.longitude;
        $scope.repo = ghs.getRepo( "xrd", "spa.coffeete.ch" );  // ❺
        $scope.repo.read( "gh-pages", "cities.json",
          function(err, data) {  // ❻
            $scope.cities = JSON.parse( data );  // ❼
            // Determine our current city
            $scope.detectCurrentCity();  // ❽

            // If we have a city, get it
            if( $scope.city ) {
                $scope.retrieveCity();
            }

            $scope.$apply(); // ❾
        });
    });
...
```

❶ We extract the GitHub library into an AngularJS factory. This allows us to inject our mocked GitHub object inside our tests; if we had placed the GitHub instance-creation code inside our controller, we would not have been able to easily mock it out in our tests.

❷ We extract the geolocation support into an AngularJS factory. As we did with the GitHub library mock, we can now inject a fake one into our tests.

❸ Our new controller "injects" the various objects we need. We have extracted the GitHub API object and a Geo object into dependencies, and this syntax finds the proper objects and provides them to our controller. You'll also notice a slightly different syntax for creating the controller: `controller( "CtrlName", [ 'dependency1', 'dependency2', function( dependency1, dependency2 ) {} ] );`. This style works even if JavaScript minification were to occur; the previous incarnation we saw would not have survived this process because AngularJS would not have known the dependency name after it had been mangled by a minimizer.

❹ We extract the functionality into a function called `init`, which we can explicitly call from within our tests.

❺ Set the username and load the repository. If you are putting this into your own repository, modify this appropriately, but you can use these arguments until you do post this into your own repository.

---

❻ We use the `read` method to pull file contents from the repository. Notice that we use the `gh-pages` branch since we are storing our single-page app and all the data there.

❼ Once our data is returned to us, it is simply a string. We need to reconstitute this data to a JavaScript object using the `JSON.parse` method.

❽ After we retrieve our data from the repository, we can use the data inside the cities array to determine our current city.

❾ Since we are calling outside of AngularJS and returning inside a callback, we need to call `scope.$apply()` like we showed in prior examples.

We are now ready to write our geocoding implementation.

Geocoding Support

We'll build functions to retrieve the data for a city from the GitHub API, find the location of the user using their browser's Geolocation feature, use the user's current location to determine what cities they are close to, implement a distance calculation function, load the city once close proximity cities are determined, and finally, add a function to query the user for their GitHub credentials and annotation data.

First, we can implement the city-loading functions:

```
$scope.retrieveCity = function() { ❶
    $scope.repo.read( "gh-pages", $scope.city.name + ".json",
      function(err, data) {
        $scope.shops = JSON.parse( data );
        $scope.$apply();
    });
}

$scope.loadCity = function( city ) { ❷
    $scope.repo.read( "gh-pages", city + ".json", function(err, data) {
        $scope.shops = JSON.parse( data );
        $scope.$apply();
    });
...
```

❶ `retrieveCity` retrieves a list of shops in the same way we retrieved the list of cities by reading from the repository object. After loading the data into the scope, we need to call `$apply()` to notify Angular.

❷ `loadCity` uses the city name to load city data.

Next, we can implement the functionality to calculate distances between the current user and available cities:

```
$scope.getCurrentLocation = function( cb ) { ❶
    if( undefined != Geo ) {
        Geo.getCurrentPosition( cb, $scope.geolocationError );
    } else {
        console.error('not supported');
    }
};

$scope.geolocationError = function( error ) { ❷
    console.log( "Inside failure" );
};

$scope.detectCurrentCity = function() {  ❸
    // Calculate the distance from our current position and use
    // this to determine which city we are closest to and within
    // 25 miles
    for( var i = 0; i < $scope.cities.length; i++ ) {
        var dist = $scope.calculateDistance( $scope.latitude, ❹
                                             $scope.longitude,
                                             $scope.cities[i].latitude,
                                             $scope.cities[i].longitude );

        if( dist < 25 ) {
            $scope.city = $scope.cities[i];
            break;
        }
    }
}

toRad = function(Value) { ❺
    return Value * Math.PI / 180;
};

$scope.calculateDistance = function( latitude1,   ❻
                                     longitude1,
                                     latitude2,
                                     longitude2 ) {
    R = 6371;
    dLatitude = toRad(latitude2 - latitude1);
    dLongitude = toRad(longitude2 - longitude1);
    latitude1 = toRad(latitude1);
    latitude2 = toRad(latitude2);
    a = Math.sin(dLatitude / 2) * Math.sin(dLatitude / 2) +
        Math.sin(dLongitude / 2) * Math.sin(dLongitude / 2) *
        Math.cos(latitude1) * Math.cos(latitude2);
    c = 2 * Math.atan2(Math.sqrt(a), Math.sqrt(1 - a));
    d = R * c;
    return d;
    ...
```

❶ We build a `getCurrentLocation` function we will call within our code. We use the injected `Geo` object that has our `getCurrentPosition` function (which inside our tests will be the mocked function, and inside our real code just layers an abstraction on top of the native browser interface).

❷ We need to provide an error callback to the `getCurrentPosition` call, so we implement that, which logs it to the console.

❸ Then we build `detectCurrentCity`; we will look over the list of cities and see if we are in one.

❹ We iterate over the list of cities and calculate whether they are within 25 miles of our current location. Each city is stored with its own latitude and longitude data. When we find a city, we store that in the scope as the official current city and exit the loop.

❺ To calculate distance, we need to build a radian conversion function.

❻ Finally, we build our distance calculation function.

At first glance, the calculate distance function looks confusing, no? This was code I developed after reading a post on geocoding using a stored procedure within the PostgreSQL database, and I converted the code to JavaScript. Unless you are a geocoding geek, how do we know this works as advertised? Well, let's write some tests to prove it. Add these lines to the bottom of your *coffeetech.spec.js*, just within the last `});` closing braces:

```
describe( "#calculateDistance", function() {
    it( "should find distance between two points", function() {
        expect( parseInt(
        scope.calculateDistance( 14.599512,
        120.98422,
        10.315699,
        123.885437 ) * 0.61371 ) ).
    toEqual( 354 );
        });
});
```

To build this test, I searched for "distance between Manila" and Google autocompleted my search to "Cebu." It says they are 338 miles apart. I then grabbed latitude and longitudes for those cities and built the preceding test. I expected my test to fail as my coordinates were going to be off by a few miles here or there. But the test showed that our distance was 571. Hmm, perhaps we calculated in kilometers, not miles? Indeed, I had forgotten this algorithm actually calculated the distance in kilometers, not miles. So, we need to multiply the result by 0.621371 to get the value in miles, which ends up being close enough to what Google reports the distance to be.

City Data

Let's seed our application with some starting data and write out the *cities.json* file:

```
[
  {
    "longitude": -122.67620699999999,
    "latitude": 45.523452,
    "name": "portland"
  },
  {
    "longitude": -122.323837,
    "latitude": 47.662613,
    "name": "seattle"
  }
]
```

Now that we have our geocoding implementation complete and sample data in place, we can move on to acquiring credentials from the user.

Adding Login

If we want people to fork a repository on GitHub, we need to have them log in to GitHub. So, we need to ask for credentials:

```
...

$scope.annotate = function() {
    user = Prompt( "Enter your github username" )
    password = Prompt( "Enter your github password" )
    data = Prompt( "Enter data to add" );
};

...
```

We can now expose the new data inside the *index.html* file like so (omitting the obvious from the HTML):

```
<body ng-app="coffeetech">

<div class="container" ng-controller="GithubCtrl" ng-init="init()">

<h1>CoffeeTe.ch</h1>

<h3 ng-show="city">Current city: {{city.name}}</h3>

<div class="row">
<div class="col-md-6"><h4>Shop Name</h4> </div>
<div class="col-md-6"><h4>Lat/Lng</h4> </div>
</div>
<div class="row" ng-repeat="shop in shops"> ❶
<div class="col-md-6">     ❷
```

```
{{ shop.name }}  ❸
</div>
<div class="col-md-6"> {{ shop.latitude }} / {{ shop.longitude }} </div>
</div>
</div>
```

❶ ng-repeat is an AngularJS directive that iterates over an array of items. Here we
   use it to iterate over the items in our *portland.json* file and insert a snippet of
   HTML with our data interpolated from each item in the iteration.

❷ Bootstrap makes it easy to establish structure in our HTML. The col-md-6 class
   tells Bootstrap to build a column sized at 50% of our 12-column layout (the
   default for Bootstrap layouts). We set up two adjacent columns this way. And if
   we are inside a mobile device, it properly stacks these columns.

❸ Using AngularJS two-way data binding we insert the name of the shop.

Errors Already?

If you run this in your browser, you will not see the shops for our city displayed.
Something is broken, so let's investigate. I recommend using the Chrome browser to
debug this, but you can use any browser and set of developer tools you like. For
Chrome, right-clicking the page anywhere and selecting "Inspect Element" at the bottom (or by the keyboard shortcut "F12" or "Ctrl-Shift-I" on Windows or Linux or
"Cmd-Opt-I" on Mac) will bring up the developer console. Then select the console
window. Refresh the browser window, and you'll see this in the console:

```
Uncaught TypeError: Cannot call method 'select' of undefined
```

If you click the link to the right for GitHub.js, you'll see something like Figure 9-3.

Figure 9-3. An unexpected error

You see at the point of error that we are calling `select` on the tree. `select` appears to be a method defined on an underscore character. If you use JavaScript frequently, you'll recognize that the underscore variable comes from the Underscore library, and `select` is a method that detects the first matching instance inside an array. Under the hood, the GitHub.js library is pulling the entire tree from the repository, then iterating over each item in the tree, then selecting the item from the tree that matches the name of the file we have requested. This is an important performance implication to consider; the GitHub API does not provide a way to directly request content by the path name. Instead, you pull a list of files and then request the file by the SHA hash, a two-step process that makes two (potentially lengthy) calls to the API.

How do we fix the error telling us `select` is undefined? Did we forget to include underscore.js? Reviewing the documentation on GitHub.js, we see that it states underscore.js and base64.js are required. We forgot to include them. Oops! To include these, run these commands from the console:

```
$ wget http://underscorejs.org/underscore-min.js
$ wget https://raw.github.com/dankogai/js-base64/master/base64.js
```

Then, add the libraries to your *index.html* so that the JavaScript includes look like this:

```
...

<script src="angular.js"></script>
<script src="underscore-min.js"></script>
<script src="base64.min.js"></script>
<script src="github.js"></script>
<script src="coffeetech.js"></script>
...
```

Now we can build out some faked data and start envisioning the structure of our data that will eventually come from our users.

Displaying (Soon-to-Be) User-Reported Data

So far we have built a database of cities and coffee shops in those cities. Google Maps or Apple Maps already provide this information. If we layer additional information on top of this data (like quirky information about the coffee shop), however, then we might have something that someone might find useful once they have found the coffee shop on their favorite mapping application.

So, to start, let's add some fake data to our coffee shop information. Add a file called *portland.json* that looks like this:

```
[
    {
        "information" : [
```

```
            "offers gluten free desserts",
            "free wifi",
            "accepts dogs"
        ],
        "longitude" : -122.643074,
        "latitude" : 45.52292,
        "name" : "Very Good Coffee Shop"
    },
    {
        "latitude" : 45.522181,
        "name" : "Very Bad Coffee Shop",
        "longitude" : -122.63709
    },
    {

        "name" : "Mediocre Coffee Shop",
        "latitude" : 45.520437,
        "longitude" : -122.67846
    }
]
```

Notice that we added an array called `information` to our data set. We'll use this to allow simple search. Add the search feature to our *index.html*:

```
...

<div class="container" ng-controller="GithubCtrl" ng-init="init()">

<h1>CoffeeTe.ch</h1>

<input style="width: 20em;" ng-model="search"
        placeholder="Enter search parameters..."/> ❶

<h3 ng-show="city">Current city: {{city.name}}</h3>

<div class="row=">
<div class="col-md-6"><h4>Shop Name</h4> </div>
<div class="col-md-6"><h4>Lat/Lng</h4> </div>
</div>
<div class="row" ng-repeat="shop in shops | filter:search"> ❷
<div class="col-md-6">
{{ shop.name }}

<div ng-show="search"> ❸
<span ng-repeat="info in city.information">
<span class="label label-default">city.data</span>
</span>
</div>

</div>
<div class="col-md-6">
<a target="_map" ❹
    href="http://maps.google.com/?q={{shop.latitude}},{{shop.longitude}}">
    Open in map ({{shop.latitude}},{{shop.longitude}})
```

```
</a>
</div>
...
```

❶ We add a search box that binds to the `search` model in our scope.

❷ We add a filter on the data to display that searches through all data inside each item in our `shops` array.

❸ If we are searching (the model variable `search` is defined) then we show the extra information.

❹ We alter our lat/lng information to point to a Google Maps page.

Now if we type the word "gluten" in our search box, we filter out anything except shops that match that, and we see the information pieces formatted as labels underneath the shop name (Figure 9-4).

Figure 9-4. Filtering coffee shops using the term gluten

User-Contributed Data

Now that we have a functioning application, let's allow people to add information themselves and help build our database. Just beneath the link to the map link, add a button that will allow us to annotate a coffee shop with extra information.

To make a contribution, users will fork the repository, make a change, and then issue a pull request from the fork to the original repository. Forking means we create a copy of the original repository in our GitHub account. All these steps are possible from within our webapp using the GitHub.js library. Of course, if someone is going to fork a repository into their account, we must ask the user to log in, so we will prompt them for their username and password. If you are grimacing at the thought of a webapp asking for GitHub credentials, don't fret—we'll find a safe way to achieve the same thing shortly.

The implementation we will use starts with adding an annotate button to our HTML:

```
<button ng-click="annotate(shop)">Add factoid</button>
```

Let's add some tests. Add another file called *coffeetech.annotate.spec.js* with these contents:

```
describe( "GithubCtrl", function() {

    var scope = undefined, gh = undefined,
     repo = undefined, prompter = undefined;

    function generateMockPrompt() {
        prompter = { prompt: function() { return "ABC" } }; ❶
        spyOn( prompter, "prompt" ).andCallThrough();

    }

    var PR_ID = 12345;
    function generateMockRepositorySupport() { ❷
        repo = {
            fork: function( cb ) {
                cb( false );
            },
            write: function( branch, filename, data, commit_msg, cb ) {
                cb( false );
            },
            createPullRequest: function( pull, cb ) {
                cb( false, PR_ID );
            },
            read: function( branch, filename, cb ) {
                cb( undefined,
                    JSON.stringify( filename == "cities.json" ?
                        CITIES : PORTLAND ) );
            }
        };
        spyOn( repo, "fork" ).andCallThrough();
        spyOn( repo, "write" ).andCallThrough();
        spyOn( repo, "createPullRequest" ).andCallThrough();
        spyOn( repo, "read" ).andCallThrough();

        gh = { getRepo: function() {} }; ❸
        spyOn( gh, "getRepo" ).andCallFake( function() {
            return repo;
        } );
        ghs = { create: function() { return gh; } };
    }

    ...
```

It looks similar to our previous tests where we mock out a bunch of items from the GitHub.js library.

❶ We added a mock prompt. We will be prompting the user for username, password, and the annotating data, and we will use the native browser prompt mechanism to do this.

❷ We added three new methods to our mock GitHub object: `fork`, `write`, and `createPullRequest`. We verify that these are called.

❸ When we call the `getRepo` function we want to spy on it so we can assure it is called, but we also want to return the fake repository we provide inside our test, and this syntax does that.

We have some setup code that is called in a before function to load the mock objects and establish a controller and scope for testing:

```
...

var $timeout;  // ❶
beforeEach( inject( function ($controller, $rootScope, $injector ) {
    generateMockRepositorySupport();  // ❷
    generateMockPrompt();
    $timeout = $injector.get( '$timeout' );  // ❸
    scope = $rootScope.$new();
    ctrl = $controller( "GithubCtrl",
        { $scope: scope,
          Github: ghs,
          '$timeout': $timeout,
          '$window': prompter } );
} ) );
...
```

❶ According to the documentation for `fork` in the GitHub.js library, this method can take a little time to return (as long as it takes for GitHub to complete our fork request, which is nondeterministic), so we need to set a timeout in our app and query for the new repository. If we are using AngularJS, we can ask it for a mocked and programmatic timeout interface, which we can control inside our tests.

❷ We generate our mocked GitHub method calls and spies, and we follow that by mocking our prompt calls.

❸ As mentioned earlier, we need to get `$timeout`, and we can use the injector to retrieve the mocked one AngularJS provides for testing using this call.

Now we can write our tests for the annotate function:

```
...
describe( "#annotate", function() {  ❶
    it( "should annotate a shop", function() {
        scope.city = PORTLAND
        var shop = { name: "A coffeeshop" }
        scope.annotate( shop );  ❷
        expect( scope.shopToAnnotate ).toBeTruthy();❸
        expect( prompter.prompt.calls.length ).toEqual( 3 );
        expect( scope.username ).not.toBeFalsy();
        expect( scope.annotation ).not.toBeFalsy();

        expect( repo.fork ).toHaveBeenCalled();  ❹
        expect( scope.waiting.state ).toEqual( "forking" );  ❺
        $timeout.flush();❻

        expect( scope.forkedRepo ).toBeTruthy();  ❼
        expect( repo.read ).toHaveBeenCalled();
        expect( repo.write ).toHaveBeenCalled();
        expect( repo.createPullRequest ).toHaveBeenCalled();
        expect( scope.waiting.state ).toEqual( "annotated" );
        $timeout.flush();❽

        expect( scope.waiting ).toBeFalsy();
    });

});
...
```

❶ We create a new describe block to organize our tests, calling it #annotate. We then implement one it function, which is the single test we are creating: "annotate a shop."

❷ After setting up the preconditions that our scope object should have a city selected, and creating a shop to annotate, we then call our annotate method.

❸ Once we have called annotate, our code should request our credentials for the GitHub API, and then ask us for the information to use in annotating the shop. If this were happening in the browser, we would get three prompts. Our test mocks out the prompt object here, and we should therefore see three calls made to our mocked prompt object. We also validate some state we should see on the scope object like holding a username and annotation for usage later.

❹ We should then see the first of our GitHub API calls being made: GitHub.js should issue a request to fork the repository.

❺ We should then enter in our waiting state; we will tell the user we are waiting and our UI will use the `scope.waiting.state` to notify them of that.

❻ Once we have flushed the timeout that simulates completion of the fork, we will then see our code storing the result of the forked repo into the scope.

❼ Next, we can observe the other GitHub API calls that perform the annotation.

❽ We flush again to resolve the timeouts, and then finally, after everything is done, we should no longer be telling the user they are in a waiting state.

If you are still running Karma in the background, you'll see the tests fail with:

```
Chrome 32.0.1700 (Mac OS X 10.9.1) GithubCtrl #annotate should
annotate a shop FAILED
        TypeError: Object #<Scope> has no method 'annotate'
            at null.<anonymous> (/.../coffeetech.spec.js:80:19)
```

Now, let's implement this functionality in our *coffeetech.js* file. Add these lines to the bottom of the file, but before the last closing braces. The function `annotate` actually does two things: makes a fork of the repository for the user, and then adds annotation information to that repository using the GitHub API once the fork has completed:

```
...
$scope.annotate = function( shop ) { ❶
    $scope.shopToAnnotate = shop;
    $scope.username = $window.prompt( "Enter your github username (not email!)" )
    pass = $window.prompt( "Enter your github password" )
    $scope.annotation = $window.prompt( "Enter data to add" ); ❷
    gh = ghs.create( $scope.username, pass );  ❸
    toFork = gh.getRepo( "xrd", "spa.coffeete.ch" );  ❹
    toFork.fork( function( err ) {
        if( !err ) { ❺
            $scope.notifyWaiting( "forking",
              "Forking in progress on GitHub, please wait" );❻
            $timeout( $scope.annotateAfterForkCompletes, 10000 );❼
            $scope.$apply();
        }
    } );
};
    ...
```

❶ We start by creating our annotation function. As we specified in our tests, this function takes a `shop` object, an object into which annotations about the shop are added.

❷ We prompt the user three times: username and password on GitHub, and the text they want to annotate. If this seems like a really bad way to do things, don't worry, we'll fix it in a moment.

❸ We create a new GitHub object with the username and password provided. We leave it as an exercise for the reader to contend with mistyped or incorrect credentials.

❹ The GitHub.js library allows you to create a repository object (meaning create a local reference to an existing repository) using the `getRepo` function. Once we have this, we can issue a `fork` to the repository.

❺ If we did not get an error, we still need to contend with the fact that forking takes a nondeterministic amount of time. So, we schedule a timeout in 10 seconds, which will check to make sure our request completed. As this operation is happening inside the browser, we have no way of registering for a notification, and as such, must poll GitHub to determine whether our fork has completed. In the real world, we probably would need to redo this request if we see it fail as this could just mean it was still pending on GitHub.

❻ We register a message using a key called `"forking"` which we can use inside our HTML template to display to the user that our fork has completed. We'll build this function out soon; it basically stores the value and a string for display, and allows us to clear it when the message is no longer valid.

❼ Finally, we call the method `annotateAfterForkCompletes`, which adds data to our new forked repository once the process is fully complete.

Let's now build the code to annotate our repository after the fork has completed:

```
...

$scope.annotateAfterForkCompletes = function() {❶
    $scope.forkedRepo = gh.getRepo( $scope.username, "spa.coffeete.ch" );
    $scope.forkedRepo.read( "gh-pages", "cities.json", function(err, data) {
        if( err ) {
            $timeout( $scope.annotateAfterForkCompletes, 10000 );
        }
        else {
            $scope.notifyWaiting( "annotating",
              "Annotating data on GitHub" ); ❷
            // Write the new data into our repository
            $scope.appendQuirkToShop();

            var newData = JSON.stringify( $scope.shops, stripHashKey, 2 ); ❸
            $scope.forkedRepo.write('gh-pages', $scope.city.name + '.json', ❹
                            newData,
```

```
                          'Added my quirky information',
                          function(err) {
            if( !err ) {
                // Annotate our data using a pull request
                var pull = { ❺
                    title: "Adding quirky information to " +
                        $scope.shopToAnnotate.name,
                    body: "Created by :" + $scope.username,
                    base: "gh-pages",
                    head: $scope.username + ":" + "gh-pages"
                };
                target = gh.getRepo( "xrd", "spa.coffeete.ch" ); ❻
                target.createPullRequest( pull,
                    function( err, pullRequest ) { ❼
                        if( !err ) {
                            $scope.notifyWaiting( "annotated",
                                "Successfully sent annotation request" );❽
                            $timeout(
                                function() {
                                    $scope.notifyWaiting( undefined )
                                }, 5000 );
                            $scope.$apply(); ❾
                        }
                    } );
            }
            $scope.$apply();
        });
    }
    $scope.$apply();
} );
```

...

❶ Once we have verified the fork has completed, we need to get the new forked
repository. We use the username provided to our code when the user logs in to
build the repository object. We then read the *cities.json* file from the repository; if
we retrieve this file successfully (we don't see the err object evaluating to true)
then we know we are ready to start editing data.

❷ We notify the UI that we are annotating and tell the user they will need to wait
while the annotation request is in progress.

❸ JSON.stringify converts our annotated shop object into a JSON object. If you
have used JSON.stringify before, you might not know about the other two
parameters (beyond just the object you want to serialize) you can provide to this
function. These two extra parameters allow us to filter the object and specify certain elements to ignore when serializing and how and if to indent the resultant
JSON. So, we provide the stripHashKey function to remove the $$hashKey

Angular tracking data, and an indentation count. The indentation count makes it much easier to read a pull request, because the diff'ing algorithm can diff line by line rather than as a long JSON string, which is how `JSON.stringify` serializes by default.

❹ We then write data back to the forked repository using the `write` function. If this succeeds, the error value will be undefined inside the callback function as the last parameter.

❺ If our error was undefined, we are in a position where we can make a pull request back to the original repository. To make a pull request, we create a pull request object we need to provide to the pull request method inside of GitHub.js.

❻ We then get a reference to the target of the pull request, the original repository.

❼ We then issue the pull request against the target. This takes the pull request specification object we created earlier, and a callback function that has an error code if the request failed, and otherwise, a pull request object.

❽ Once the request has succeeded, we can notify the UI that the annotation process has completed, and then issue a timeout to remove that from the UI after 5000 milliseconds, or 5 seconds.

❾ Any time we are inside a callback in a third-party library (like GitHub.js) we, as mentioned before, need to use `$apply()` to notify Angular that our scope object has changed.

We have three convenience methods to implement:

```
...

$scope.appendQuirkToShop = function() { ❶
    if( undefined == $scope.shopToAnnotate.information ) {
        $scope.shopToAnnotate.information = [];
    }
    $scope.shopToAnnotate.information.push( $scope.annotation );
};

function stripHashKey( key, value ) { ❷
    if( key == "$$hashKey" ) {
        return undefined;
    }
    return value;
}

$scope.notifyWaiting = function( state, msg ) { ❸
    if( state ) {
```

```
            $scope.waiting = {};
            $scope.waiting.state = state;
            $scope.waiting.msg = msg;
        }
        else {
            $scope.waiting = undefined;
        }
    }
    ...
```

❶ The `appendQuirkToShop` function creates an empty array if it is not yet defined and then adds the annotation to the list of annotations. We don't want our code to crash if we try to add an annotation to an object for which there is an undefined array reference.

❷ We define a transformation function that we used with the `JSON.stringify` function. AngularJS adds a tracking attribute (`$$hashKey`) to our objects when we use the `ng-repeat` directive, and this function filters that out so that our pull request data is clean.

❸ `notifyWaiting` (obviously) notifies users. We create a waiting object, and then update the state (which our app will use to hide or display messages) and then a message itself. If we provide an empty message, we will clear the object, effectively removing the message from the UI.

Now we need to expose the status message in our UI by modifying the HTML:

```
...
<input class="ctinput" ng-model="search"
       placeholder="Enter search parameters..."/>

<h3 ng-show="city">Current city: {{city.name}}</h3>

<div ng-show="waiting">
{{waiting.msg}}
</div>
...
```

Accepting Pull Requests

When someone makes an annotation to a shop, the owner of the original repository gets a pull request notification on GitHub (Figure 9-5).

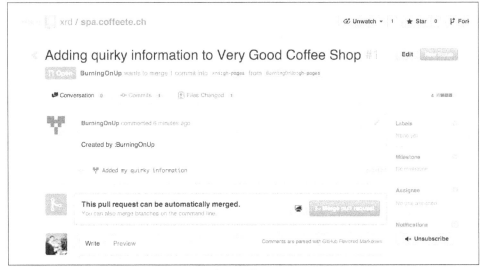

Figure 9-5. Adding information through a pull request

Now we can review changes through GitHub's integrated online diff tool (Figure 9-6).

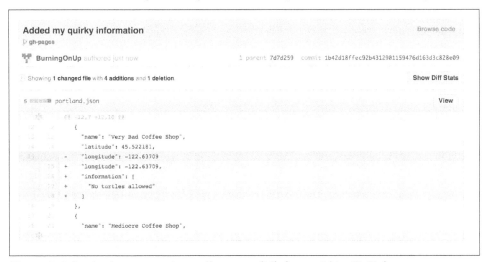

Figure 9-6. Reviewing annotation pull request diffs from within GitHub

Here we see a clear "diff" of the changes our contributor made: they added an annotation that tells us "no turtles allowed." We might want to consider a different location the next time we have a date with Morla. The diff is clear in that the green information is easy to read, which is a benefit we get when we use the JSON.stringify function with the third parameter set to something other than undefined. Unfortunately, the first line differs only by the extra comma, but this is still a very readable diff.

Toward a Safe Login Implementation

If I saw this app in the wild I would never use it to submit data. The app asks for my GitHub username and password. Asking for my username and password implicitly asks me to trust the authors of this application. Trust in this case means that I trust them to not maliciously use my credentials for nefarious purposes, and also asks me to trust that they are not doing something stupid that would allow an attacker to insert themselves into the middle of the authentication process and steal my credentials. GitHub is a large part of my online identity and I would never provide these credentials to a web application.

Fortunately, we have an alternative to asking for passwords: OAuth.

When we use OAuth, our users enter their credentials directly into GitHub. If our users have turned on two-factor authentication, GitHub can still authenticate them (while our naive implementation could not be modified to accept this type of authentication process). Once we have entered our credentials, GitHub decides whether we are who we say we are, and then returns us to the application that requested access.

There are many benefits to using OAuth. GitHub provides the application with what is called an OAuth token that encapsulates exactly what services on GitHub we have access to, and whether that access is read-only or whether we can add data in a read-write manner. This means our requesting service can ask to modify only parts of our data within GitHub; this provides a much higher level of trust to users as they know the application cannot touch the more private parts within GitHub. Specifically, this means we could ask for access only to gists and not request access to our repositories. One important point about OAuth tokens is that they can be revoked. So, once a specific action has been taken, we can destroy the token and revoke access. With simple username and password access, the only way to revoke access is to change the password, which means any place you have saved that password (password managers or other applications that log in via username and password) need to update their settings as well. With OAuth we can revoke a single token at any time (and GitHub makes it easy to do this) without affecting access to other services.

Let's modify our application to use OAuth.

Authentication Requires a Server

Up until now we have been able to publish all our files into GitHub, and they are hosted for us by GitHub. Sadly the authentication component cannot be hosted on GitHub. Somehow we need to safely authenticate our user into GitHub and retrieve an

OAuth token. There is currently no way to do this strictly client side (using only static HTML and JavaScript running in the browser). Other authentication providers like Facebook do provide pure JavaScript login functionality in their SDKs, but GitHub, citing security concerns, has not released anything that does authentication purely on the client side as of yet.

Somehow we have to involve a server into our authentication process. The most obvious choice we have is to run a small authentication server, delegate authentication to it, and once authentication is completed, jump back in our application hosted on GitHub. We provide code (written in NodeJS, JavaScript for the server side) to do this in the associated repository for this chapter. But creating even a simple authentication system has a baseline of complexity that seems like overkill. If we could instead delegate this authentication to a third party, we could reduce a massive amount of code and complexity from our system.

Fixing Authentication with Firebase

Instead of writing our own server to manage authentication and talk to the GitHub API, we will delegate that authentication to Firebase. Firebase is a real-time communication toolset that integrates well with our choice of AngularJS. By far the simplest and safest option, Firebase offers AngularJS bindings (called "AngularFire") and an integrated GitHub authentication component (called "Simple Login"). Together they resolve the authentication issue for us, and keep all our code hosted on GitHub. Delegation of our authentication component is easy with Firebase: we just modify our existing GitHub application, provide the credentials and GitHub OAuth scope to Firebase, and then our application offloads user management to Firebase.

First, we need to create a new GitHub application. In the top-right corner on GitHub.com, click on the "Account settings" link, and then navigate to the "Applications" link toward the bottom. Click the "Developer Applications" tab in the right center column and then click the "Register new application" button. Make sure "Authorization callback URL" is set to *https://auth.firebase.com/auth/github/callback*. Then save the application by clicking the "Register application" button as shown in Figure 9-7.

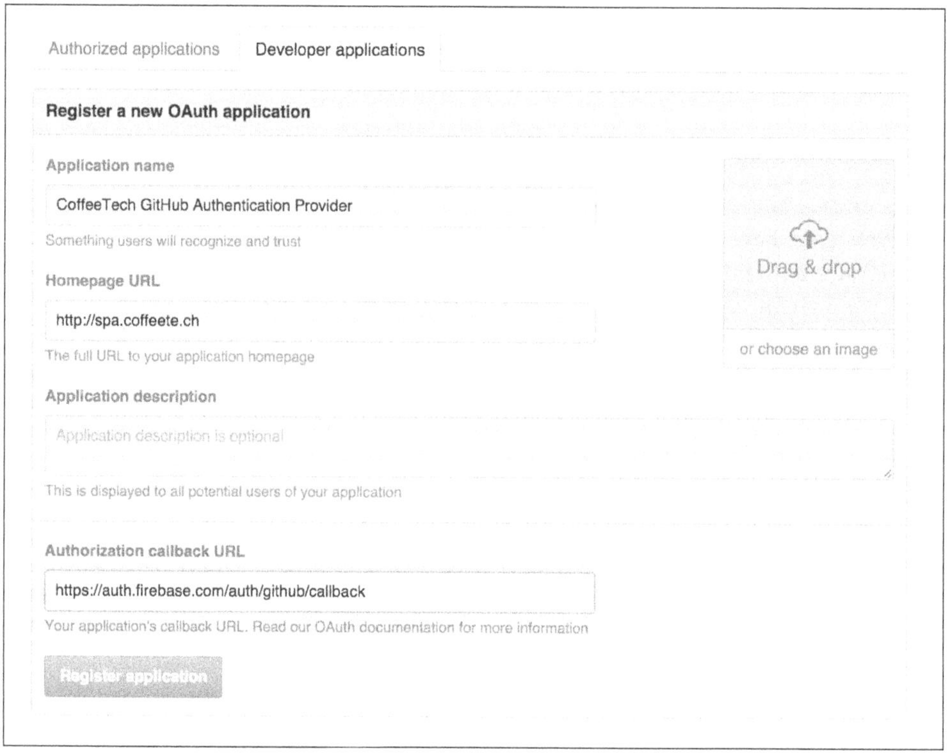

Figure 9-7. A new GitHub application for OAuth

Now, create an account on Firebase. Once you have done this, create a new app called "CoffeeTech" inside Firebase. The APP URL needs be unique, so use "coffeetech-<USERNAME>", replacing USERNAME with your GitHub username. Once you have created the app, click the "View Firebase" button. You'll then see a settings screen, and click "Simple Login" and then "GitHub" as shown in Figure 9-8.

Figure 9-8. Creating the Firebase hosted login

Then, copy your GitHub client ID and secret to the sections inside the Firebase Simple Login settings for the GitHub provider. Make sure the "enabled" checkbox is checked to enable the provider.

We've now established a login application on GitHub, configured it to use the Firebase service, and have properly configured Firebase to use that GitHub application. We want all functionality, especially external services, to be covered by tests, so we'll write that test coverage next.

Testing Firebase

Since we load Firebase from its CDN, we first need to mock out the Firebase constructor using a simple shim. Put the following into a file called *firebase-mock.js*:

```
var Firebase = function (url) {
}

angular.module( 'firebase', [] );
```

To test our code, we make the following changes to our *coffeetech-annotate.spec.js*:

```
beforeEach( module( "coffeetech" ) );

var mockFirebase = mockSimpleLogin = undefined;
function generateMockFirebaseSupport() { ❶
    mockFirebase = function() {};
    mockSimpleLogin = function() {
        return {
            '$login': function() {
                return { then: function( cb ) {
                    cb( { name: "someUser",
                          accessToken: "abcdefghi" } );
                } };
            }
        }
    };
}

var $timeout;
beforeEach( inject( function ($controller, $rootScope, $injector ) {
    generateMockRepositorySupport();
    generateMockPrompt();
    generateMockFirebaseSupport(); ❷
    $timeout = $injector.get( '$timeout' );
    scope = $rootScope.$new();
    ctrl = $controller( "GithubCtrl",
        { $scope: scope,
          Github: ghs,
          '$timeout': $timeout,
          '$window': prompter,
          '$firebase': mockFirebase,
          '$firebaseSimpleLogin': mockSimpleLogin } ); ❸
} ) );


describe( "#annotate", function() {
    it( "should annotate a shop", function() {
        scope.auth = mockSimpleLogin( mockFirebase() ); ❹
        scope.city = PORTLAND
        var shop = { name: "A coffeeshop" }
        scope.annotate( shop );
        expect( prompter.prompt.calls.length ).toEqual( 1 ); ❺
        expect( scope.shopToAnnotate ).toBeTruthy();
        expect( scope.username ).not.toBeFalsy();
        expect( scope.annotation ).not.toBeFalsy();

        expect( repo.fork ).toHaveBeenCalled();
        expect( scope.waiting.state ).toEqual( "forking" );
        $timeout.flush();

        expect( scope.forkedRepo ).toBeTruthy();
```

```
expect( repo.read ).toHaveBeenCalled();
expect( repo.write ).toHaveBeenCalled();
expect( repo.createPullRequest ).toHaveBeenCalled();
expect( scope.waiting.state ).toEqual( "annotated" );
$timeout.flush();

expect( scope.waiting ).toBeFalsy();
```

❶ We add a `generateMockFirebaseSupport()` function that creates the mock firebase and simple login objects.

❷ We call this method to initialize the mocks.

❸ In our test we use the `$controller` method instantiator to inject these mock objects instead of letting AngularJS inject the real ones. We should modify our other spec file as well now that we are changing the required injections for any controller.

❹ We change our `#annotate` test and create the `auth` object (normally created inside the initialization).

❺ We prompt only once for the data to annotate (we don't need to prompt for username and password any longer).

Implementing Firebase Login

Now, add Firebase support to our AngularJS application. Add the references to the Firebase support libraries right after AngularJS is loaded:

```
<script src="angular.js"></script>
<script src='https://cdn.firebase.com/v0/firebase.js'></script>
<script
  src='https://cdn.firebase.com/libs/angularfire/0.6.0/angularfire.min.js'>
</script>
<script
  src='https://cdn.firebase.com/js/simple-login/1.2.5/firebase-simple-login.js'>
</script>
```

We need to adjust our *coffeetech.js* file in a few ways. First, import the Firebase into our AngularJS module. Also, our original GitHub service expected username and password as parameters, but we are now using a slightly different signature for OAuth tokens:

```
var mod = angular.module( 'coffeetech', [ 'firebase' ] );

mod.factory( 'Github', function() {
    return {
        create: function(token) {
            return new Github( { token: token, auth: 'oauth' } );
```

```
        }
    };
});
```

When we instantiate our controller, we need to inject `Firebase` and `FirebaseSimple`
`Login` and initialize them inside our `init` method:

```
mod.controller( 'GithubCtrl', [ '$scope', 'Github', 'Geo', '$window', '$timeout',
    '$firebase', '$firebaseSimpleLogin',
    function( $scope, ghs, Geo, $window, $timeout,
        $firebase, $firebaseSimpleLogin ) {

    $scope.init = function() {

        var ref = new Firebase( 'https://coffeetech.firebaseio.com' );
        $scope.auth = $firebaseSimpleLogin( ref );

        $scope.getCurrentLocation( function( position ) {
            $scope.latitude = position.coords.latitude;
```

Then, when we annotate, we need to provide the `auth` token returned from Firebase.
But it is gratifying to see that little else needs to change in our flow:

```
$scope.annotate = function( shop ) {
    $scope.shopToAnnotate = shop;

    $scope.auth.$login( 'github', { scope: 'repo' } ).then(
      function( user ) { ❶

        $scope.me = user;
        $scope.username = user.name;

        $scope.annotation = $window.prompt( "Enter data to add" ); ❷

        if( $scope.annotation ) {
            gh = ghs.create( $scope.me.accessToken ); ❸
            toFork = gh.getRepo( "xrd", "spa.coffeete.ch" );
            toFork.fork( function( err ) {
```

❶ We call the `$login` method on our `auth` object created using the Firebase Simple-
   Login service. It returns a "promise," which is an interface that has a `then()`
   method that will be called if the `$login()` succeeds. `then()` calls our callback
   function, giving us a user object.

❷ We still need to prompt the user for one piece of information—the data to annotate. You can imagine other ways to get this information, using modal HTML5
   dialogs, but this will work for us for right now. At least we are only prompting
   once instead of three times!

❸ Once we are ready to fork we need to create our user object using the token.

After we make these changes, we can click the "Add factoid" button and we'll get a dialog like Figure 9-9 indicating we are logging in to GitHub (via the Firebase Simple-Login).

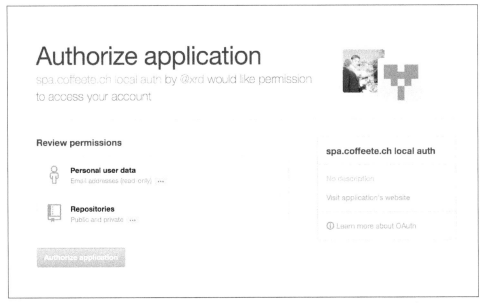

Figure 9-9. The final step in the permission flow for GitHub access using Firebase

After you authorize the application, the execution flow is identical to the prior authentication flow (using username and password). As an optimization we could check for previous logins before calling $login() again, but we don't do that here, meaning the login dialog momentarily pops up each time we click the button.

Once users have logged in, they will be redirected to the application, and we'll notify them that they have submitted a pull request with their contribution. Since their contribution is associated with their GitHub account, they will receive standard pull request notifications when their contribution is accepted, so we don't need to implement that ourselves.

Summary

We've built an application in JavaScript that requires no server and provides users with a searchable coffee shop database that accepts contributions in a very safe and secure way using the Pull Request API. We were able to completely ignore all the administrative features of a data entry system, delegating all these to GitHub. Our single-page app permits us to focus on one thing: making a powerful and useful application.

GitHub Enterprise

Most people understandably equate GitHub (the company) with GitHub.com (the website), but it's interesting to note that they're not one and the same.

The GitHub website, as important as it is to modern open and closed source software development, is not the only product that GitHub (the company) produces. The single largest other product from that team is called GitHub Enterprise, and it's a version of the GitHub software that can be deployed inside a corporate firewall—like having your own private GitHub.com.

The two products are very similar from a user's point of view, but there are some important differences. It can sometimes be hard to imagine the kinds of difficulties that Enterprise is designed to solve, but keep in mind that it's for large teams.

Installation

Using GitHub Enterprise isn't as easy as signing up for an account. You're responsible for all the infrastructure and maintenance, including installation, updates, system maintenance, keeping the machine running, and so on. However, if your company is considering Enterprise, it's likely you already have specialists who are already doing this for other services.

The GitHub team has also made it pretty easy for them. The software comes as a pre-packaged virtual machine in a variety of formats, so you'll likely find something that fits into your infrastructure. Once the machine is running, most of the configuration can be done with a web interface, but there are some tricky bits like network configuration and port forwarding that aren't easy for the layperson to get right.

Administration

Since you're in control of the environment in which Enterprise runs, you now have a lot of concerns that the typical GitHub.com user does not. GitHub Enterprise has an administration interface for dealing with these issues, which doesn't exist on Git-Hub.com. It allows management of things like system resources, reports, search, and many others.

Also, while GitHub.com has its own user system, GitHub Enterprise can optionally plug in to your organization's existing authentication system. This allows a company's IT organization to manage user identities in one single place, rather than having to duplicate a lot of effort when a new team member hires on. It also eases the initial transition, when perhaps thousands of people will need new accounts. Several systems are supported, including LDAP and SAML, as well as plain old email and password.

Endpoints

The complete GitHub API is also available on an Enterprise instance; you just need to send your requests to *https://<hostname>/api/v3* instead of *https://api.github.com/*. You can imagine that some users have accounts on both an Enterprise instance as well as GitHub.com, and many applications have started supporting this scenario.

Full Hostnames Versus Mount Points

One of the main differences between GitHub.com and an Enterprise setup is often in the way that hostnames are set up. GitHub.com has several hostnames for various content served. An incomplete list includes:

github.io
    Hosting Jekyll blogs for users and project pages

gist.github.com
    Hosting gists

raw.githubusercontent.com
    Hosting raw pages (unprocessed files)

For a variety of reasons, Enterprise GitHub installations often don't retain the same mapping. An Enterprise installation might look like:

github.bigdevcorp.example.com/pages/xrd/somerepo
    Hosting gh-pages sites *github.bigdevcorp.example.com/gists*: Hosting gists

As you can see, Enterprise installations often map the subdomains to a subdirectory rather than a different hostname. This simplifies the setup of the Enterprise installation. But it means that some tools require reconfiguration.

For the command-line Gist tool (*https://github.com/defunkt/gist*), you need to export an environment variable that specifies the Gist URL:

```
$ export GITHUB_URL=http://github.bigdevcorp.example.com/
```

For the command-line Hub tool (*https://github.com/github/hub*), you need to use a different variable—GITHUB_HOST:

```
$ GITHUB_HOST=github.bigdevcorp.example.com hub clone myproject
```

Command-Line Client Tools: cURL

We show in Chapter 1 how to use cURL to make a request against the API on the main GitHub.com site. If you wanted to do this against an Enterprise site, your request would look a little different:

```
$ curl -i https://github.bigdevcorp.example.com/api/v3/search/repositories?q=@ben
```

Example Request Using a Client Library

If you use a client library, most provide a way to configure the library to use a different endpoint, as is required when you are using an Enterprise GitHub instance.

This book documents connecting to GitHub using five different languages: Ruby, Java, JavaScript, Python, and C#. Here are examples in each language. With these snippets in hand, any example in the book can be converted to work against a GitHub Enterprise server.

Ruby Client Configuration

For the Octokit Ruby library, use code like this:

```
github = Github.new
          basic_auth: 'login:password',
          endpoint: 'https://github.bigdevcorp.example.com/api/v3/'
puts github.repos.list
```

Java

For the EGit Java library, this code specifies an Enterprise endpoint:

```
GitHubClient client = new GitHubClient("github.bigcorpdev.example.com");
UserService us = new UserService(client);
us.getUser("internaluser");
```

When you create a new GitHub-backed service object of any type, you parameterize the service constructor with the customized client object.

Also, note that this library is specifically configured for version 3 (v3) of the API (you cannot specify another version). If you need to use a newer version of the API, you will need to make sure you are using the correct version of the EGit libraries. And, unfortunately, there is no way to use an older version of the API with this Java client if you have an outdated Enterprise server that for some reason cannot be upgraded.

JavaScript

The JavaScript library we write about in this book (GitHub.js) uses the following syntax to specify a GitHub Enterprise backend:

```
var github = new Github({
  apiUrl: "https://github.bigdevcorp.example.com/api/v3"
  ...
});
```

Python

The agithub client we use in Chapter 4 does not permit parameterizing an Enterprise endpoint when creating the GitHub client. To use an Enterprise endpoint you need to define a new class that overrides the built-in `agithub.Github` and then use that new client in place of the built-in one:

```
class GitHubEnterprise(agithub.API):
    def __init__(self, api_url, *args, **kwargs):
        props = ConnectionProperties(
                    api_url = api_url,
                    secure_http = True,
                    extra_headers = {
                        'accept' :    'application/vnd.github.v3+json'
                        }
                    )

        self.setClient(Client(*args, **kwargs))
        self.setConnectionProperties(props)

g = GitHubEnterprise('github.mycorp.com', 'myusername', 'mypassword')
```

C#

The default behavior of the Octokit library is to connect to GitHub.com, but it's relatively straightforward to give it another API host instead. Simply replace the instantiation of the `GitHubClient` object with something like this:

```
var ghe = new Uri("https://github.myenterprise.com/");
var client = new GitHubClient(new ProductHeaderValue("my-cool-app"), ghe);
```

Management API

Enterprise servers have a special additional API section that isn't available on GitHub.com, called the Management Console API. It allows you to do things like check settings, maintain SSH keys, manage your license, and so on. Nearly anything you can do from the web management console, you can do through the API (so you can script management tasks when desirable).

Documentation

Documentation for the Enterprise API is available at *https://developer.github.com/v3/enterprise*.

Ruby, NodeJS, (and the Shell) at GitHub

The founders of GitHub all had deep ties and contributions to the Ruby programming language, so we cover it more than other languages in this book.

In recent years, NodeJS (JavaScript for the server side) has grown in popularity, and JavaScript has always been an interesting language because it works on both the client side and server side. GitHub has offered several popular open source projects written in NodeJS.

For these reasons, this appendix gives a little more detail on using these two languages.

In addition, some fluency with the shell is beneficial. There are many GUI programs that hide the command line from you, but to truly dive deep into the GitHub API, it is worthwhile to use the command line inside a shell. These examples all work with bash (the Bourne Again Shell), but are careful not to use any advanced features of bash (so they should convert to other shells if you strongly favor another shell).

GitHub and Ruby

When the history of GitHub is documented, the Ruby language will take its place as a major character. Tom Preston Warner (one of the three founders of GitHub) built the initial libraries for using Git with Ruby, a library called Grit. You can host blogs on GitHub for free, and this tool called Jekyll is built using Ruby. Gollum, the technology that powers GitHub wikis, is built using Grit and runs on Ruby.

To understand GitHub, it is best to understand a little bit of Ruby. You can use many of the tools used at GitHub by simply installing Ruby, and not knowing any Ruby syntax. This book will not require you to become an expert in Ruby, but will ask you to read through Ruby code. We write in a literal, readable way, so that anyone with basic software developer skills and mastery of the English language should be able to understand the tools we are using. Ruby is not a perfect language, but is a useful addition to a developer's toolkit because of its focus on developer productivity.

Installing Ruby

There are many ways to get Ruby but not all of them are created equal. As a long-time user I have experienced the pain of using a preinstalled Ruby or one from a package manager, and generally these installation methods provide a suboptimal experience. If you are not familiar with Ruby, use this appendix to get through installation with the least friction and trouble.

You might already have a version of Ruby installed. Mac OS X comes bundled with Ruby and various flavors of Linux do as well (or provide a quick and easy installation through the built-in package manager like "apt-get"). However, I recommend that you use the method of installation described here rather than using the stock installed version of Ruby you might already have on your system. Often Ruby packages require a specific version of Ruby, though they may work with other versions. The problem is that you might encounter subtle bugs that have never been seen before, and using the methods described here will make it trivial to install any version of Ruby that you need side by side with any other version. You can guarantee you are using the correct version, and the method described here will not interfere with any other previously installed version of Ruby you already have on your system.

To install Ruby, use RVM. RVM stands for Ruby Version Manager. RVM allows you to install multiple versions of Ruby on your machine and have them interoperate without conflict. You will probably only need to install a single version of Ruby to use the examples in the book. And RVM makes it so that if you choose to install another version, you will not have to reconfigure any applications that relied on the other versions installed.

Installation of Ruby using RVM depends on your operating system. If you are using Mac OS X or Linux, your installation will probably be as simple as running these commands from a shell:

```
$ \curl -sSL https://get.rvm.io | bash -s stable
```

This will install RVM and Ruby.

If you are running Windows, you can use RVM to install Ruby, but your instructions are a little more complicated. Refer to the documentation to do so. A better option is to consider installing something like VirtualBox (a virtual machine manager). If you do this, you can install RVM inside a Linux Virtual Machine (VM). Windows is, sadly, a second-class citizen with Ruby and RVM and, for this reason, it is often better to install RVM inside a host system like Linux, which has a wider community around it to support you. VirtualBox and Linux are free as in beer and as in speech, so you can try them out without cost (other than your time). There are many native gems for Ruby that don't properly compile if the host system is Windows, so you can save yourself considerable time by just using a completely free (as in beer) option like VirtualBox and a Linux virtual machine running on Windows instead of fighting with running everything directly on Windows.

Important Ruby and RVM Concepts

Here are a few tips when using Ruby and RVM:

Gemfile
Ruby packages libraries in a format called a gem. A gemfile is a manifest that describes which gems your application needs. Gemfiles make it simple to install all the required libraries: run the `bundle` command from a shell prompt and all libraries will be installed, which can include downloading from the network and building from source if compilation is required.

.ruby-version or .rvmrc
These two files tell your application (or shell) which version of Ruby to use. Often applications will include this file as a part of their package. If you use RVM, it will either switch to that version of Ruby or prompt you to install that version. Imagine that you have an application that only runs on Ruby 2.1.3. You can create a file called *.ruby-version*, which contains the string `ruby-2.1.3` and when your application starts, it will automatically use that version of Ruby. There are other Ruby-based tools (like the zero-configuration web server Pow) that are aware of files like *.ruby-version* and will properly use the correct version of Ruby if they see this file.

config.ru
This is a file used to run Ruby applications using Rack. Rack is a web server interface, compatible with many application servers. If you see a *config.ru* file, you can run this application with many different servers. These can be powerful frontends used in production on many large sites on the Internet, or they can be minimal servers used just on a single laptop; Rack makes it easy to set up a server.

Potential Problems Installing Ruby

Missing system tools
If you are running Mac OS X, you need to install Xcode and the command-line tools. If you are a software developer, you probably have these already installed. If not, review online documentation to install these. If you are running Linux, you might not have installed the compiler chain; you can install all the build tools you will ever need using this command: `sudo apt-get install build-essential`.

This can take a while, but will ensure you have all the tools necessary for building RVM and any binary gems.

Missing developer libraries

There are some libraries that support Ruby (readline support, as an example, which allows you to use command-line history inside of an interactive Ruby shell) that are not always installed or available to the RVM tool. RVM has greatly improved in detecting the correct libraries, and there are often notes that tell you how to properly configure these libraries. Make sure to read the output printed to the screen as you install Ruby using RVM for special instructions specific to your platform.

GitHub Is Excited about NodeJS

NodeJS is the server-side version of JavaScript. JavaScript is the only ubiquitious client-side programming language for the Web. Between Ruby and JavaScript, you can build any web application you need. Tools like Hubot show the benefits of using a language like JavaScript running on the NodeJS platform, which facilitates building "fast, scalable networked applications."

NodeJS Installation

The nodejs.org web page offers various binary installers. These are generally the best way to install the most recent version of NodeJS.

Node Version Manager

NVM stands for "Node Version Manager" and is a direct correlate to RVM. Like RVM, NVM allows you to install multiple versions of NodeJS on a single machine and switch between them seamlessly. This can be very useful when using a tool like NodeJS that is iterating rapidly (and whose modules are also often tested against only a very new version of NodeJS). NVM runs on OS X or Linux. To install, run these commands from a shell prompt:

```
$ curl -o- \
https://raw.githubusercontent.com/creationix/nvm/v0.25.3/install.sh | \
bash
```

This will install NVM for you. You then might need to run `source ~/.bash_profile` to load the NVM scripts. Once this is completed, you are able to run NVM commands:

```
$ nvm install 0.10 # Install version 0.10
$ nvm use 0.10     # Use version 0.10
```

There are many more commands available with NVM, all of which can be found at the repository where the tool is hosted (*https://github.com/creationix/nvm*).

package.json

Much like Ruby has a Gemfile that indicates required libraries, so too does NodeJS have an equivalent file. In NodeJS, this file is called *package.json*. To install all required libraries for any project, use the npm tool (installed by default when you install NodeJS using NVM). Running npm without any arguments will install all libraries specified by the application if there is a *package.json* file included with the project. If you want to add a package to an existing *package.json* file, you can append --save to the npm command and npm will update *package.json* for you once the installation of the package has completed.

Command-Line Basics and the Shell

Though most chapters have focused on a specific programming language (aside from Chapter 1), all of the chapters contain command-line invocations. There are a few intricacies when using the shell you might not be familiar with that we will explain here, with an actual example of each.

Shell Comments

If you type a hash character (#) into a shell command, the rest of the line is considered a comment. This makes it easy to document commands on the same line:

```
$ cat file.txt # This prints out the file "file.txt"
```

This command ends after the file.txt string. We use this often throughout the appendix to document shell commands.

Providing Variables to Commands

When a process runs in the shell, it runs within an environment, and this environment can be configured with key/value pairs. These are called environment variables. A common reason for this is that you can write a program that reads passwords from the environment variables and then specify them at runtime rather than in the source code. You specify environment variables either as key/value pairs joined by an equal sign in front of a command, or by using the export command to persist them across commands:

```
$ PASSWORD=MyPwd123 myProgram  # myProgram retrieves the variable PASSWORD
$ export PASSWORD=MyPwd123
$ myProgram # PASSWORD is now a persisted key value
```

Splitting Commands into Multiple Lines

The shell invokes commands when you hit the Enter key. But there are times when you want to break a command into multiple lines for readability. In this case, break each line up using the backslash character:

```
$ git log -S http
...
$ git \
log \
-S \
http
...
```

Though not the most compelling command to break into multiple lines, this example shows two commands that do exactly the same thing.

Piping Output to Successive Commands

Shell commands were written long ago in an era when programs fulfilled upon a small set of functionality, in stark contrast to today's monolithic GUI programs. Each program generally did a few simple things and then passed information to another program for further processing. Programs then needed an elegant way to pass data between each other, and the pipe was born. Pipes facilitate communication between processes: one command's output becomes another command's input.

```
$ cat /etc/mime.types | grep http
application/http
application/vnd.httphone
application/x-httpd-eruby        rhtml
application/x-httpd-php
phtml pht php
application/x-httpd-php-source        phps
```

This invocation uses the `cat` program to output the file */etc/mime.types*, and then passes this information to the `grep` program, which looks inside the input to find all lines that contain the string `http`.

Redirection

Similar to the pipe, shells support redirecting output to files using the > and >> characters. > will overwrite an existing file (or create a new file if it does not exist) while the double >> string will append to a file:

```
$ cat /etc/mime.types | grep http > saved-output.txt
```

After running this command, the file *saved-output.txt* will contain the same text as was produced in the prior example for the pipe. The file will be overwritten if it existed already.

Index

B

BASH, xvi
body parser middleware, 205
Booleans, 157
Bootstrap, 132, 221, 237
build_commit() method, 42

C

C#, 85, 262
caching
    and scraping, 119-123
    tags, 16
callback, 213, 219
chat robot (see Hubot)
CLR (Common Language Runtime), 85
CNAME file, 109
code reviews, 183-188
code search, 58
code snippets, 36
coffee shop database app, 220-257
    accepting pull requests, 248
    and coffeetech.js. file, 231-233
    AngularJS application using GitHub.js, 222-233
    application database structure visualization, 225
    city data for, 236
    displaying data, 238-248
    error handling, 237-238
    geocoding support, 233-235
    login for, 236
    mapping hostnames, 221
    safe login implementation for, 250-257
    setup, 220-222
    support libraries for, 221
    test data for, 231
    testability of app, 226
    user-contributed data for, 240-248
CoffeeScript
    characteristics, 182
    extension boilerplate, 184
    indentation in, 182
    Jasmine support tests, 185
Collaborators API, unifying usernames via, 214
combined status, 84
command line
    basics, 269
    editing Gollum from, 39
    gists from, 25

Jekyll command line tool, 126-128
    launching Hubot from, 216
    parsing JSON from, 3
    piping output to successive commands, 270
    providing variables to commands, 269
    redirection, 270
    shell comments, 269
    splitting commands into multiple lines, 270
commit (Android app example), 167
Commit Status
    example app, 85-97
Commit Status API, 81-98
    and Visual Studio, 86
    combined status, 84
    creating a status, 85
    development environment for app, 86-89
    libraries for, 86
    OAuth flow, 91-95
    raw status, 83
    sending request, 89-91
    status handler, 96-97
    statuses in, 82-85
    Xamarin Studio, 87-89
comp pages, fixing linking between, 51
conditional HTTP headers, 16
conditional requests, 16
config.ru, 267
continuous-integration service, 82
core rate limits, 14
CORS, 19
createBlob function, 166
createCommit() function, 167
createServices() function, 164
create_controls method, 71, 73
credentials, 69
CSS
    for Jekyll blogs, 132-134
    Gollum limitations with, 37
cURL, 1
    and GitHub Enterprise, 261
    and rate limit retrieval, 15
    debugging switches for, 5-6
    installing, 2

D

debugging, cURL switches for, 5-6
describe functions, 186
Destroy() method, 70
directed acylic graphs (DAG), 165

LoginPanel class, 72

M

MacBooks, xvi
Management Console API, 263
Markdown, 35
    and Jekyll, 99
    and Jekyll markup, 106
    link tag, 36
Maven, 161
Mechanize, 116-119
meta–tools, ix
Mono, 85
MonoDevelop, 87

N

Nancy library, 86-97
network calls, synchronous, 70
NodeJS, xv
    and Express.js, 205
    and Hubot, 175
    and package.json, 269
    GitHub and, 268
    installation, 268
    version manager, 268
node–github module, 209
notifications, 181
NuGet, 88
numerical values, in search queries, 56
NVM (Node version manager), 268

O

OAuth, 9-11
    and Commit Status API, 82
    authorization process outline, 91
    benefits of, 250
    flow for Commit Status API, 91-95
    for coffee shop database app login, 250-257,
        255
    scopes, 9-11
    simplified flow, 11
    tokens, 9-11, 9, 189-191
OAuth2, 11
Octokit, 28
    and GitHub Enterprise client configuration,
        261
    using hypermedia data from, 30
Octokit NuGet, 88

Octokit Ruby, 28
OkHttp library, 142
onCreate function, 156
onPostExecute() function, 160
onView function, 152
operating system prerequisites, xvi
operators, search API, 55
Organizations API, xiii
output tags, 128

P

package.json, 269
password authentication, 8
pipes, 270
post requests, handling PR notifications as,
    194-216
posts, blog, 123-126
privacy, Jekyll, 107
public gists, 24
published variable, 105
publishing Jekyll blogs, 135
pull requests
    and response object, 213
    and user list from Hubot brain, 200
    assigning an active chat room user to,
        196-200
    code reviews via, 183-188
    handling notifications as post requests over
        HTTP, 194-216
    responding to, 208-213
    securing webhook, 203-208
    sending data via webhook, 201-203
    testing Hubot with, 191-193
    unifying usernames via Collaborators API,
        214
    with coffee shop database app, 248
PyInstaller, 65, 79
Python
    2.7 vs. 3, 65
    AGitHub library, 65
    and code for search API application, 66-79
    and Git credential helper, 67
    and GitHub Enterprise, 262
    as implementation language for search API
        application, 64-66
    PyInstaller, 65
    WxPython project, 65

Slack API, 197-200
sorting, search query results, 56
source code management (SCM), ix
spyOn function, 229
standard error, 4
status codes, 11-15
    improper JSON (422), 13
    invalid payload (400), 12
    no change (304), 14
    successful creation (201), 13
status handler, 96-97
String type, 157
subdomain, DNS setup with, 109
switches, cURL, 5-6
synchronous network calls, 70

T

target SDK, 139
testing
    Android app, 147-153, 169-171
    coffee shop database app, 226
    Firebase, 253-255
text format, 21
themes, Jekyll, 107
titles, scraping, 116
tokens, OAuth, 9-11, 9, 189-191
total_count field, 55
tree (for Android app), 166
Tumblr, 112

U

UI tests, 151-153
Unbuntu Linux virtual machine, xvi
unit tests, 147-150
uploading ZIP files, 40
user search, 60
username authentication, 8
    benefits of, 8
    downsides to, 9
usernames, unifying via Collaborators API, 214
Users API, xiii

V

Vagrant, xvi
variables, providing to commands, 269
VirtualBox, xvi, 266
Visual Studio, 86
Void type, 157

W

watch switch, 107
Web content
    accessing, 17-21
    accessing with JSON–P, 18
    CORS requests, 19
    response format specification, 20
    retrieving formatted content, 20
webhook
    for Hubot, 187
    securing, 203-208
    sending PR data via, 201-203
wikis (see under Gollum)
withId function, 152
Wordpress
    importing database as XML file, 111
    importing into Jekyll blogs from, 110
    importing with direct database access, 110
write_review_file method, 51
WxPython project, 65
WxWidgets, 71

X

Xamarin Studio, 87-89
XHR (XmlHttpRequest), 17
X–GitHub–Media–Type header, 7
X–RateLimit–Limit, 7
X–RateLimit–Remaining, 7
X–RateLimit–Reset, 7

Y

YFM (YAML Front Matter), 104

About the Authors

Chris Dawson comes from a family of public school teachers. From an early age, computers provided an always fascinating and often frustrating complement to learning and teaching for Chris. Notably inconspicuous at several notable startups and technology companies like Apple, Virage and RealNetworks, Chris gratefully had the opportunity to live on three continents and experience the power and dynamism of diverse communities. As such, it is with great relish that Chris has been participating in and documenting one of the most exciting learning communities of the 21st century: GitHub.

Ben Straub is a lifelong developer, and enthusiast of the craft of making great software. He's written software for over 15 years, has authored several books, and has recorded educational software training videos. He enjoys reading, taking his kids on bike rides, chocolate, dogs, those little notebooks you carry around with you, photography, a good weekend hack, traveling, writing, food, craftsmanship, a great pen, Markdown, music, movies, and talking to amazing people.

Colophon

The animal on the cover of *Building Tools with GitHub* is a beagle, a small- to medium-sized breed of dog (*Canis familiaris*). The modern beagle breed was developed in Great Britain in the 1830s, and was originally created to track small game animals, such as rabbits. Hunting by using beagles to track prey is known as "beagling."

Beagles are part of the hound family of dog breeds, but compared to other hounds beagles are small, with shorter legs and snouts. Beagles are most commonly tricolored (white, black, and brown), but can occasionally be found with only two of the three colors.

Beagles are well-regarded as household pets because of their even demeanor and high intelligence. They have made appearances in popular culture since Elizabethan times, from the works of Shakespeare to modern cartoon strips.

Many of the animals on O'Reilly covers are endangered; all of them are important to the world. To learn more about how you can help, go to *animals.oreilly.com*.

The cover image is from *Lydekker's Royal Natural History, Vol. 1*. The cover fonts are URW Typewriter and Guardian Sans. The text font is Adobe Minion Pro; the heading font is Adobe Myriad Condensed; and the code font is Dalton Maag's Ubuntu Mono.

Learn from experts.
Find the answers you need.

Sign up for a **10-day free trial** to get **unlimited access** to all of the content on Safari, including Learning Paths, interactive tutorials, and curated playlists that draw from thousands of ebooks and training videos on a wide range of topics, including data, design, DevOps, management, business—and much more.

Start your free trial at:

oreilly.com/safari

(No credit card required)

Ingram Content Group UK Ltd.
Milton Keynes UK
UKHW030245180423
420317UK00010B/703